Keith Thomson is Professor of Natural History at the University of Oxford and Director of the Oxford University Museum. A zoologist and palaeontologist, he was previously a professor at Yale University and Dean of the Graduate School of Arts and Sciences, President of the Academy of Natural Sciences of Philadelphia, and Distinguished Scientist-in-Residence at the New School for Social Research. He is the author of *Living Fossil* (Norton), *The Common but less Frequent Loon* (Yale), *Treasures on Earth* (Faber and Faber), and a book on the relationships between science and religion will be published by HarperCollins in 2004.

HMS *Beagle*

The Story of Darwin's Ship

KEITH STEWART THOMSON

Drawings by Townsend Moore

PHOENIX

A PHOENIX PAPERBACK

First published in the United States in 1995
by W. W. Norton & Company, Inc., New York
This paperback edition published in 2003
by Phoenix,
an imprint of Orion Books Ltd,
Orion House, 5 Upper St Martin's Lane,
London WC2H 9EA

A CIP catalogue record for this book
is available from the British Library.

ISBN 0 75381 733 0

Printed and bound in Great Britain by
Clays Ltd, St Ives plc

Contents

Contents

Preface

A STORY, WHETHER THE HISTORY OF A SHIP, THE COURSE OF a battle, a life, or a fable, whether told once or repeated over generations, is always told by an individual. The same story in the mind or hand of each person is different. For Charles Darwin the story of HMS *Beagle* was a story of scientific inquiry and an adventure, in retrospect a particularly intellectual adventure. For Robert Fitzroy, it was a larger story of man against nature and himself, a story of will. For Midshipman Musters it was a story so short that his death from yellow fever was perhaps scarcely noticed except, of course, by his mother and by the late Byron. For many seamen the *Beagle* was their whole life, spent boy to man in an uncomfortable ninety-foot brig, three times around the world.

For me the story of HMS *Beagle* is a story of connections—of lives, of ideas, of natural science, and the opening and closing of distances in the nineteenth century. It is certainly a story full of the strangest coincidences, as perhaps all life is. These chance connections continued right up to the time of preparation of the final drafts of the manuscript.

I had known from the beginning that natural history was not solely the pursuit of Charles Darwin and not only the *Beagle*'s second voyage. The *Beagle*'s surgeon (assistant surgeon at first) for all the voyages was Benjamin Bynoe. The specimens of animals and plants that he collected in Australia included examples of many species entirely new to science. His bird specimens were used by John Gould in the preparation of his great monograph *The Birds of Australia* (1840–48). Only recently, however, had I discovered that many of those Bynoe/Gould specimens were included in the magnificent ornithology collections of my own institution, the Academy of Natural Sciences. (As our collections include some twenty-eight million specimens, I do not know them all intimately.)

Immediately after I discovered that just a few yards from my office were bird skins collected by Bynoe on the *Beagle*'s third voyage, I asked to see them. The ornithology staff told me that on that very same day the world's authority on Gould's work, Dr. Clemency Fisher from Liverpool, was visiting the academy to study the Bynoe materials! She soon informed me that we have specimens from not only Bynoe but also the other officers of the *Beagle*, like Stokes, Helpman, and Wickham. The gap between 1840 and 1993 closed in a second.

I started to learn the story of HMS *Beagle* because my profession is that of a biologist, and I have a strong interest both in the history of science (which must include Darwin) and in ships and the sea. My story of HMS *Beagle* is partly the story of how my researches into the *Beagle* progressed. I soon realized that it is impossible to tell the full story of this ship. There is so much still to be learned, particularly about the life of Robert Fitzroy, the *Beagle*'s enigmatic captain from 1828 to 1836, and his interactions with Darwin. The lives of these two opposite-leaning intellectuals were bound up together for six years, and we know almost nothing of that relationship. Similarly, no physical relic of the ship survives—no splinters of timber preserved from the sacred decks upon which Darwin walked, no brightly painted figurehead. But that is a central factor in the *Beagle* story—the wonderful paradox. The *Beagle* was, in Darwin's words, "not a particular ship," just ninety-odd feet of oak and tar, not worth saving for posterity. My aim has therefore been to recover as much as possible of the ship from books and archives in order to set the context for all the wonderful things that were done during her three voyages.

Acknowledgments

THIS BOOK SIMPLY WOULD NOT HAVE BEEN POSSIBLE WITH-
out the generous assistance of the staffs of the National
Maritime Museum in Greenwich, England, and the libraries of
Cambridge University, University College London, Yale University, Harvard University, and particularly the reference and
interlibrary loans staff of the Academy of Natural Sciences. My
work began during a sabbatical leave at University College
London and continued at Yale University and the academy.

At the beginning of the project David Stanbury of London
generously shared with me his knowledge and great love of the
Beagle. At the end of the project Townie Moore's eagle eye, as
he prepared from my untidy sketches the elegant drawings that
grace this book, brought many details of the *Beagle*'s physical
makeup into clear focus at last. In between, I depended a great
deal upon access to the National Maritime Museum collections
of ship's drafts, through the courtesy over the years of David
Lyon, Arthur Waite, and David Topliss.

Peter Gautrey of the Darwin Archive of Cambridge University Library generously shared his knowledge of the Darwin
correspondence, happily now becoming available through a
magnificent complete edition, and first showed me the sketch,
annotated by Darwin, of the *Beagle*'s poop cabin. His successor, Adam Perkins, was equally generous in providing informa-

tion. Sir Geoffrey Keynes allowed me access to the Philip Gidley King sketches of the *Beagle,* prepared for Murray's publishers. The curators of the Latrobe Library of the State of Victoria, Australia, allowed me access to the unpublished diary of Benjamin Helpman. Mr. Edward Carson, librarian and archivist at Customs House in London, enthusiastically searched out references to the *Beagle* in the Customs and Excise Maldon letter books. Mr. Arthur C. Wright, curator of the Central Museum, Southend-on-Sea, drew my attention to a watercolor of a brig similar to the *Beagle,* in its collection.

I am grateful to the National Maritime Museum for permission to publish three original drawings from its archives, to the Syndics of Cambridge University Library for permission to quote from Charles Darwin's *Correspondence* and *Diary* and for permission to reproduce two drawings from its archives, to HMS Customs and Excise for permission to use and quote from the Maldon letter books from 1845 to 1865, and to the Central Museum, Southend-on-Sea, Essex, for permission to reproduce a watercolor by J. G. Ford from its collections.

Among those who have corresponded with me concerning the work have been James Martens, Charles Blake, John Lyman, and Richard Freeman. I am grateful to my father-in law, Don K. Price, Stan Rachootin, John Maisey, Amy McCune, and Townsend Moore and two anonymous reviewers for helpful critical readings of various versions of the manuscript. Sheryl Harris, as "Curator of Disk Drives" at the Academy of Natural Sciences, performed her usual heroic efforts in keeping the text legible.

My family has (mostly) been tolerant of the time that my preoccupation with the *Beagle* has taken away from them. So with great pleasure I dedicate this book to Linda, Jessica, and Elizabeth Rose.

Postlude and Prologue

... almost a gale ... we first lowered the top-gallant
yards and then struck the masts. ... The *Beagle* glided
over the waves, appearing as if by her own choice she
avoided the heavy shocks. As the night came on, the sky
looked very dirty, and the waves with their white crests
dashed angrily against the ship's sides. In the middle
watch however the wind fell and was succeeded by a
calm; this is always the worst part of a gale, for the ship,
not being steadied by the wind pressing on the sails, rolls
in a most uncomfortable manner between the troughs of
sea.

Charles Darwin, *Diary*,
July 10, 1832

AS ON MOST MORNINGS FOR A HUNDRED YEARS PAST AND A
hundred years to come, on June 14, 1845, the early-morning
sun, watery enough at the best of times, had difficulty penetrating the smoky haze from the coal fires of London's homes and
industries. But as soon as there was any visibility at all, a
ninety-foot naval "sloop" edged away from her mooring at
Sheerness Dockyard and slowly moved with the tide down

toward the mouth of the Thames. After a long and glorious history, but showing all the signs of nineteen years of continuous service, HMS *Beagle,* a tiny ship by any standards and under the command of a mere mate, was making one last voyage. She had a small crew and a minimal selection of sails, mildew-stained and repaired, but she would not really need anything more than that.

All around her in the crowded estuary were signs of the changing world of ships—particularly the steam tugs towing large sailing merchantmen upstream into the Pool of London. As he guided *Beagle* down the oily smooth river, the same river where she had been launched twenty-five years before, George Wrake stood where Lieutenant Robert Fitzroy had once stood to take *Beagle* around Cape Horn, to the distress of Charles Darwin's ever-queasy stomach. The *Beagle*'s temporary skipper probably knew something of the fame and the history of the old ship, although Darwin's fame (or notoriety) as the proponent of the theory of evolution was still twenty years away.

Except for her obvious wear and tear, there was nothing about the *Beagle* to suggest that she had sailed around the world, to Terra del Fuego and Cape Horn twice, and around Australia, or that she had been the vehicle for history-making science. To George Wrake this was just another of those converted brigs. He has seen them before—packets or survey ships, with a mizzenmast added and a fancy poop cabin. They had a bad reputation; "coffin brigs" they called them. Always sinking.

The *Beagle* was dark and dirty. Her rigging was worn and frayed in places but still basically sound. Her deck lacked that scrubbed-clean look that Fitzroy had insisted on. Belowdecks, after the ship had been battened down for nearly two years, the air was rank. Those musty smells were the product of eighteen years at sea, almost all below the equator. In freezing storms and sweltering heat, men had lived and died down there. Fifty, sixty, or even seventy living together in a space less than ninety feet long and twenty-four feet wide. The old *Beagle* creaked and groaned, and she moved out from the sheltered dock into the gentle waves of the river.

Steadily the old ship came to life again. A gusty westerly breeze picked up, and amid showers of rain she quickly became a real ship again, the sound of the water swirling under her stern gradually rising in volume as she headed down the estuary toward the open sea. She once again began that familiar rise and fall with the waves, moving very easily in these sheltered waters. But all too soon she turned north, out of the bustle of the river, into the quiet of the Essex marshes. Under the barest minimum of sail she crept forward to where she would end her career. Right from the beginning of her career the *Beagle* had made history, but today this last voyage ended quietly and slowly in the reeds and mud of a tiny coastal creek. Unobserved.

The reader will be surprised to learn that she belongs to that much-abused class, the "10-gun brigs,"—*coffins,* as they are not unfrequently designated in the service, notwithstanding which, she has proved herself, under every possible variety of trial, in all kinds of weather, an excellent sea boat.

—John Lort Stokes,
  Discoveries in Australia;
  with an Account of the Coasts
  and Rivers explored and
  surveyed during the Voyage
  of HMS Beagle *in the*
  years 1837, 38, 39, 40, 41,
  42, 43 (1846)

HMS *Beagle*

ONE

Searching for the Beagle

"AFTER HAVING TWICE BEEN DRIVEN BACK BY HEAVY SOUTH-west gales, His Majesty's Ship *Beagle,* a ten-gun brig, under the command of Captain Fitzroy, R.N., sailed from Devonport on the 27th of December, 1831." So begins Charles Darwin's account of one of the most famous and important of all scientific voyages. Given that fame, it ought already to be quite easy to list some basic facts about HMS *Beagle*. But this turns out to be quite difficult.

Nothing remains of HMS *Beagle*. There are not even many contemporary illustrations of her. For such a famous ship she has remained remarkably mysterious—invested, in fact, in a great cloud of misinformation. Of course, the work accomplished on board—Darwin's natural history, and his first evolutionary musings, the coastal surveys of South America and Australia, the exquisitely accurate fixing of a chain of longitudinal measurements around the world, to say nothing of the fascinating lives of the men who served on her—all these are in a great sense independent of the *Beagle* herself. Great naval vessels like HMS *Victory* or USS *Constitution* are preserved because they have become part of the history they participated in. HMS *Beagle,* on the other hand, was a simple working ship, as Darwin himself observed, "not a particular ship."

For professional biologists like myself, the life and career of Charles Darwin are a continuous fascination; there are so many contradictions. On the one hand, we have the young Darwin fearlessly exploring on horseback across South America; on the other, we have Darwin the reclusive, hypochondriac, Victorian gentleman with a bushy white beard, preoccupied with enemas and "water cures." The same man who dared to theorize on a grander scale than any other biologist was also concerned with the lives of earthworms and barnacles. One of the greatest puzzles about Darwin is the fact that he accomplished so much so early, in the isolation of the "Voyage of the *Beagle*" when he was only just out of the university.

Darwin's geological and biological accomplishments while on board HMS *Beagle* for nearly six years are so great that one naturally wonders just what life was like on that ship. And the first thing that anyone notices about the *Beagle* is how tiny she was—a rather dumpy-looking naval brig, only some ninety feet long. The second is that she was not a brig at all, but a bark. She had three masts, not two.

Several years ago I innocently started to delve beyond the few obvious facts known about HMS *Beagle*, just to see what I could discover. I found myself drawn into a fascinating story, a story of not one but three extraordinary voyages of exploration, a story of changing naval history and world politics. It was also a story, like Darwin's own, that was full of paradoxes and contradictions. HMS *Beagle* was a brig, but perhaps a bark. She was eventually sold to Japan as a training ship, or perhaps she became a coast guard watch vessel. She was extensively altered for the Darwin voyage, or perhaps the changes were made for the earlier voyage. Darwin and Captain Fitzroy quarreled during the whole voyage, or perhaps they were close friends. Darwin was invited as the expedition's naturalist, or perhaps he was only Fitzroy's "companion." There was a challenge here.

I decided to try to bring together the whole story of this interesting ship. That meant starting with trying to assemble an accurate physical description of her.

Plans

First, I did what countless others had done before. I wrote to the National Maritime Museum in Greenwich, England, to ask what information concerning the *Beagle* it had in its magnificent collections of plans, models and archives. Alas, I received its customary answer: "Unfortunately we have no model or plans of the . . . vessel, nor can we suggest any literature to help with your query." Luckily a second inquiry produced a more hopeful answer. Plans of sister ships, such as HMS *Cadmus*, which would give the basic hull dimensions were available, and I was welcome to come and explore the collection of plans. But although it was well known that the *Beagle* had been extensively modified during her career, "the plans of the conversion of the *Beagle* must have been removed from the Admiralty very many years ago."

Lois Darling of New York had preceded me in this quest and, using the *Cadmus* plans, had attempted a reconstruction of the ship.[1] But even the meager results of my researches so far already told me that many items in her account of the *Beagle* and her model (based on a New England whaler) were wrong. She showed windows in the stern, for example, and was wrong in imagining that the *Beagle*'s mizzenmast was added during the preparations for the second (Darwin) voyage. In fact, most published sources on the *Beagle* had obvious errors and contradictions.

Perhaps I would have given up the search early except for a stroke of luck. As a newcomer to the world of ships' architecture, let alone the confusing details of cordage and rigging, but as an expert in museums, I knew I needed at least to make a visit to Greenwich to search among those plans. My first thought was to get some basic hull details from the *Beagle*'s sister ships, and by now I had done quite a lot of library research on the sister ships, the "coffin brigs" of the so-called Cherokee Class of 10-gun brigs.

In those days the press of business at Greenwich and the exigencies of funding were not what they are today. Visitors were welcome, and the staff of the Department of Ships willingly allowed me to poke around under their watchful eyes. I spent several delightful days pulling out the plans of various sister ships to the *Beagle* (I was to learn there were very many sisters).

The museum's collection of ships' drafts at that time was stored in a series of archival boxes. The staff showed me the basic plan labeled "HMS *Cadmus*" that they had shown to others. Then I explored further. In another box was a complicated document, number 3974. It was a copy, dated November 26, 1809, of the original (1807) plans for the 10-gun brigs. The Admiralty had at some time stamped it with the name *Cadmus,* but there was no proof that it was actually for any particular ship. Indeed, much more interestingly, the hull lines had been altered several times in different-colored inks, and on both faces of the sheet were long lists of annotations, dating from 1817.

These plans were much more interesting than I could ever have hoped. Among the many corrections and notes written on the face and back of this sheet, I was able to make out the following words: "16 July 1817. Copies agreeably to the alterations in green and yellow (except the alterations in yellow in the water lines and stations of the forebody & in the dimensions) were sent to Deptford for the Alacrity & Ariel, to Woolwich for the Barracouta, Beagle. . . ."

Beagle! By a stroke of luck I had found a set of plans that either formed the master copy from which the plans for various brigs, including the *Beagle,* had been copied and sent to the respective dockyards or was a summary copy recording the changes that had been specified for those ships. In either case, here, after all, was a starting point, an exact specification of the *Beagle*'s lines as she was first built, at Woolwich. Plainly written on the back of the plan is a complete list of vessels constructed from this plan. It shows that the *Beagle* and several of her sisters had been altered from the original design for the 10-gun brigs by having the bulwarks raised about six inches at the stem, falling away to four inches at the stern.

The museum staff was delighted at this discovery, which I included in a short article summarizing my research so far, written in 1976.[2] Subsequently, I shared all the information I had discovered with David Stanbury, perhaps the most persistent of all diggers after information about the *Beagle*,[3] and Lois Darling. The latter was rather distressed that she had missed the key plans at the National Maritime Museum and other basic sources such as John Edye's 1832 *Naval Calculations,* which gives a lot of basic information about the 10-gun brigs.[4] To my surprise, she subsequently wrote three rather hostile articles updating her 1954 paper.[5,6]

There is another draft at the National Maritime Museum (number 4056), dated July 1817, specifying modifications by Sir Robert Seppings to the construction of the frames of the 10-gun brigs, with new diagonal bracing. This is also a kind of master copy and bears the annotation that a copy was sent to Woolwich for the building of *Beagle.*

These plans seem to be as close as we are likely to come to original plans for the *Beagle,* the only alternative being the possibility that one day the copy that went to Woolwich Dockyard in 1819 might eventually come to light. The plans allow us to reconstruct the hull of *Beagle* as she was originally built, which is the starting point for our reconstruction of the ship.

Here, then, was a beginning. In the physical sense it was a plan to refer to. Of course, it was only a plan of the original hull, not of the later modifications. But psychologically it was a marvelous boost; it suggested that further research would be rewarded, and soon I was deep into the history of the *Beagle.* I quickly found that there was a lot of information to be gathered from looking at all her sister ships, many of whom had been modified in just the ways that *Beagle* had.

The 10-Gun Brig

I knew, even before I received that first letter from the National Maritime Museum, that to understand HMS *Beagle,* I would first have to understand the whole class to which she belonged. Whereas information about the *Beagle* was only available in snippets here and there, I could bring the ship completely to life by pulling together a mass of data about the class as a whole.

The basic design for the *Beagle,* as for the class as a whole, was that of a brig. A brig is a smallish vessel, usually not more than 150 feet overall, with two masts. Each mast is square-rigged—that is, with square sails rigged symmetrically from side to side. Obviously such a ship can sail well "before the wind" but is restricted in the face of a headwind or a wind coming from a narrow angle to the bow. For this reason the mainmast is also rigged with a large fore-and-aft sail, the driver or spanker. The brig design is a highly functional one. Shipyards around the North Atlantic produced thousands of merchant brigs in the nineteenth century.

These brig-sloops (anything carrying less than twenty guns was often referred to as a sloop) were a curious group of vessels. In comparison with great ships of the line of the Napoleonic Wars they were hardly worth mentioning as warships. Later, however, when smaller vessels were needed for the peacetime Navy, they turned out to be useful after all. But they were always controversial.

The "tens" had a nickname, hardly an affectionate one. They

A 10-gun brig. HMS *Lyra* in 1815, detail from an engraving published in 1818; see note 29.

were called coffin brigs because of a reputation for sinking. One has to wonder, if they were so small, despised, and apparently dangerous, why on earth did Charles Darwin entrust himself to one of these lowly vessels for nearly six years and a voyage around the world, starting with months of close inshore work around Cape Horn? In fact, the *Beagle* turned out to be extremely safe during the Darwin voyage. Perhaps this is due to the skill of her officers, particularly Fitzroy, and men. Perhaps it is due in part to the fact that she was heavily modified from the original brig design.

Over the years the basic design for the 10-gun brig was frequently modified. The *Beagle* herself was rebuilt twice. As we shall see in the following chapters, these modifications were often aimed at fitting the brigs for different types of service—particularly packet vessel and survey ship. Some of these brigs were even transformed from sailing ship to paddle-driven steamer. But a lot of the changes were concerned with improving basic handling. So here is another paradox: If these vessels were so inferior, why did they survive so long in so many different guises? If the basic design was so flawed, why did the Admiralty not give up on it and work with other designs?

TWO

The Origin of the Beagle

HMS *BEAGLE* WAS BUILT AT WOOLWICH NAVAL DOCKYARD on the river Thames and launched as a typical member of the 10-gun brig class. In later chapters we shall need to discuss in detail the fact that she never sailed as a brig but was converted to a bark—square-rigged on the fore and mainmasts and with a smaller mizzenmast that had no square sails, only a fore-and-aft driver. The fact remains, however, that she was built as a quite standard brig. So our first task is to describe what the *Beagle* looked like in this first incarnation.

Unfortunately the *Beagle* was not important enough for special notice to have been taken of her when she was launched. But we can confidently reconstruct what she must have been like from the specifications of her sister brigs.

The original design for the 10-gun brigs, by Sir Henry Peake (surveyor to the navy), called for vessels of 235 tons burthen (the older builder's measure of capacity) and 297 displacement when loaded. They were all 90 feet 4 inches from stem to stern-post (which works out to about 99 feet from beak to stern rail) and 73 feet 7 inches in the keel. Their maximum breadth was 24 feet 6 inches. When fully laden, a typical 10-gun brig drew 11 feet 5 inches forward and 12 feet 6 inches aft.

These were, then, quite small sloops but heavily armed with

eight 18-pounder carronades and two 6-pounder long guns. As typical brigs they had two masts—fore and main—each of which was made up of three parts: lower, top, and topgallant. Each mast was rigged with a full complement of square sails (mainsail, topsail, and topgallant), together with the driver on the mainmast carried in addition to a main driver. (See Appendix A for specifications of masts, yards, and sails.)

There was a minimum of external decoration; none of the elaborate scrollwork seen on ships of the line graced the appearance of a lowly 10-gun brig. There was no figurehead. Although many later artists have sketched the outline of the head of a beagle dog in their illustrations of the *Beagle,* I suspect that they have been misled by the shape of the beak shown in the illustrations for the 1890 edition of Darwin's *The Voyage of the Beagle*. All the brigs were painted in the standard Navy fashion of the time, with black sides and a broad white stripe around the upper parts. Probably some of them also had small touches of gold and scarlet around the beak and the stern.

There were six gunports along each side, two in the stern and one in each bow, all the guns being carried on the main deck. The main deck was flush, interrupted by neither a forecastle (apart from a tiny locker in the bow) nor a poop deck. In the stern were two tiny "boxes," containing on the starboard side a flag and signal locker and on the port side a water closet. The ship's wheel and binnacle were completely exposed on deck. Also on deck were two large hatches (fore and main), gratings allowing air to the galley, a chimney for the stove, and the capstan. Not a distinguished design!

A very noticeable feature of the 10-gun brig, as far as the landlubber is concerned, is the extremely limited illumination for the lower deck, apart from the two large hatches and companions, and a ladderway just aft of the mainmast. There were no skylights. We know that for the second voyage of HMS *Beagle,* there were bull's-eyes (brass-mounted glass disks) let into the deck to provide a little light to the cabins below. Presumably these were originally present in all the 10-gun brigs. Ventilation was just as bad a problem. Apart from air that may have reached the lower deck via the companions and hatches, it must

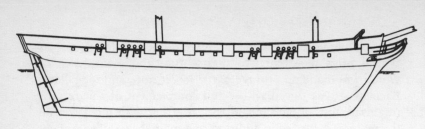

H.M.S. BEAGLE, AS LAUNCHED-ELEVATION

0   10   20   30 FT.

HMS *Beagle* launched in 1820 as a 10-gun brig, elevation; after the
Admiralty drawings.

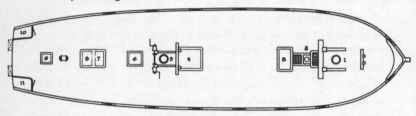

H.M.S. BEAGLE, AS LAUNCHED-MAIN DECK PLAN

0   10   20   30 FT.

1 FORE MAST	4 MAIN HATCH	7 LADDER WAY	10 FLAG LOCKER
2 GRATING & CHIMNEY	5 MAIN MAST	8 COMPANION	11 WATER CLOSET
3 FORE HATCH	6 COMPANION	9 SCUTTLE to BREAD	

HMS *Beagle* launched in 1820 as a 10-gun brig, main deck plan; based
on Admiralty drawings of sister ships.

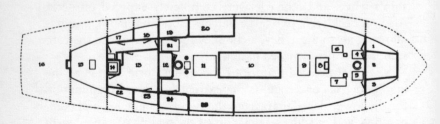

H.M.S. BEAGLE, AS LAUNCHED-LOWER DECK PLAN

0   10   20   30 FT.

1 BOS'N'S CABIN	6 SCUTTLE to COALS	12 STEWARD'S ROOM	19 BOS'N'S STOREROOM
2 GUNNER'S CABIN	7 SCUTTLE to DRY	13 MESS ROOM	20 STORE BIN
3 CARPENTER'S CABIN	PROVISIONS	14 SCUTTLE to MAGAZINE	21 SCUTTLE to SPIRITS
4 SCUTTLE to BOS'N'S	8 GALLEY	15 CAPTAIN'S CABIN	22 1ST LIEUTENANT'S CABIN
STORES	9 FORE HATCH	16 BREAD ROOM	23 2ND LIEUTENANT'S CABIN
5 SCUTTLE to	10 SAIL ROOM	17 MASTER'S CABIN	24 CAPTAIN'S STORE ROOM
CARPENTER'S STORES	11 MAIN HATCH	18 SURGEON'S CABIN	25 CARPENTER'S STORE ROOM

HMS *Beagle* launched in 1820 as a 10-gun brig, reconstruction of lower
deck plan; based on Admiralty drawings of sister ships.

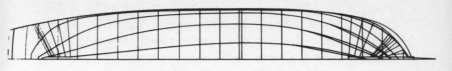

H.M.S. BEAGLE, AS LAUNCHED-SHEERLINE

HMS *Beagle* launched in 1820 as a 10-gun brig, sheer lines; based on Admiralty drawings.

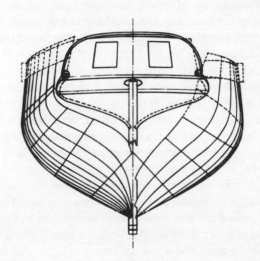

H.M.S. BEAGLE, AS LAUNCHED-SECTION

0   10   20   30 FT.

HMS *Beagle* launched in 1820 as a 10-gun brig, sections; based on Admiralty drawings.

have been pretty dark and dismal down below. In fine weather a system of canvas screens could be erected in order to direct fresh air below, but in wet and stormy weather, with everything battened down and the galley fire out, what conditions there must have been! One is hard put to imagine which would be worse: being battened down in the penetrating cold of a North Atlantic winter gale or in the stifling heat of a tropical storm.

The general picture of crowding and discomfort in the lower deck is not alleviated by closer examination of the arrangements down there. The headroom was only fifty-three inches! The captain had his cabin right at the stern. Behind it, in the oddly shaped space where the stern quarters raised up, was storage for the bread, reached by the scuttle in the deck above. The companion for the captain's cabin reached down to where a marine sentry stood guard, covering both the magazine and the entry to the captain's cabin. Along the port side of the passage leading forward were marked off the tiny cabins for the master and surgeon. In the center of the vessel was the messroom, and from this, on the starboard side, were the cabins for the first and second lieutenants. Abreast the mainmast were grouped sleeping spaces for the purser, the steward's room, and the access to the spirit room and well, and the gunner's storeroom. The main part of the lower deck was taken up with the large sail bin, the carpenter's and boatswain's store bins, and the general sleeping and eating area for the crew. Forward of the fore hatch was the galley, and right at the bow were the boatswain's, carpenter's, and gunner's cabins. The sleeping spaces marked on the plans were, of course, not really well-defined cabins but were temporary canvas and wood enclosures that could be removed when necessary.

Belowdecks were the usual holds and stores reached via two large hatches and several smaller scuttles, giving access to the spirits, coal bins, carpenter's stores, etc., as noted on the plans.

Given the fact that some sixty-five officers, men, and boys lived in these close quarters, it is evident that some highly structured social organization was necessary. The social code that applied relatively easily on ships of the line was enforced rigorously on these smaller vessels as well, and indeed, on these smaller and cramped vessels it was vital for iron discipline. It is important to remember that the captain lived separately from the rest of the officers, in his cabin, alone except when he invited any of them to share his table. The other officers ate in the messroom. The purser and surgeon messed in this "wardroom." But beyond this there was no separate gun room, no marines' quarters, no separate messes for the warrant officers (gunner, carpenter, boatswain). A complex arrangement for the division of space and also the time of eating was necessary in order to maintain the vital separations requisite to the delicate hierarchy among the noncommissioned officers and men, boys, and servants. Each person on board will have come to know his fellows extremely well.

We have some idea of the stores that would have been carried on a fully equipped 10-gun brig, and they are not impressive. The 10-gun brig could carry nineteen tons of water. (Iron casks were introduced into the navy in 1815 and were a vast improvement over wooden casks, whose contents were usually completely fetid after a few days.) She would have carried about six tons of coal and wood for the galley and could take on about six and a half tons of provisions, spirit, and slops. The latter is also a relatively small figure: an 18-gun brig (complement of 120) could load more than twenty-three tons. For the fighting ship, the weight of gunner's stores, powder, shot, and cases, etc. amounted to another ten tons. Also on board were about two thousand yards of spare canvas for sails and about two tons of spare masts, yards, and gear lashed to the main deck. Typically a brig would have carried three main *bower* anchors (two with iron cables), one smaller *stream* anchor, and a small *kedge* anchor.

Despite the seeming bulk of these stores and spare equipment, they would have lasted only for about three months. The 10-gun brigs were really not capable of extended cruises away from well-established bases of supply. When these little vessels came to be used for various survey works in the 1820s, 1830s, and 1840s, this lack of range was a great problem. On her first survey cruise the *Beagle* was accompanied by a "mother ship," the *Adventure,* which carried more ample stores. On her second and third voyages the *Beagle* worked alone, and this added a major burden to the already almost overwhelming responsibilities of her captains (Pringle Stokes, her first commander, committed suicide before the first voyage was completed).

The Brig at Sea

Given proper materials in construction, 10-gun brigs like the *Beagle* were in fact rather sturdy, especially when built according to the method of diagonal bracing introduced by the distinguished naval architect Sir Robert Seppings. Indeed, even the skeptical James in his *Naval History* records the strength of the 10-gun brig *Frolic,* which "after lying eight hours on her beam ends, upon the rock of Sable Island, beating violently, got safely into Halifax Harbour"[1] And Fincham in his *Marine Architecture* states "the vessels of this . . . class were good sea boats, although they were not fast sailors. . . ."[2] Even this is unfair: Eight to nine knots for a vessel of this sort was pretty fast.

The problem was their handling characteristics. The first 10-gun brigs had not been in service more than a few years before they acquired the sobriquets "coffin brig" and "half tide rocks." Admiral Sir Bartholomew J. Sulivan, who served on the *Beagle* as a midshipman and lieutenant (from 1830 to 1836) and whose recollections we shall draw on heavily in this book, summarized the situation very simply. They were "very deep-waisted . . . so that a heavy sea breaking over them was the more dangerous."[3]

By *deep-waisted,* Sulivan means that the gunwales were very high compared with the length of the ship. This deep-waisted-ness, coupled with the fact that the top of the rail was only some six feet above the waterline (or less when the ship was heavily laden), and the flush deck without a forecastle, made them dangerous in high seas. Without a forecastle to turn aside waves that broke over the bow, this class of ship had a tendency to ship a lot of water and, having done so, to labor with this heavy weight trapped on deck by the high bulwarks, wallowing and losing steerageway with the risk of turning broadside on to the weather. A second wave, shipped before the first had cleared the deck, would then bring the ship to a standstill; a third would have her completely at its mercy, and the vessel would likely founder. Therefore, very careful sailing was necessary in bad weather. Some minimum sail had to be retained until the last, in order to keep under way. There was no room for laxness or carelessness in handling. This then was the coffin brig—something like a sailing spoon. This problem is undoubtedly the reason that later 10-gun brigs like the *Beagle* were built with an even higher bulwark, especially at the bow. Paradoxically, however, this may have made the situation worse rather than better by increasing the deep-waistedness.

Ample confirmation of the difficulty of handling the 10-gun brigs is given in the written reports of those who served in them and in the silent testimony of the wrecks. Of 107 10-gun brigs built between 1808 and 1845, none was lost to enemy action (except for the *Redpole* of 1808, which was sunk by the pirate *Congress* in 1828), but fully 26 were wrecked or sank from unknown cause.

In addition to the fatal weakness of handling in bad weather, various writers have noted their poor sailing qualities. It is difficult to get these various comments in perspective because other accounts, particularly those of Fitzroy (admittedly with the *Beagle* rerigged as a bark) emphasize their excellent qualities as sea boats. Probably Fincham is correct when he explains:

[T]he dullness of their sailing is sufficiently accounted for by the armament and other weights which were put on board of them being too great, in relation to the power of sail which their dimensions would allow them to carry. To have given scope for the production of excellence in these vessels, when their armament had been determined on, larger dimensions should have been given them; but as the armament in these brigs was of too small a caliber to furnish them with sufficient power against the enemy, they might, with sufficient dimensions, have been armed with 24 instead of 18 pounder carronades; and dimensions suited to this description of armament would have enabled them to carry such a quantity of sail as would have rendered them a far superior class of vessels to what they ever were.[4]

This is at odds with another criticism of the 10-gun brigs (see page 39): that they should have had bigger guns. However, these brigs, carrying their guns on the (upper) deck, rather than below, held the center of gravity rather high. It would have been impossible to carry heavier guns; that would have rendered them far too unstable—regardless of "dullness" of sailing.

Basically the 10-gun brigs were small vessels whose armament was probably just a little too heavy to be carried well and too light to make a powerful fighting ship. Later members of the class such as HMS *Beagle* could sail in peacetime with lighter armament on their decks, and except when very heavily laden with stores, they were probably not bad sailors in favorable seas. But in really rough waters they were always the "diving ducks" that Charles Darwin remembered, with a tendency to a particularly nasty roll.[5]

THREE

His Majesty's Coffin Brigs

THE PROBLEM FOR THE CONTEMPORARY RESEARCHER IS that HMS *Beagle* was a small working vessel, not very different from more than a hundred others in her class, the Royal Navy's 10-gun brigs (later called Cherokee Class) built between 1808 and roughly 1845. None of them was particularly distinguished, and most were altered and even completely rebuilt during their careers.

If this history of the *Beagle* were the biography of a person, I would not be able to trace an intimate lineage from this noble statesman to that ne'er-do-well, actress, or great lady. Rather, I would be writing vaguely about "decent peasant stock of the eighteenth century." The *Beagle* and her sister "half tide rocks" (sailing more below the water than above) bore no relationship to the great ships (like HMS *Victory,* for example) that we normally associate with the Royal Navy. She was merely a workhorse brig in basic design and distinctly unfashionable. Brigs as a type had in fact only recently been allowed into the Royal Navy.

One of the reasons that the navy broke down and started building brigs in addition to their traditional three-decker ships of the line and fast sleek frigates was the fact that the brig was a familiar tried and true design. From the collier brigs of the

British east coast, where Captain Cook learned his seamanship, to the large merchant fleets that were to fan out all over the world throughout the nineteenth century, the brig remained a solid, undramatic, but reliable and economical vessel. Brigs were popular in merchant service because they were simple to build, simple to rig, and easy to sail with a small crew. Merchant seamen pressed into the Navy found them familiar. Brigs could easily be built by the many small merchant yards around the country, allowing a rapid build-up of naval power in times of war without taxing the already burdened naval dockyards that were, in any case, better equipped and more suitable for building larger ships. Brigs were, in short, sensible.

Overall, a less glamorous group of vessels can hardly be imagined. But by the second decade of the nineteenth century, just as brigs were the predominant merchant type, so we find the 10-gun naval brigs engaged in every aspect of the changing world of the early to mid-nineteenth century, from straight warfare to the suppression of piracy, from the introduction of steam power to the navy to the establishment of the colonial outposts of the peacetime empire. Therefore, as I probed further and further into the history of the *Beagle,* I found that she and her sister ships provided a snapshot history of the whole Royal Navy of the first half of the nineteenth century.

It was a time of transition from sail to steam, and sure enough, several of the *Beagle*'s sisters actually ended up as steam tugs. It was a transition from the Napoleonic Wars to Pax Britannica, from Georgian to Victorian Britain. In the Royal Navy in the first decade of the nineteenth century everything changed, from the ships and the men to their missions. From the military role of the ship of the line to the problem of impressment, events were occurring, or had already occurred, that were greatly to change the future shape of the navy.

Whereas in past history, and again later, naval actions had been fought between ships of the line on the high seas, the wars with France (1794–1802, 1803–15) brought a change in the nature of naval warfare. The French fleets were largely block-aded in their home ports by British fleets. The classic ships of the line were not often used in battle, as huge moving castles bristling with firepower, but became set pieces in a chess game. (It has been stated that the conditions of repair and manning of some of the older *British* vessels were such that it is as well they were not put to the test.) In any case, with the big ships in stalemate, the naval war was conducted in large part by a host of smaller vessels. Frigates and smaller "sloops of war" were both the "eyes and ears of the fleet" and also fighting elements, swooping down on coastal shipping and the smaller cruisers of the enemy and engaging in action often very close to the coastline. It was in this context that brigs entered the service in large numbers.

Brigs and Carronades

As is so often the case, a powerful agent of change was technology. The changing spectrum of naval set pieces and impromptus was made possible in part by the development of a new naval gun—the carronade, named after the town in Scotland (Carron) where they were first cast in 1779 under the design of General Robert Melville. Carronades were small, short, and wide-barreled, with a relatively short recoil. They were capable of delivering an extremely powerful blow, although only at relatively short range because their accuracy decreased rapidly with distance. Carronades usually did not exceed 32-pounders.[1]

Up to this point naval guns had essentially been fieldpieces, artillery brought on board. These long guns were heavy and needed big ships and many men. The invention of the carronade was a tremendously important advance in naval armament. Because carronade guns were half the weight of an equivalent long gun, a ship that would normally carry eighteen long 32-pounders could now carry a dozen carronades as well and, at close quarters, would therefore have more than three times the effective firepower, as the powerful "smashers" or "devil guns" were brought into play. A smaller vessel that could carry only a few heavy long guns could now be armed as heavily as a small frigate.

There were, of course, many disadvantages to the carronade. One was finding the right gun carriage for the short but powerful recoil. Another was range. Whereas the 32-pounder long gun might be used effectively at a range of more than half a mile, the range of a 32-pounder carronade was far less. This meant that all ships had to carry some long guns anyway, usually as stern and bow "chasers" because otherwise they would be undefended against an enemy who could stand out of range of the carronades and then pick them to pieces with his long guns—in theory, at least. In fact, accuracy with long guns was never a strong point of any navy. Despite the stirring accounts of heroes of fiction, use of any gun from a rolling ship on a moving target in the heat of battle was not at all easy before the invention of gyroscopic stabilizers. For that reason, even though they were armed solely with long guns, earlier ships normally fought at close range anyway, using not only round shot but also grape and chain shot, the purpose of which was to dismast the enemy, bring down his rigging, sweep his decks clean, and effect maximum damage to the superstructure.

The carronade was specifically designed for short-range action, and now even a small vessel could have a very powerful firepower and could take on a large merchantman or moderate-size man-of-war or privateer. Carronades made the brig a practical fighting design. So, with the enthusiastic endorsement of the first lord of the Admiralty, Lord Melville, new classes of smallish sloops of war, armed almost exclusively with carronades, quickly came into being in the first decade of the new century. And with them came, eventually, HMS *Beagle*.

Melville's policy was, of course, not without its severe and persistent critics in an organization as traditional and conservative as the Royal Navy. For example, Sir John Briggs, writing later in his history of naval administration, concluded that this era was an "era of donkey-frigates, over-masted sloops, and coffin gun-brigs ... rendered memorable, in naval annals, by the substitutions of carronades for long guns, whereby the numerical strength of a man-of-war was increased at the expense of her fighting efficiency."[2]

However, the logic of arming smaller ships with carronades

was inescapable, and construction proceeded apace. The new brigs were cheap to build, were easy to handle with a small crew, and could operate in shallow waters as well as deep. In oceanic operations they were restricted only by their limited capacity to carry stores. Armed with from ten to eighteen guns, they became the workhorses of the navy. They were used in escort duties, on reconnaissance work, on routine patrols, as packets, even as troopships. Naval historians sometimes did not bother to record the names in their accounts of major naval battles; most of these smaller vessels came in single and light actions rather than squadron or fleet actions.

The increase in smaller vessels began, naturally enough, with traditional ship-rigged designs, some flush-decked, some quarter-decked, such as HMS *Dart* (launched 1796; 129 feet, carrying twenty-eight 32-pounder carronades). They were fast and powerful. But very soon after the onset of the Napoleonic Wars, the brig began to come into service, one of the most successful patterns being the 100-foot 18-gun brig-sloop (Cruizer Class), of which 110 were laid down between 1797 and 1826. Each carried a powerful battery of two 6-pounder long guns and sixteen 32-pounder carronades. These new gun brigs gave long and effective service.

After the eighteens came 16- and 14-gun brig-sloops, and these remained the smallest brig-sloops, larger only than gun brigs and cutters, until 1808. On February 1, 1808, HMS *Achates* was launched, the first of a new class, the 10-gun brig-sloop, armed with two 6-pounder long guns and eight 18-pounder carronades.[3]

The 10-gun brig was unpopular from the very first. James, in his *Naval History of Great Britain,* sourly remarked: "This was the first time the British Navy could boast of a 10-gun sloop-of-war. [They] ... were inferior in force to the generality of gun brigs, and not superior, except in point of size, to many of the 10-gun schooners or cutters." He continues: "Surely, if the number of guns must be limited to 10, the carronades should have been at least 32 pounders. The size of the vessels, 235 tons, was quite equal to that caliber, and no one can dispute that they would have been more effectively armed. In addition to all this, the whole class turned out very dull sailors; proving that as little judgment had been employed in modelling the hull as in establishing the armament."[4]

By January 1, 1808, some 26 of the 10-gun brig-sloops were already on order, and in 1808 alone 31 came into commission. Between 1808 and 1838 a total of 107 Cherokee Class brigs, or vessels based on the original design, were built. Considering their poor reputation, it is a little difficult to see why. Much bigger than schooners of similar armament, they had a far greater range. But in comparison with the 18-gun brigs, they lacked both firepower *and* range.

The records show that of 114 10-gun brigs ordered (only 107 were actually built), 38 were built at private yards.[5] As might be expected, with one exception (*Briseis* of 1829) all private building of 10-gun brigs was done before 1815, during the pressure of wartime. After that all shipbuilding for the navy was at the royal dockyards. The navy-built brigs had a slightly better record of service.[6]

HMS *Beagle* was launched at Woolwich Naval Dockyard on May 11, 1820, as a typical 10-gun brig. The third vessel of the Royal Navy to bear the name *Beagle* (Appendix B), she was not originally destined for any particular purpose: just a very ordinary, small sloop of war to be put into service as necessary.

FOUR

Sister Ships:
"This Worthless Class"

COFFIN BRIG OR HALF TIDE ROCK, HMS *BEAGLE* WAS HARDLY
one of those dashing ships of the sort canonized in romantic fiction. There were no daring raids under the enemy's guns
at midnight, no all-out gun battles, ambushes, chases, or muti-
nies. HMS *Beagle* and her sister ships were designed as the most
basic of small naval vessels, whose use in war or peace would
be in backing up the larger and faster frigates and more ponder-
ous ships of the line. Of the 33 wartime tens, none played a
major part in the war with France, although they saw a small
share of action.

Two examples will serve to show the role of the coffin brigs
as men-of-war. Apparently the first significant action involving
a 10-gun brig was on January 1, 1809, when the *Onyx* (Captain Charles Gill) was cruising in the North Sea. They spotted
and tackled the Dutch 16-gun brig-sloop *Manly* (in fact, a British vessel that had been captured in a previous action). After
two and a half hours of fighting at close quarters the *Manly*
struck her colors, to be taken in and returned to the Royal
Navy. The *Onyx* suffered only three casualties.

In April 1809 two 10-gun brigs (*Redpole* and *Lyra*) took part
in the historic action at Basque Roads. Lord Cochrane was in
charge of the fire and explosion ships that made the initial

attack on the boom defenses. The *Lyra* and *Redpole* merely carried signals to guide the attacking vessels. Incidentally, of the British vessels to suffer damage in this prolonged battle, one of the worst hit was named *Beagle,* an 18-gun brig-sloop of the Cruiser Class that was the immediate predecessor of the vessel with which this book is primarily concerned. Other actions involving the 10-gun brigs are summarized in Appendix C.

The 10-gun brigs were more useful in peacetime, in the period between 1814 and 1840. But first they had to escape extinction. At the end of the wars with France and the United States, the building of ships for the navy slowed down greatly. There was a flurry of building new frigates in 1812 and 1813, after the British vessels had shown to poor advantage in comparison with the new ships of the United States, but this was the last major shipbuilding effort for some time. No 10-gun brigs were added to the service between 1809 and 1814. But then one was added in each of the years 1814, 1815, and 1816. By this time nine had already been lost by wreck.

Between 1818 and 1819 eight of the brigs were sold as part of a general reduction of the navy, having outlived their period of usefulness and starting to need extensive repairs.*

In 1819 a period of further construction of the 10-gun brigs began; an amazing total of sixty-three more was built between 1819 and 1834. Although James in his *Naval History* finds it "surprising indeed that the navy-board should continue adding new individuals by dozens at a time ... to this worthless class,"[1] Briggs states flatly that the navy in 1830 consisted of "nothing more than a few old but serviceable 120 and 80 gun ships, many 74's and 60's and too many 46 gun frigates, donkey-frigates of 26 guns, over-masted sloops (the 18 and 16 gun brig-sloops) and the coffin-brigs (the 10's); of the last named, several foundered annually, and hence the name."[2]

However, the 10-gun brigs, manned by a relatively small complement yet relatively well armed, had turned out to be a

---

* Nonethless, excluding the extensions of life that many of the brigs got through harbor service, being cut down for use as barges and so on, the average life of a 10-gun brig in the naval service was twenty and a half years.

handy size of vessel for peacetime use. They could "show the flag" with only a modest investment in manpower and material, and Seppings's "diagonal bracing" had produced a very sturdy vessel after all. And there turned out to be two particular services for which the 10-gun brigs were of great usefulness. Both were directly related to the new role of the peacetime navy. Small vessels were needed by the navy to operate the mail Packet Service (not then conducted by the Post Office) and for the surveying and exploratory work of the Hydrographic Office.

The Packet Brig

Given all that has been said about the coffin brigs, they do not strike one as the ideal vessels to make safe and sure passage from Falmouth to Halifax, Nova Scotia, or across the Bay of Biscay and around into the Mediterranean with His Majesty's mails. However, the Packet Service probably did not need larger ships at this time, and the comfort of the few passengers was certainly not a prime consideration. For those with money to pay there were more comfortable ways of traveling—on the big merchant ships. (Transatlantic travel, at least, was not as popular in the 1820s as it was to become in the 1850s, when the great new steamships and the propaganda associated with them brought the development of the big transoceanic companies.) The volume of mails was probably small, and it was better to have more frequent regular services of small scope.

Up to about 1824 the navy had operated the Packet Service with hired vessels, but after that the 10-gun brigs became the backbone of the service. Not only did this keep large numbers of ships in service, but also a relatively large number of naval officers and men remained on active duty. It cannot have been a particularly desirable assignment. But in the peacetime navy, with everything cut back, the alternatives were few. With only a small nucleus of regular ships in commission, an aspiring young officer had only available the Packet Service, the Coast Guard Service, or, in a very few rare number of cases, special assignments such as those having to do with exploration and hydrographic survey, a point to which we shall return.

The Packet Service was dull and frequently dangerous, especially on the Falmouth to Halifax run and it is said that the 10-gun brigs originally got their name coffin brigs because of the large numbers of them that foundered while in the Packet Service in the North Atlantic.[3] The records show, however, that of the thirty-three brigs that were at any time in the Packet Service, only seven were lost at sea, roughly the same percentage as for the class as a whole. The actual dangers of operating a 10-gun brig of the Packet Service were probably no greater than for any other mission. Very likely, however, the loss of packet vessels would have received much more attention in the press, and this may have contributed to giving the class a bad name.

In one of the peak years, 1826, nineteen packet ships operated out of Falmouth. Seventeen of these were 10-gun brigs of the Cherokee Class. In 1833, eighteen of the nineteen ships in the Packet Service were 10-gun brigs. Most of these ships went into the packet duty without being specially adapted in any way. However, at least eight 10-gun brigs were completed in the dockyards or rebuilt with special modifications for the Packet Service, and as we shall see, some of these more or less experimental modifications turned out to be useful in the redesign of the *Beagle*.

In all cases the armament was reduced: Brigs on packet duty carried only from three to six guns. As the total weight of guns, powder shots, and gunner's stores on a fully equipped 10-gun brig was over eighteen tons, cutting this in half not only greatly improved their capacity to carry passengers and mails but got some of the weight of the guns off the deck, lowering the center of gravity with good effect on the sailing qualities.

Existing plans for HMS *Barracouta* show that the lower deck of the packet version of the 10-gun brig was very different from that of a man-o'-war. The captain was crammed into the former midshipman's cabin on the starboard side, and the large cabin at the stern was now the "lady's cabin" with two bed spaces on either side and a separate passage down from the upper deck. Eight bed spaces for male passengers were arranged in what had originally been officer's spaces on either side of the gun room. Fewer officers' cabins were needed, anyway, because the packet brig sailed only with a captain, master, mate, and surgeon. However, there was now some illumination for the lower deck. Two skylights had been added: one over the main "lady's cabin" and one over the messroom, at the cost of one of the principal companions of the original brig.

The 10-gun brigs continued to be the mainstay of the Packet Service as long as the navy operated it, but after 1830 an important change occurred. One of the regular runs was between Falmouth and the Mediterranean, to Malta and Corfu. From there the mails went overland to the Red Sea and thus to India. This route was therefore a key link in the communication within the empire. A brig normally took three months to sail to Corfu from England. But for the past fifteen or more years steam had begun to come into its own. On February 5, 1830, the first steam vessel made the run from Falmouth to Corfu *and back again* in only forty-seven days. The ship was HMS *Meteor,* a paddle vessel built at Deptford Dockyard in 1824. Apparently the next vessel to leave Falmouth after the *Meteor* was the *Osborne,* a hired sailing vessel. She left on March 6. Next HMS *Echo,* another steam paddle vessel, left on April 6. The *Meteor* set off again in May, and both the *Echo* and the *Meteor* reached Corfu before the *Osborne.* Indeed, the *Meteor* was back in England again only nine days after the *Osborne* reached Corfu.

Very soon after these experiments with the use of steam vessels, the following steamers were in regular monthly service between Falmouth and Corfu: *African, Carron, Columbia, Confiance, Echo, Firebrand, Hermes, Messenger,* and *Meteor.* Eventually all this led to the formation of the Peninsular Steam Navigation Company.

The point of mentioning these events here is to draw attention to a curious fact. The steam paddle vessels *African, Columbia, Confiance,* and *Echo*—some of the earliest steam vessels to be built for the navy—were all none other than modified versions of the much-despised *10-gun brigs,* sister ships of the *Beagle.*

10-Gun Brigs as Paddle Vessels

Despite the Royal Navy's reluctance to accept steam power, the effectiveness of steam vessels was well demonstrated. And if there were strong objections to the commissioning of a steam-powered man-of-war, there could be little doubting the utility of a steam vessel as a tug and as a coastal packet. The first steam vessel *built* for the navy was the paddle tug HMS *Comet,* a small vessel (115 feet, 238 tons, 80 horsepower). She was built in 1822 although she did not figure in the navy list until 1831. The tug *Monkey* was purchased for the navy and in use in 1821. HMS *Lightning* was built in 1823.

Sir Robert Seppings, whose name we have already seen in reference to his famous redesigning of the methods of ship construction, was surveyor of the navy at this time and not reluctant to experiment with steam vessels. In the next few years several paddle vessels were built by the relatively simple expedient of modifying existing designs for sailing vessels and installing modest auxiliary power-steam—driven paddle wheels with engines of up to about 90 horsepower. And once again Sir Henry Peake's tough little 10-gun brigs were found to serve a new useful purpose.

HMS *Dee* was ordered as a 10-gun brig and laid down at Woolwich in 1824. Orders were given for remodeling in May 1825, and she was launched on August 30, 1825, as the paddle vessel *African*. She was of 295 tons and 90 horsepower. On March 28, 1827, the *Confiance* was launched as a paddle vessel for the Packet Service. Like the others, she had two engines and, in this case, only 50 horsepower. She was later made over as a tug in 1842 and continued in service until 1872—a remarkable record. On May 28, 1827, the *Echo* was launched as a paddle vessel although in this case the design had been very heavily modified. She was lengthened to 112 feet and broadened to 28 feet in the beam. She also became a tug (in 1830) and lasted until 1885 before being sold out of the service. On July 1, 1829, the *Columbia* was launched, with even more drastic modification, being lengthened to 130 feet overall. She became a survey

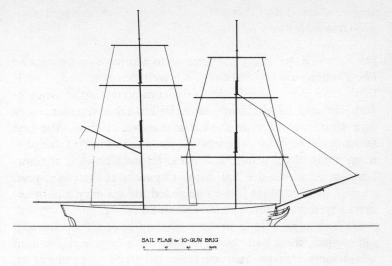

SAIL PLAN for 10-GUN BRIG

HMS *Beagle* as a 10-gun brig, basic sail plan; see Appendix A.

vessel in 1842 and was reduced to a coal hulk in 1857, at Halifax, Nova Scotia. The last two named are perhaps only barely to be considered members of the Cherokee Class. The *Falcon* (1820) was also fitted with an engine (in 1833), but this was evidently not a success, for it was taken out the next year. Finally, the *Alban* (1926), a 110-foot paddle vessel, was also modified from an original brig design, very similar to the old 10-gun brigs.

So far we have traced a remarkable history for a class of vessel that was so denigrated by contemporary sailors and authors: from simple brig-sloop to packet vessel to remarkably serviceable and long-lived paddle vessel. There remains one last use of the class to be mentioned specifically. I have reserved it until last because here I return to the main emphasis of the work. Without doubt the most significant use of 10-gun brigs was in surveying and exploratory work under the Hydrographic Office of the navy. This can only attest to the basic handiness, durability, and certainly flexibility of the design. Some of the tens were specially modified for the hydrographic work, and among this group we find the most famous of all the 10-gun brigs: HMS

Beagle, which, for all her active service life, was rerigged as a three-masted bark.

The Hydrographic Survey

With the end of the Napoleonic Wars came an enormous expansion in world trade, the cornerstone of which was the Pax Britannica. The role of the navy in maintaining and expanding this growth was crucial, for most commerce between nations was conducted via the high seas. The tasks of the navy were severalfold. First there had to be peace and stability. Unarmed merchant ships loaded with raw materials or manufactured goods had to be able to make their way to and from Europe unmolested. There had always to be a British war vessel within call—if only a small sloop of fewer than twenty guns—or at least there had to be the *possibility* that one would appear over the horizon at the propitious moment.

But safety at sea for merchant fleets was not just a matter of military safety. In order to open up new trade routes, it was necessary that all the hazards of navigation be fully known, the vagaries of weather and current fully documented, coasts and harbors fully charted. The Hydrographic Office of the navy had been engaged in basic surveying work for many years, but in the period 1808–60, under the successive leadership of Thomas Hurd, Sir William Parry, and Francis Beaufort, its work proceeded at an extraordinary rate. During this time major expeditions were sent out to survey Africa, India, South America, Australia, the Pacific islands, and the Malay archipelago. They brought back detailed charts that, in some cases, remained the authoritative maps of those areas for a hundred years. But Their Majesties' survey ships were not simply charged with charting out coastlines and rivers; they were expected to conduct complete expeditions of exploration. Their officers were chosen for their ability to survey the natural resources of the lands they saw as well as to estimate the potential value of the harbors and rivers. They also established important relations with the local officials, political connections that would be important in the future. Thus we will see that on the first two voyages of the *Beagle* quite a lot of time was spent in making contacts with South American rulers, so that future British ships would have access to supplies and stores as they operated so far from their home stations.

There is one factor above all that made the work of the Hydrographic Office so important at this time. Accurate and safe operations on the high seas depended not only on well-built ships, well-trained men, and good maps and charts but on accuracy of navigation. In modern times, with radio beacons, computers, radar, and space satellites, it is difficult to imagine the problems faced by the navigators of a hundred years ago. They had to work basically with a sextant and a good chronometer, the sun, and the stars. With these they could fix their position pretty well, especially since there were good patent logs to estimate the speeds of the ships and the distances traveled. And all this was a vast improvement over the situation a hundred years before that. But accuracy of position fixing is only half the battle; the other half is knowing exactly where one's destination is. In 1820 existing world maps contained many remarkable errors, dangerous errors—not just a matter of rocks and islands not marked on the charts but also errors in the given position of features, large and small. The more precisely one comes to navigate, the more one needs an accurate chart to work with. It is no good knowing one's position on the surface of the earth to an accuracy of one mile when the chart may have a feature marked with an accuracy of only five miles. For example, we will see that during the *Beagle*'s second voyage Captain Fitzroy discovered that Bahia, Brazil, was actually four miles from where contemporary French charts placed it. Merchantmen sailing closely competitive schedules, who cannot always afford to be cautious and wait for good weather to check their position, cannot operate safely under such conditions. Therefore, a major goal of hydrographic research was the establishment of exact positions by latitude and longitude as well as surveys of the geography of coastlines.

Finally, exploration work involved the searching out of new resources, new markets, and new possibilities for colonial settlement. So we see expeditions to Africa, South America, and Australia aimed at expansion of the world's commerce as well as conducting the survey work aimed to facilitate its transactions. And the most remarkable feature of all, as many have pointed out, is that the information gained in all this very costly and time-consuming effort was not held secret by one government for the use solely of its own (British) trade and its own ships. The results were freely published for the world to use.

Ships of many different types (large and small) were involved in the survey work, and excellent accounts of the period are given in books by Day[4] and Ritchie.[5] As far as I can discover, the following 10-gun brigs were used in survey and exploration work: *African* (ex-*Dee*), *Barracouta, Beagle, Britomart, Chanticleer, Columbia, Echo, Fairy, Lyra, Saracen*, and *Scorpion*. Their activities give a flavor of the sort of survey work that was being pushed ahead during this time.

The paddle steamer *Echo* seems to have been the first steam vessel ever used in survey work—in a survey of the river Thames, 1827–1828. The *African* (also a paddle vessel) was used on the Gambia River in 1828. The *Columbia* was used briefly for survey work in 1842. The *Fairy*, an unmodified brig, was an important vessel in the survey of British coasts for ten years until she was lost with all hands in a terrible storm off Lowestoft in 1840. The *Scorpion* (in 1848) and the *Saracen* (in 1854) were also used in overseas surveys. But five 10-gun brigs had an involvement in survey and exploration of particular significance to our story.

HMS *Barracouta* has been mentioned before as a packet brig. She was launched in 1820 and commissioned on October 2, 1821, to take part with HMS *Leven*, a sixth rate of twenty guns built in 1813, in a major expedition to survey the eastern coast of Africa, particularly Mozambique and Madagascar. The expedition was then extended by order of the Admiralty to include a large part of the Arabian coast and also the western coast of Africa. They did not return to Britain until 1826. The leader of the expedition was Captain W. F. W. Owen, and the *Barracouta* was commanded by Captain William Cutfield.

At the end of the first month of her surveying career the *Bar-*

racouta was at Lisbon. Here she was rerigged as a bark, just as the *Beagle* was to be later. "While at Lisbon the *Barracouta* was rigged as a bark, on account of the particular service of survey; by removing the main-boom, which would certainly have obstructed those operations, she was rendered more manageable with a reduced crew, which to us, was a very material consideration, as our boats would very commonly be detached for the critical examination of the coasts and rivers."[6] Reading Owen's narrative also confirms what we know of the performance and capabilities of the 10-gun brig. One problem was, of course, the lack of hold capacity. "The *Barracouta* had not stowage for three months, without carrying it upon deck."[7]

The expedition showed that such a brig, even when rerigged for efficiency of operations, would not be a very good vessel to send on a solo surveying expedition. She would need a mother ship to carry stores for the long periods of time that any such expedition would be away from bases of supply. And yet, as we shall see, for two of her three long surveying voyages HMS *Beagle,* also rigged as a bark, was sent out alone.

There is no room here to recount all of the adventures of the *Leven–Barracouta* expedition. In terms of the work completed it was a great success, with more than three hundred charts produced covering the major part of the African and Arabian coasts and half of the major rivers. The cost in human life, mostly through disease and fever, was appalling.

Successive 10-gun brigs had the name HMS *Britomart*. The first was a standard brig, built in 1808 and sold out of the service in 1819. The second, built in 1820, under the command of Captain Owen Stanley, accompanied HMS *Alligator* (a sixth rate of twenty-eight guns) on an expedition to Australia under the command of Sir James Gordon Bremer in 1838. As we shall see in Chapter 11, the careers of the *Beagle* (her third voyage) and the *Britomart* were closely connected during the years 1838 to 1842.

One task of Bremer's expedition was to establish a settlement at Port Essington on the northern coast of Australia (Chapter 13). In addition, Stanley and the *Britomart* became involved in a series of diplomatic and quasi-military maneuvering with a

French colonizing expedition, the prize at stake being the rights to New Zealand. The resulting victory for Stanley settled the matter, neatly demonstrating the role of a small ship in showing the flag at the right time and place and of a resourceful British officer in assuming a heavy responsibility on the spot—a fine example of Pax Britannica in full stride.

HMS *Britomart* herself came to a sad end. Docked at Singapore in late 1841, with no immediate assignment, she was discovered to be rotten beyond repair. Stanley was left waiting for new active orders for nearly eighteen months until word came to sell the vessel off.

HMS *Chanticleer* was built in 1808 (not 1814, as is frequently stated) and not finally broken up until 1871. Throughout this long career her path constantly crossed that of the *Beagle*. In 1815 she had been involved in the attack on Guadeloupe (see Appendix C). In 1828 she was converted to a survey vessel and sent around the South Atlantic for three years (for a twenty-year-old vessel she must have been well built). Like the *Barracouta*, the *Chanticleer* was also rerigged as a bark for this survey work.

The *Chanticleer*'s mission came to be known as the Pendulum Voyage. Very briefly, the Royal Society, during the time that Parry was hydrographer to the navy, was very keen to set up a World Scientific Cruise along the lines set down by, among others, Captain Basil Hall. The work would entail "observations of longitude at salient points, magnetic variation observations, wind and current observations, measurement of tides and tidal streams, height measurements of coastal mountains, details of nautical supplies obtainable at foreign ports, and more observations for the length of a second pendulum so that a true Figure of the earth might finally be established."[8] What this means is that scientists had come to realize that the earth was not a true sphere. One way to measure the true shape was to measure minute variations in the force of gravity at different points over the earth's surface. The available way to measure that, in turn, was through making extraordinarily precise measurements of the motion of a pendulum at different points.

Captain Henry Foster was the obvious choice to head the expedition, and the little *Chanticleer,* with fifty-seven men and an armament of two guns, sailed in April for the South Atlantic. Foster was one of the most eminent of the young officers in the navy. He was extremely gifted in mathematics and had sailed as an astronomer with Parry's third voyage to the Northwest Passage (1824–25). During this expedition he had made such distinguished, scientific contributions that he was awarded the Copley Medal of the Royal Society.

The story of the "pendulum" expedition is set out in Webster's *Narrative of a Voyage to the Southern Atlantic Ocean in the Years 1828, 1829, and 1830, Performed in H. M. Sloop Chanticleer under the Command of the Late Captain Henry Foster F.R.S. etc.*[9] In their solo voyage of three years' duration they went from England down the east coast of South America to Cape Horn, then across to the Cape of Good Hope and back to northern South America, and back via the West Indies. All along they established their little laboratory stations where the pendulums were carefully set up and their motions minutely observed while, at the same time, general surveying was conducted and elaborate chronometric measurements were made. Tragically Foster died just before the last turn for home, in a canoe exploration in the Chagres River of Panama.

While the *Chanticleer* was at Cape Horn, she was provisioned by HMS *Adventure,* which was then acting as mothership to the *Beagle* in the latter's first surveying voyage (1826–30).* Because of the usual problems of capacity, "*Chanticleer*'s officers and men had been on short rations for some months and many luxuries were made available to them by Captain King and his men. Among these were tins of Donkin's Preserved Meats which have now found a secure place in vessels sailing from England for extended voyages." It enabled the *Chanticleer*'s crew "to have a joint of mutton cooked in London, to

---

* Captain John Harvey Boteler in his *Recollections* notes that he was also charged to meet up with the *Chanticleer* at Maranhão on the west coast of Brazil to deliver more instruments. He never did meet up with them, but the vessel in which he made the attempt was, of course, another 10-gun brig, the *Onyx.*[10]

eat fresh and good at Cape Horn, which is more than entered the minds of men formerly."[11]

Another of the 10-gun brigs to be involved in major surveying expeditions was HMS *Lyra*. The *Lyra,* like the *Chanticleer,* was one of the earliest 10-gun brigs, having been launched on August 22, 1808. She participated in the Battle of the Basque Roads (1809) and in actions in Spain (1812) and France (1813). In 1816 the British government decided to send an embassy to China as a first step toward developing possible diplomatic and mercantile ties between the two countries. In the end the venture was a failure and the ambassador, Lord Amherst, returned home. To make matters worse, on the way home the frigate *Alceste,* flagship of the little expedition, was totally wrecked although without any loss of life. The *Lyra* was the escort chosen to accompany the *Alceste,* and while the ambassador was negotiating in China the two ships were set to explore and survey the coast of Korea.[12]

The narratives of all these voyages, written for a general readership at home, are fascinating for the close attention that the officers paid to every aspect of geography, natural history, and the habits and customs of the people (Appendix D). This leads us to a final, very important matter: the quality of the officers in the surveying expeditions.

The British Navy over the years 1815 to 1830 had undergone a great reduction in both ships in commission and numbers of officers and men. The navy cannot have been a career that a young man would enter with great hopes of rapid advancement. Wars provide not only great adventure and a chance to show one's mettle but also fast promotion. In the dwindling peacetime navy of the 1820s and 1830s, the prospect for a young officer was only long delays between commissions and long delays between promotions. One's most likely command would be a small brig on routine coastal patrol or the monotony of the Packet Service. During this period a large number of officers were on half pay ashore. Some found positions with the Coast Guard Service, from which they were at least within easy reach for active duty should the call come.

The navy was in a great period of transition, as Lewis's book of that name has so clearly set out.[13] Yet despite the many problems, the navy continued to attract some extraordinarily able young men into its service. For these men some of the most exciting possibilities in naval service turned out to be the surveying and exploration work. To be on one of these voyages, to explore and chart the unknown, was a great prize and a great opportunity. They were remarkable men: well read and versatile in many skills. Luckily for us, many of them were most fluent in writing, and their books make easy and fascinating reading even now. Many of them were accomplished artists and have left us a pictorial record of the world they saw. The ships' surgeons often claimed places in the history of biology. Thomas Henry Huxley (surgeon of HMS *Rattlesnake*) was one. Benjamin Bynoe, surgeon of HMS *Beagle* for all three of her voyages, was another. But in fact, all officers were keen explorers of every part of the observable world. I was reminded vividly of this when doing research for this book at the National Maritime Museum. While I was going through the notebooks of John Lort Stokes (midshipman on the first voyage, mate and assistant surveyor on the second voyage, and subsequently commander of the *Beagle* for the latter part of the third voyage), the brilliantly colored skin of a bird fell out of the folds of one book, pressed like a flower between pages of detailed measurements. A special breed of men went to sea in these very undistinguished little ships.

In summary, while the 10-gun brigs may indeed have been ordinary little ships, they accumulated a record of extraordinary interest. The first ones entered the service in 1808 as simple brigs. Apart from the paddle vessel versions, the last 10-gun brigs to see active service were the *Griffon* and the *Rolla,* both of which were still in commission in 1847. The last brig to be sold out of the navy was the *Tyrian;* she survived until August 1892! Built in 1826, the second 10-gun brig to bear that name, she served as a packet brig, then as a quarantine hulk, and finally as a coast guard depot ship. For her last forty-five years she was not exactly in active service, but at least the hull survived for sixty-six years. Several of the regular 10-gun brigs served safely for twenty-five to thirty years. The greatest number of 10-gun brigs in the service at one time (including those in commission, on Packet Service, on coast guard harbor and other uses, and under repair) was sixty-nine, for the years 1831 and 1832. Not until 1860 did the total number fall below twenty.

The most famous of all the surveying brigs was the forty-first, HMS *Beagle* (1820–70).

FIVE

Rebuilding HMS Beagle

W HETHER THE LORDS OF THE ADMIRALTY WERE BEING
prudent or profligate in launching seven new 10-gun
brigs in 1820, we shall never know. However, after the *Beagle*
was launched at Woolwich Naval Dockyard on the Thames on
May 11, 1820, she was not immediately put into service.
Instead of being commissioned, she lay at Woolwich in ordinary (we might now say "in mothballs"). And there she stayed
for five full years. Even so, by a strange quirk of fate, even
before she was first commissioned, she achieved a minor place
in history—one small mark of fame. For the celebration of the
coronation of King George IV in July 1820 there was a splendid
review of naval vessels in the Thames. The spanking new *Beagle*
was fitted out for the parade, and in passing up the river, she
became the first man-of-war ever to pass fully rigged under the
(old) London Bridge. It is a minor distinction and certainly no
one would then have predicted that the name of this little ship
would eventually become a household word the world over.

Were it not for this episode of the coronation review, HMS
Beagle would never have sailed as a brig at all. When orders
for her first commission came in 1825, she was returned to the
dockyard to be rerigged as a bark and to have changes made

to her upper deck. All this was in preparation for work as a survey vessel.

To remind the reader, a brig has two masts and a bark three. On a brig both masts are square-rigged, and the mainmast also has a large fore-and-aft sail. On a bark the fore and mainmasts are square-rigged only; neither has a fore-and-aft sail. The mizzenmast, by contrast only carries a fore-and aft sail and no square sails. The mizzen driver was smaller than that on a brig as the boom was necessarily much shorter (Appendix A).

There has been a great deal of misunderstanding and misinformation about the structural transformations of the *Beagle*. Many authors have fallen into the quite understandable trap of assuming that everything important about the ship occurred in connection with the second (Darwin) voyage—by far her most famous.[1] It was not unreasonable to think that it might have been Fitzroy, the most innovative of her skippers, who would have ordered such changes. The errors were compounded by the fact that the *Beagle* was indeed rebuilt again before the start of the second voyage, under Fitzroy's eagle eye. But the records show quite clearly that the major features of her reconstruction were established prior to the first voyage.

Not only does the official *Narrative* of the first voyage state flatly that the *Beagle* was reconfigured as a bark for her first voyage, but there is ample independent firsthand corroboration. Just before he joined the *Beagle* as a midshipman, B. J. Sulivan was serving on HMS *Thetis*. In his autobiographical sketch he writes: "December 11, 1827, was the day on which I

10-gun brig converted to bark for the Packet Service, elevation; based on Admiralty drawings for HMS *Barracouta*.

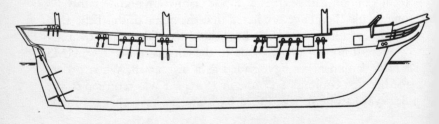

10-GUN BRIG, FITTED AS PACKET - ELEVATION

0   10   20   30 FT.

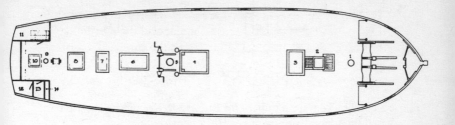

10-GUN BRIG, FITTED AS PACKET-MAIN DECK PLAN

0   10   20   30 FT.

1 FORE MAST	5 MAIN MAST	9 MIZZEN MAST	12 WATER CLOSET
2 GRATINGS & CHIMNEY	6 SKYLIGHT	10 SCUTTLE to BREAD	13 PACKAGES
3 FORE HATCH	7 LADDER WAY	11 COMPANION to	14 FLAG LOCKER
4 MAIN HATCH	8 SKYLIGHT	LADIES' CABIN	

10-gun brig converted to bark for Packet Service, main deck plan; based
on Admiralty drawingts of HMS *Barracouta*.

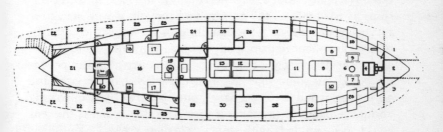

10-GUN BRIG, FITTED AS PACKET-LOWER DECK PLAN

0   10   20   30 FT.

1 CARPENTER'S STORE ROOM	8 SCUTTLE to COALS	16 MESS ROOM	25 STEWARD'S BERTH
2 GUNNER'S STORE ROOM	9 GALLEY	17 SCUTTLE to SPIRITS	26 SURGEON'S CABIN
3 BOS'N'S STORE ROOM	10 SCUTTLE to DRY PROVISIONS	18 SCUTTLE to HOLD	27 GUNNER'S CABIN
4 SCUTTLE to STORES	11 FORE HATCH	19 SCUTTLE to MAGAZINE	28 MESS TABLES
5 SCUTTLE to CARPENTER'S STORES	12 SAIL BIN	20 LADIES' WASH ROOM	29 CAPTAIN'S CABIN
6 FORE MAST	13 PURSER'S STORES	21 LADIES' CABIN	30 MASTER'S CABIN
7 SCUTTLE to BOS'N'S STORES	14 MAIN MAST	22 LADIES' BED SPACES	31 MATE'S CABIN
	15 SIDEBOARD AROUND MAIN MAST	23 PASSENGERS' BED SPACES	32 COOK'S CABIN
		24 TWO PASSENGERS' BED SPACES	

10-gun brig converted to bark for Packet Service, lower deck plan;
based on Admiralty drawings of HMS *Barracouta*.

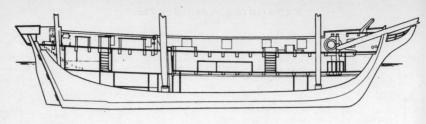

10-GUN BRIG, FITTED AS PACKET- SECTION

10-gun brig converted to bark for Packet Service, midships section; based on Admiralty drawings of HMS *Barracouta*.

first saw the *Beagle,* in which I served so long afterwards. I find that date in my log: exchanged numbers with H.M. Barque *Beagle:* 0.40 A.M., anchored near H.M.B. *Beagle.*"[2]*

The rerigging of the *Beagle* as a bark comes as no surprise in view of the previously noted alterations of the *Chanticleer,* the *Barracouta,* and many of the 18-gun brigs. Naval architects reported that brigs were found to sail much better by having the mizzenmast added: "It then became the fashion to rig our ships as barques . . . the government thought it was better for surveying purposes."[3] The handling of the brigs increased to barks was enhanced principally because of moving aft the leverage of the driver. They became more maneuverable and probably could sail somewhat closer to the wind. Not only did the 10-gun brigs sail better as barks, but Captain Owen in writing about the *Barracouta* makes it very clear that as barks the tens could be handled with much smaller crews.[4] This was extremely important when, as often happened, up to four separate parties of officers and men would be dispatched from the main ship in small boats to work in shallow inshore regions. A vessel that could be worked with a reduced crew was a great asset.

That the *Beagle* was rerigged as a bark in 1825 cannot be disputed. But the scope of a simple modification to bark rig

* *Thetis* at that time was with the fleet of Sir Robert Otway, commander of the South American station. Naturally enough, one of the *Beagle*'s sister ships was nearby in the form of an old friend: "On the 12th we sailed in company with HMS *Cadmus,* 10-gun brig, for a cruise off the coast of Patagonia."

10-gun brig converted to steam tug, HMS *African*, originally HMS *Dee*;
detail from a painting (probably after 1830), courtesy of the National
Maritime Museum.

should not be overestimated. After all, the *Barracouta* was
rerigged as a bark (after the start of her voyage with HMS
Leven) in about nine days, while in a foreign port, Lisbon. All
that was required was that the mainmast be reduced to square-
rigged, the main boom and driver being removed. Neither the
fore nor mainmast had to be moved or rebuilt. Simply, a small
mizzenmast was added, consisting only of a lower and top
mast, in order to carry a small driver (and, in most cases, a
mizzen gaff-topsail; see Appendix A).

Since I lacked the plans for the *Beagle,* to find the exact dimensions of the new mizzenmast and exactly where it was stepped, it was necessary to return to the National Maritime Museum and consult the files for the *Barracouta.* Sheet number 4052—"The Barracouta rigged as a bark"—shows just the information we want. The *Beagle* must have had the same, rather small mizzenmast.

The rebuilding of the *Beagle* was more thorough than that of the *Barracouta,* however, because during her refitting between September 25 and May 26 she had two other important features added: a large poop cabin and a forecastle.

In the design of navy ships of the period there was still an emphasis on flush decks. Therefore, while the bark rig was not uncommon in the survey service and was highly functional, the addition of a poop cabin and forecastle was more unusual. A flush deck gave a maximum clear area of deck for working the guns and handling the sails. For the survey service far fewer guns were carried on the main deck, however, and as the decks were rarely, if ever, "cleared for action," let alone devoted to serious combat, some of the arguments in favor of flush decks did not apply. There were, in addition, several major considerations that made the poop cabin and forecastle highly desirable.

The forecastle gave additional storage space for equipment and a place where the men could get out of the elements. Above all, the forecastle deflected large seas shipped over the bow. They would break first on the forecastle deck and then be turned off to the sides. This made the whole main deck much dryer and safer. In comparison, in the open flush-decked brig of the original design every wave that came crashing over the bows was dumped straight onto the main deck. How much of a break there was at the forecastle and poop is not clear from the information available; probably the forecastle deck was level with the rail. Without the poop deck being raised above the after bulwark, however, the poop cabin would only have had about fifty inches of headroom. Perhaps it was raised another foot.

The general lack of accommodation in a 10-gun brig showed up particularly in survey work because there was no large well-lit space for drafting, where notes could be worked up, sketches turned into finished charts, and so on. The captain had the largest cabin, but this was poorly suited to such use, even if a large skylight was to be let in for illumination. The addition of a poop cabin gave room in the *Beagle* for a large charting table to be fixed in place. It also provided accommodation for the extra surveying officers (or supernumeraries in the case of Darwin) carried on board. With a big skylight above, it was well lit and, for a ship of that size, extremely spacious, with room even for a decent library of books. Furthermore, the raised poop deck above was an excellent platform from which observations could be made, away from the work involved with running the ship.

The poop cabin sat directly over the steering gear, which on the *Beagle* was largely hidden by the huge drafting table set in the center of the cabin. Also, the mizzenmast, of course, stood straight up through the cabin. But all that extra space was still invaluable, and none of it was wasted. Despite the fancy of later reconstructions,[5] the original pair of stern gunports was not converted into windows for the poop cabin; the after bulkhead was too valuable as a place to put shelves and cabinets.

HMS *Beagle* as a bark, basic sail plan; see Appendix A.

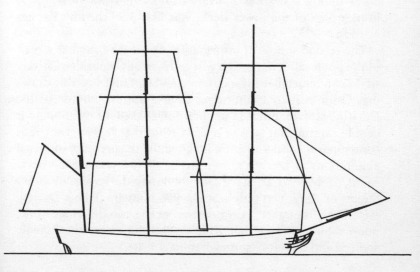

During the second surveying voyage, Charles Darwin had his quarters in the poop cabin. Basically that means he had a few drawers at his disposal and slung his hammock there. Because the poop cabin was so central to Darwin's life on board, we will leave any further discussion of its internal fittings until the chapter dealing with that voyage.

There are three major sources of information about the layout of the upper deck of the *Beagle* after she had been converted to the bark rig. All, unfortunately, derive from the second surveying voyage. The first source, which has usually been taken to be the most authoritative (perhaps because it appears so detailed), is a set of drawings made by Philip Gidley King, midshipman on the first and second voyages and the son of Philip Parker King, commander of the first. These drawings, however, are not truly contemporary. They were produced by King in 1890, more than fifty years after the fact, for John Murray's first illustrated edition of Darwin's *A Naturalist's Voyage around the World*.[6] Two of King's drawings, a side elevation of the *Beagle* and a plan of the main deck, were redrawn and published in that volume and have been extensively copied. Two others, a sketch of the quarterdeck as seen from midships and a plan of the poop cabin, were not published until 1933 (in Nora Barlow's *Charles Darwin's Diary of HMS Beagle*).[7] A fifth, a plan of the lower deck, was first published by Keynes in 1979.[8]

The second source of information about the *Beagle* is a plan of the poop cabin in the Darwin archives at Cambridge University. I can remember my excitement when I first saw this drawing. On a visit to Cambridge, Peter Gautrey, curator of the Darwin archives, put it in my hand and asked me if I thought it could confirm that it was a plan from the *Beagle*. That it is contemporary and authentic is shown by the presence of pencil annotations in Darwin's own hand.[9] It is a plan of the poop cabin, probably drafted for Darwin during the voyage by either Stokes or King (certainly not Darwin himself, as Lois Darling mistakenly thought)[10]. Comparison of the two drawings of the poop cabin confirms that King's 1890 drawings were heavily stylized and therefore somewhat inaccurate.

The third source of information is a contemporary drawing by Augustus Earle, the artist who accompanied the second voyage. This frequently republished drawing—*Crossing the Equator Aboard the Beagle*—was first published in the official *Narrative*[11] and gives a good view of the midship's section of the main deck. None of the other contemporary sketches or watercolors gives a view of the decks of the vessel.

Putting together these drawings and the plans of the other 10-gun brigs allows us to re-create a plan of the main deck, poop, quarterdeck, and forecastle. For example, from the plan in the Darwin archives we can see that the poop cabin was not located symmetrically across the stern. It was placed off center to the starboard side. Darwin's penciled annotations show that there was a short passageway down the port side, leading to lockers and a small cupboard that (as indicated by the plans of the *Cadmus* and the *Barracouta*) must have been the "water closet." Perhaps King omitted this through a sense of delicacy.

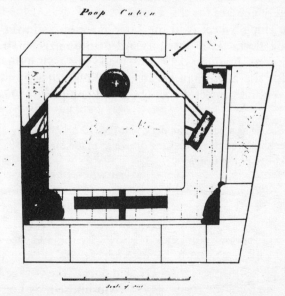

HMS *Beagle,* original drawing of the added poop cabin with pencil annotations in Darwin's handwriting; by permission of the Syndics of Cambridge University Library (DAR 44-16).

The new forecastle was presumably large enough to enclose the capstan, but we do not know exactly how big it was. When the *Beagle* was rebuilt for the second voyage, the forecastle extended almost to the foremast. This was probably the case in 1826. The fore and main hatches evidently remained in the standard position. King does not figure the smaller gratings and the galley chimney, but we can be confident in adding them to the plans. A major change to the upper deck, aft of the mainmast, was the addition of a large skylight for the gun room. We know this was in place for the second voyage, but we cannot be sure about the first. A similar skylight was added to the *Barracouta* when she was rebuilt for the Packet Service, however, so we may reasonably safely restore it. It must have made conditions for everyone below considerably more pleasant. For the same reasons we can assume that an additional skylight was provided for the captain's cabin. Such a skylight, just aft of a new "after companion" leading below to the lower deck, was definitely in place for the second voyage.

The ship's wheel is in the same position as in the *Cadmus* and the *Barracouta:* just forward of the mizzenmast. But the addition of the poop deck now made life a lot more comfortable for the helmsman because the break of the poop jutted out over and protected the wheel and compasses. Quarterdeck

HMS *Beagle* as a bark, main deck plan; based on Admiralty drawings of sister ships and the P. G. King drawings made for the 1890 edition of *The Voyage of the Beagle.*

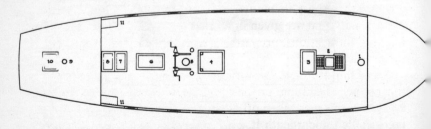

DARWIN'S BEAGLE-MAIN DECK PLAN

1 FORE MAST	4 MAIN HATCH	7 COMPANION	10 POOF CABIN SKYLIGH
2 GRATINGS & CHIMNEY	5 MAIN MAST	8 SKYLIGHT	11 POOP DECK
3 FORE HATCH	6 SKYLIGHT	9 MIZZEN MAST	COMPANIONS

companions on either side gave access to the poop deck. Under each companion was a tiny cabin for an officer, and under both starboard and port companions were signal flag lockers as well.

For the first surveying voyage, the *Beagle* carried six guns, according to Commander King's official *Narrative,* although we don't know what they were. There must have been at least one signal gun of small caliber, but was this one of the six? Probably the six were 6-pounder boat carronades with perhaps one or two 6-pounder long guns, enough for the *Beagle* to have given a good account of herself should there have been a threat of force against the expedition or the need to exert a policing action of any sort.

We also do not know the exact number of small boats carried by the *Beagle* for the first voyage, although we know there were several, including a largish broad-beamed cutter (carried on skids amidships) and two or three large boats (two at least had ten oars), from which work was carried out in shallow waters (the narratives mention a "gig," "cutter," "yawl," and a "whale-boat" at various points).

There are no records that allow us to restore in any detail the new arrangement of cabins and other spaces on the lower deck of the *Beagle* for the first voyage. Luckily we have much better information about her layout for the second voyage. Therefore, we will leave discussion of the lower deck and the hold until Chapter 6.

The *Beagle*'s first sail complement has been restored in the figures here both from contemporary sketches (second voyage) and those of her sister ships. However, strong cautions must be given with respect to many of the illustrations of the *Beagle* "in full sail" that are given in modern books. These are mostly fanciful illustrations prepared after the 1890s specially for those volumes.

According to the *Admiralty Progress Book,* the *Beagle* had the copper sheathing on her bottom replaced on March 4, 1825, but this was taken off again and an extra layer of planking installed underneath it, on September 25, 1825. The total cost of the fitting out of the *Beagle* for the first surveying voyage was £5,913.

Commissioned at Last

What were the *Beagle*'s voyages actually for? Too often readers become preoccupied with Charles Darwin and think that the prime purpose was natural history. Not so. *Beagle*'s first commission was intimately bound up with the changing history of South American politics.[12] The end of the Napoleonic Wars brought about somewhat of a power vacuum in South and Central America, with Spain separated from its former colonial possessions. The countries of South America were struggling for full independence, as Britain had discovered during a short-lived occupation of Buenos Aires in 1806–07. Not only were France, Britain, and the United States vying for influence in South America, but Britain was jockeying to establish a dominant position in European power and politics. Both missions depended on developing the British economy, particularly through exports, and in maintaining the dominant world naval presence.

Great Britain had never had a large trade with South American countries before, but they were potential sources of minerals and other raw materials and possible markets for the trade in manufactured goods upon which the expansion of British industry depended. While the United States was a growing rival for influence in South America, it had neither a comparable need for raw materials nor comparable naval power. The British government wanted particularly to control Portuguese industrialization of Brazil and to keep the French out of South America. The United States, with the Monroe Doctrine of 1823, asserted a dominant protective role for the Americas. George Canning, the British foreign secretary, was able to secure a prominent place in trade with South American nations by the adroit recognition of Argentina, Colombia, and Mexico in late 1824. As the United States lacked Britain's naval authority, a compromise understanding developed.

Ironically, although vast sums of British capital were quickly invested in South America, the bubble burst in 1826. The capacity of these countries to absorb manufactured goods was limited, and their mineral wealth had been greatly exaggerated. Be this as it may, the new era of British-South American relationships opened on the standard pattern. A naval presence was called for, to maintain freedom of the seas while packets and merchantmen began to move throughout South American waters.[13]

A major immediate problem was the lack of information on all aspects of navigation. The coastal waters of southern South America had been mapped, if at all, by the Spanish, French, and Portuguese, whose military charts were inaccurate, incomplete, and mostly unavailable. It was the task of the Hydrographic Office to fill the gaps. A major effort of basic surveying was called for. Not only was a total survey of the coasts, harbors, and navigable rivers of South America needed, but also special attention had to be paid to one of the most dreaded and difficult regions of the world: Cape Horn. Cook, among others, had established that the best route "west" from the South Atlantic to the Pacific was not to buck the westerly storms of the roaring forties directly but to go eastward with them, right around the southern end of the world. But the westward passage around Cape Horn or through the Strait of Magellan had to be charted. Around the cape there were important sealing and whaling grounds, and both British and American vessels were constantly in these waters. There was a particular need to look for safe alternate routes westward through the maze of waterways in Tierra del Fuego. At the same time, with the establishment of shore bases (on the Falkland Islands, for instance) came a flood of new political and practical problems for which naval presence was also needed, especially in view of the strong competition between the British and American vessels.

The work of naval surveying expeditions to South America, therefore, would be manifold. They would be carried out in unknown and downright risky waters: surveying and charting, finding safe harbors and convenient places for supply and watering, observing weather and current patterns. Accurate information was needed about the nature of the country inland, in terms of topography, natural history and agriculture, population, and resources (starting with water, fuel, and food for the ships). The surveying officers would also have to act as a police force as necessary and generally represent the British government and promote British interests. Theirs would, in many cases, be the all-important first contacts with local government officials.

The French had sent out a small mission under Baron Roussin in 1818, to survey the coast of Brazil and maintain a presence there.[14] The British took over the survey of Argentina, Patagonia, Tierra del Fuego, Chile, and Peru. Later the United States finally sent out its own first South American mission, the Wilkes expedition (1838–42), modeled in part on the second *Beagle* voyage.[15]

It is important that the difficulty and hardship of surveying work in such regions be emphasized. Too often the casual reader of nineteenth-century travel works comes away with the impression that voyages like those of the *Beagle* were romantic adventures in warm tropical seas. Instead they were hard and unglamorous, unremittingly devoted to capturing detailed information. These expeditions had well-defined practical jobs to do in what were known in advance to be appalling conditions in the high southern latitudes. The first expedition labored for five years and still did not complete the basic survey work around Tierra del Fuego. It had many tragic episodes, including the suicide of the *Beagle*'s captain. Its work was continued in the second expedition, in which Darwin took part, and that again led to the third and last expedition.

Orders

As the first volume of the official *Narrative* states, in September 1825 "the Lords Commissioners of the Admiralty directed two ships to be prepared for a survey of the southern coasts of South America; and in May, of the following year, the *Adventure* and the *Beagle* were lying in Plymouth Sound, ready to carry the orders of their Lordships into execution."[16] Captain Philip Parker King was appointed to lead the expedition from on board the *Adventure*. The captain of the *Beagle* was Commander Pringle Stokes.

Philip Parker King was an extremely experienced officer. He entered the service as a first class volunteer in 1807, serving on the frigate *Diana*. He saw action in the war, was promoted to midshipman in 1808 and to master's mate of the *Hibernia* (110 guns) in 1810. Thereafter he served on the *Centaur* (74), *Cumberland* (74), *Adamant* (50), *Caledonia* (120, Sir Edward Bellow's flagship) and then as lieutenant on the *Trident* (64) and *Elizabeth* (74) until July 1815. His next commission and his first command came in February 1817, when he was given charge of an expedition to survey the western and northern coasts of Australia. The expedition, with the brig *Bathurst* 10 and then the cutter *Mermaid*, both of which were purchased for the expedition at Port Jackson (Sydney), lasted from 1817 to 1821 and was a great success.[17] King was promoted to captain in 1821 and elected fellow of the Royal Society in 1824.

King was the son of Philip Gidley King, former governor of New South Wales and the father of another Philip Gidley King, who continued the chain by shipping as a midshipman on the *Beagle*'s second surveying cruise. After the first surveying voyage of HMS *Beagle*, Philip Parker King retired to New South Wales as manager of the Australian Agricultural Company and became a prominent figure in Australian government. He was active in the legislature and was promoted to rear admiral in 1855, one year before his death.

Of the career of Pringle Stokes, commander of the *Beagle*, we have less information. He had not previously been involved with survey work but had been preparing for it by studying mathematics in Edinburgh. He had served as a lieutenant on the *Owen Glendower* based at Chatham (1822–23) and was promoted to commander on December 26, 1823. The *Beagle* was his first command.

King and Stokes were appointed to their ships on September 7, 1825, and the work of fitting out the ships began. HMS *Adventure* had been launched as HMS *Aid* in 1809; she was a transport brig of 314 tons, 105 feet 6 inches long and 26 feet

10 inches beam, nominally carrying ten 12-pounder carron-ades. She went into survey service in March 1817, and her first work was in the Adriatic and then later in the Mediterranean under the command of W. H. ("Mediterranean") Smyth, one of the most distinguished surveyors in the naval service at the beginning of the nineteenth century.[18]

The *Aid* was renamed the *Adventure* in 1821. Although she was not much longer than the *Beagle,* she was an extremely roomy vessel and able to carry ample stores to make up for the lack of space in the *Beagle.* The *Beagle,* on the other hand, was smaller and marginally handier than the bulky and relatively more clumsy *Adventure.*

Of special internal fittings, equipment, or stores of the *Beagle* for the first surveying voyage, we have little direct information although we do know that the expedition was well supplied with the relatively new preserved meats, soups, and vegetables. These are the kinds of supplies that were transferred to the *Chanticleer* in 1829 (see page 53), and the name Donkin Cove, given to a remote region of Otway Water (discovered by Fitzroy in Tierra del Fuego), evidently stems from Donkin's brand of preserved meats.*

A gastronomic criticism of these preserved delicacies was given by W. H. Webster, surgeon of the *Chanticleer:* "The preserved mutton is excellent and makes an admirable pie; but the beef is insipid and over-boiled. The soups are capital and afforded us many an excellent meal; the sight moreover of fresh English meat on the table went far to cheer us amidst our gloomy solitude. There is decidedly too much fat mixed with the meat in general. . . ."[19]

From Webster we also get an idea of the contemporary medicine chest. Sulfate of quinine was available (eight to ten grains daily in a little port wine), and lime juice, for relief of scurvy. But the paucity of supplies of fresh food or the preserved food ("a small half-pint canister of soup was a man's allowance for two days") made sickness the rule rather than the exception for

---

* Kilner and Moorsom was the rival contemporary brand. The British equivalent of Ball jar for home canning to this day is the Kilner jar. But we have no record of a Mount Kilner or a Moorsom Gulf to honor that innovative company.

vessels working for long periods in the high southern latitudes. The *Beagle* and *Adventure* were obviously better supplied than the *Chanticleer,* but even so, widespread sickness nearly brought the expedition to disaster. Ironically, while the *Adventure* supplied the *Chanticleer* with the provisions she needed, scurvy had already broken out on the *Adventure.*

Of scientific equipment carried by the expedition, the most important was the chronometers. Chronometric measurements were to be a major element in their survey work because so much depended upon accurate fixing of longitude. Latitude could be fixed by celestial observation alone, but accurate fixing of longitude requires timekeeping—not just approximate but accurate to better than a second.

On May 16, 1826, the expedition received its first instructions:

> By the Commissioners for executing the Office of Lord High Admiral of the United Kingdom of Great Britain and Ireland, &c.[20]
>
> Whereas we think fit that an accurate Survey should be made of the Southern Coasts of the Peninsula of South America, from the southern entrance of the Rio de la Plata, round to Chiloe; and of Tierra del Fuego; and whereas we have been induced to repose confidence in you, from your conduct of the Surveys in New Holland; we have placed you in command of His Majesty's Surveying Vessel the *Adventure;* and we have directed Captain Stokes, of His Majesty's Surveying Vessel the *Beagle,* to follow your orders.
>
> Both these vessels are provided with all the means which are necessary for the complete execution of the object above-mentioned, and for the health and comfort of their Ships' Companies. You are also furnished with all the information, we at present possess, of the ports which you are to survey; and nine Government Chronometers have been embarked in the *Adventure,* and three in the *Beagle,* for the better determination of the Longitudes.
>
> You are therefore hereby required and directed, as soon as both vessels shall be in all respects ready, to put to sea with them; and on your way to your ulterior destination, you are

to make, or call at, the following places, successively; namely; Madeira: Teneriffe: the northern point of St. Antonio, and the anchorage at St. Jago; both in the Cape Verde Islands: the Island of Trinidad, in the Southern Atlantic: and Rio de Janeiro: for the purpose of ascertaining the differences of the longitudes of those several places.

At Rio de Janeiro, you will receive any supplies you may require; and make with the Commander-in-chief, on that Station, such arrangements as may tend to facilitate your receiving further supplies, in the course of your Expedition.

After which, you are to proceed to the entrance of the Rio de la Plata, to ascertain the longitudes of the Cape Santa Maria, and Monte Video: you are then to proceed to survey the Coasts, Islands, and Straits; from Cape St. Antonio, at the south side of the Rio de la Plata, to Chiloe; on the west coast of America; in such manner and order, as the state of the season, the information you may have received, or other circumstances, may induce you to adopt.

You are to continue on this service until it shall be completed; taking every opportunity to communicate to our Secretary, and the Commander-in-Chief, your proceedings: and also, whenever you may be able to form any judgment of it, where the Commander-in-Chief, or our Secretary may be able to communicate with you.

In addition to any arrangements made with the Admiral, for recruiting your stores and provisions; you are, of course, at liberty to take all other means which may be within your reach for that essential purpose.

You are to avail yourself of every opportunity of collecting and preserving Specimens of such objects of Natural History as may be new, rare, or interesting; and you are to instruct Captain Stokes, and all the other Officers, to use their best diligence in increasing the Collections in each ship: the whole of which must be understood to belong to the Public.

In the event of any irreparable accident happening to either of the two vessels, you are to cause the officers and crew of the disabled vessel to be removed into the other, and with her, singly, to proceed in prosecution of the service, or return to England, according as circumstances shall appear to require;

understanding that the officers and crews of both vessels are hereby authorized, and required, to continue to perform their duties, according to their respective ranks and stations, on board either vessel to which they may be so removed. Should, unfortunately, your own vessel be the one disabled, you are in that case to take the command of the *Beagle:* and, in the event of any fatal accident happening to yourself; Captain Stokes is hereby authorized to take the command of the Expedition; either on board the *Adventure,* or *Beagle,* as he may prefer; placing the officer of the Expedition who may then be next in seniority to him, in command of the second vessel: also, in the event of your inability, by sickness or otherwise, at any period of this service, to continue to carry the Instructions into execution, you are to transfer them to Captain Stokes, or to the surviving officer then next in command to you, who is hereby required to execute them, in the best manner he can, for the attainment of the object in view.

When you shall have completed the service, or shall, from any cause, be induced to give it up; you will return to Spithead with all convenient expedition; and report your arrival, and proceedings, to our Secretary, for our information.

Whilst on the South American Station, you are to consider yourself under the command of the Admiral of that Station; to whom we have expressed our desire that he should not interfere with these orders, except under peculiar necessity.

Given under our hands the 16th of May 1826

(Signed)   Melville.

G. Cockburn.

To Philip P. King, Esq., Commander
of His Majesty's Surveying Vessel
Adventure, at Plymouth.

By command of their Lordships.

(Signed) J. W. Croker.

Ninety or more souls and most of the gear and stores were shoehorned into the lower deck of HMS *Beagle*. Serving under Commander Pringle Stokes in the *Beagle* as she left England were:

E. Hawes	Lieutenant
W. G. Skyring	Lieutenant and Assistant Surveyor
S. S. Flinn	Master
E. Bowen	Surgeon
J. Atrill	Purser
B. Bynoe	Assistant Surgeon
J. L. Stokes	Midshipman
R. F. Lunie	Volunteer First Class
W. Jones	Volunteer Second Class
J. Macdougall	Clerk
J. May	Carpenter

Also serving were a sergeant and nine marines and forty men and boys. Many changes occurred in this list through the voyage and of those named above only John Lort Stokes (no relation to Pringle Stokes), Surgeon Bynoe, and Mr. May returned with the *Beagle* in 1830, the others having invalided out during the voyage, except for the captain, whose demise will be noted in due course.

SIX

The First Surveying Voyage

PORT FAMINE, PORT DESIRE, SOUTH DESOLATION, HARBOUR of Mercy: Was it with faint hearts or eager anticipation that HMS *Adventure* and HMS *Beagle* sailed south from Plymouth on May 22, 1826? The heavily laden ships with their new officers and crews headed cautiously out into the Atlantic, testing their capabilities and their weaknesses. The success of the expedition, to say nothing of their very lives, would depend on how well they could learn to work together. Soon seamanship and knowledge of the handling of their vessels would be all that would stand between King or Pringle Stokes and the famous gales of the southern end of the world.

The awkward motion of the *Beagle*—her "deep, quick rolling"—soon made itself felt. With the vessel loaded deeply with stores, the decks were constantly awash as the *Beagle* rolled both gunwales under, shipping large seas from both sides as the two ships plowed across the Bay of Biscay and out into the green waters of the North Atlantic. Once they entered the warmer waters of the Gulf Stream, their pristine white sails soon became stained with huge patches of mildew. The "new" six-year-old *Beagle* was finally at sea.

The expedition called at Madeira, Tenerife, and St. Jago and then made repairs and adjustments and took on supplies at Rio de Janeiro. On October 2 they left for the Río de la Plata, where they stayed for a month. Nominally they were surveying the north side of the river between Cape St. Mary and Montevideo. In fact, it was a technical shakedown: practicing with their instruments and getting the men familiar with small-boat work, setting up the routine of surveying that they would apply all the way around Cape Horn. They left Montevideo on November 19, 1826, more or less ready to start work in earnest. According to their instructions, they were supposed to work their way steadily south from Cape San Antonio (the southerly limit of the La Plata estuary), but instead King headed straight for the southern coast of Patagonia and Tierra del Fuego. King said that he wanted to get the bad weather over as early as possible. Plunging in at the deep end, little did any of them realize how difficult it would be.

Fighting their way down through hard gales, they landed at Porta Santa Elena on November 28. Here they found an American whaling ship wrecked onshore. They set up a small observatory and spent some time investigating the natural history of the region, finding, for instance, oyster shells where no living oysters occurred. Perhaps their most useful observation was to shoot the wild guanaco, a relative of the llama, which was to provide them with welcome meat at all stages of the voyage. Bad weather prevented them even from going onshore at the appointed time for a planned observation of an eclipse of the sun.

The anchorage at Porta Santa Elena was quite exposed, but it was at least a harbor. The weather was already a focal point of their every activity, and they all were nervous about what they would encounter farther south and in the Strait of Magellan. It was already clear that the *Beagle* was the handier of the two vessels, even in really rough weather. Although she rolled and corkscrewed violently, she could be kept a little closer to the wind.

And so, already battered and demoralized by the weather, they arrived at the entrance to the strait. Even the map of the area looks forbidding. The eastern end of the strait is marked by two major hazards: the First Narrows and the Second Nar-

HMS *Beagle* in 1834, beached for repairs at the mouth of the Santa Cruz River, engraved from a drawing by Conrad Martens; see note 169.

rows, in parts less than a mile wide. Between them there is a safe anchorage at Gregory Bay, and beyond the Second Narrows there are further anchorages at Freshwater Bay and Port Famine.

The Strait of Magellan

At the First Narrows they encountered tides of thirty feet and an opposing tidal stream of six knots, together with westerly gales blowing straight into their teeth. It is a difficult place to work a square-rigged vessel, and the *Adventure* and the *Beagle* battled away for about a week, first gaining ground and then being forced back until, by using the flow of the tide to battle against the winds, they managed to get the *Adventure* through. The *Beagle* followed the next day, and they met again at a quiet anchorage under Mount Gregory. Both crews were exhausted, and already the *Beagle* was running into trouble with provisions. She had only two days' water left. She reprovisioned from the *Adventure* and also got fresh supplies of meat from the Patagonian Indians on the north shore of the strait.

The north shore between the two narrows, despite the fact that it was and is one of the most desolate and lonely places in the world, was an essential port of call for any ship working in the strait. The many sealing vessels of British and American origin that sailed in those waters often put in at Gregory Bay, and the local Indians had established a freewheeling trading exchange there.*

The local Indians traded guanaco meat and other indigenous supplies to the whalers and sealers in return for such trade goods as tobacco and, of course, liquor. They were a colorful, if unattractive, group led by a large, ebullient lady named Maria who could speak a little Spanish and knew both how to strike a bargain and how to cadge a drink. The sealers called these Patagonian Indians horse Indians to distinguish them from the canoe Indians from the southern shore of the strait— Tierra del Fuego itself. The two groups had virtually nothing in common. The Patagonians were skilled horsemen and hunted the guanaco with the bola. They had relatively few tools but belonged at least to the seventeenth century, if not the eighteenth. The Fuegians, on the other hand, were essentially still in the Stone Age.

Maria and the Patagonian Indians seemed to take a particular liking to King and his group, probably because they were less stingy with their trading than the sealers. The expedition must have puzzled the Indians; instead of catching seals, the men spent a lot of time climbing hills, looking through strange instruments, and writing numbers in books.

The *Adventure* left Gregory Bay with a pilot borrowed from a sealing schooner but still had a great deal of trouble getting through the Second Narrows. The *Beagle,* "by her better sail-

---

* As these sealers were all schooner-rigged (with fore-and-aft rather than square sails) they could work more easily in the strait and the storm-battered waters around Tierra del Fuego than the British naval ships. Throughout the narratives of these voyages we find reference to these schooners—many from Stonington, Connecticut. They passed freely where the *Adventure* and *Beagle* could not.

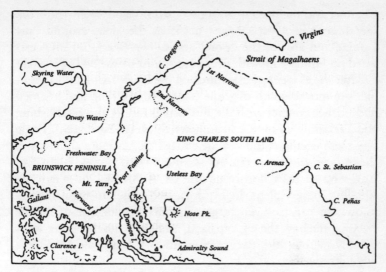

Northeast Tierra del Fuego and the entrance to the Straits of Magalhaens, as mapped by King in 1831; original spelling.

ing," got through ahead of her, and they eventually met up at Freshwater Bay (opposite Cape Monmouth) where they were to have their first contact with the canoe Indians from the islands of Tierra del Fuego.

They put into Port Famine (named for the demise of a party of Spanish settlers landed by Pedro Sarmiento, who attempted to establish a colony here in 1583) after a following gale and took the opportunity to reprovision the *Beagle* again and partially to refit her. King decided that the *Adventure* would stay in Port Famine for a period, but the *Beagle* was prepared for a hazardous voyage west to explore the distant parts of the strait. The reason for the separation is clear. It was not efficient to send both ships to the same location, and the *Beagle* was marginally easier to work in these close and dangerous waters than the unwieldy *Adventure*. Moreover, here at Port Famine was a place where King could unship the small deck boat *Hope* to explore the smaller channels in the vicinity.

The *Hope* was thus sent off to explore the St. Sebastian

Channel and the deep opening to east of Cape Valentyn. From the *Adventure* a survey was made of the areas around Port Famine and also of the "port" itself. The *Beagle* set off westward on January 15 with orders to return by the end of March.

After the *Adventure* had finished the work around Port Famine, she moved south of Cape Isidro, where King and his men had further contact with the Fuegians, trading and establishing good relations despite a little petty thievery. But here in Eagle Bay the mishaps of the voyage started. A gig and a cutter from the *Adventure* were sent across the bay to survey Porto San Antonio, an area notorious for its williwaws, or hurricane squalls. These violent, highly localized wind storms had been known to capsize even large schooners in an instant. While crossing the bay, the gig capsized, and although the cutter went quickly to their aid, two seamen and Midshipman Ainsworth were drowned.

By April 6, with no word from the *Beagle,* King began to worry. But return she did, with a tale of considerable adventure and hardship.

Immediately upon leaving the safety of Port Famine, Stokes and his men in the *Beagle* had begun a constant battle against the weather. In rounding Cape Foreward, beating continuously against the prevailing westerly gales, they tacked thirty-one times in sixteen hours. Reaching Cape Upright, they could find no anchorage and had to keep under way all night—an exhausting procedure for both officers and men, already tired and weak from poor rations. The next day they sheltered under Cape Tamar, but when they tried to go farther, the weather forced Stokes once more to turn back, giving orders to "bear up for shelter under Cape Tamar where the previous night had been passed."

Even this was a dangerous attempt; they could "hardly discern any part of the high land and when before the wind, could not avoid the ship's going too fast. While running about eight knots, a violent shock—a lift forward—heel over—and downward plunge—electrified everyone; but before they could look around, she was scudding along, as before, having fairly leaped over the rock." The collision caused a great part of her forefoot and false keel to be knocked off, as was later discovered when the *Beagle* returned to Montevideo.

After this narrow escape the men spent another full day trying to work westward but at nightfall had to return again to the same anchorage. So Stokes decided to leave the *Beagle* at Port Tamar for a while under the command of Skyring, charging him with surveying the bay from small boats. Stokes meanwhile set off in the cutter with a week's provisions and a small crew to examine the south coast. By keeping well inshore, they could at least do some work from this boat. But there was still the weather to be faced, and seven days of work in an open boat must have been hard going.

Having completed this venture, the *Beagle* and her crew again tried to work their way westward, and after being turned back once more, they eventually managed to struggle as far as the Harbour of Mercy (one can begin to see the reasons for the names of these desolate places). Here they made some contacts with the Fuegian Indians and began what can only be described as the most difficult of all their tasks: the survey of the western opening of the Strait of Magellan.

Stokes in his journal records the conditions: "The number and contiguity of the rocks, below as well as above the water, render it a most hazardous place for any square-rigged vessel; nothing but the particular duty on which I was ordered would have induced me to venture among them." It was clear that a schooner rig would be necessary to get any real work done here.

On the return trip Stokes's party spotted a small boat which at first they thought must have belonged to the Indians. But it turned out to be a ship's boat manned by men from an English sealing schooner called the *Prince of Saxe Cobourg* that had wrecked in Fury Harbour about two hundred miles south, at the entrance to the Cockburn Channel. The crew got onshore and even managed to salvage some of the skins, while sending out a series of small boats to look for help. Stokes immediately moved the *Beagle* to Port Gallant and from there sent out two ten-oared boats for the long haul of eighty miles through the Barbara Channel to Fury Harbour. Interestingly, some of the rescued men enlisted on the *Beagle,* and Bo's'n Sorrel from the *Saxe Cobourg* continued to serve as bo's'n in *Beagle*'s subsequent voyages.*

As soon as the *Beagle* met up with the *Adventure,* the two ships made their way back to Montevideo. They had little trouble making the easterly passage and shot through the Second Narrows with the wind and tide behind them. In Gregory Bay they found the Patagonian Indians riding with them along the shore and stopped to trade for meat. King, like others before and after him, carefully curried favor with these people, and this friendship (if that is the right word) was to be invaluable not only in the rest of this voyage but in the second voyage as well; the supply of fresh meat was essential.

They arrived back at Montevideo on April 24, 1827, and passed on to Rio de Janeiro for stores and to prepare for another assault upon the strait. However, King had realized that it was necessary to have a smaller vessel in order to expedite the surveying work, and he wrote to the Admiralty for permission to buy one. He had to wait for a reply, and this necessarily took a long time. The September packet arrived, and then October's, but without word. Although they had pinned their hopes on getting a small schooner, further delay was out of the question. The ships had been refitted and resupplied. The surveying officers had caught up with their paper work. So, leaving the *Beagle* to wait for the November mails, King set off down the coast to Santos for some barometric and chronometric measurements. When they returned, the permission from the Admiralty had finally arrived, and the expedition immediately set off for Montevideo, where by prearrangement they bought the schooner *Adelaide.* King put Lieutenant Graves in command of her, and she was stocked with five months' provisions. The three vessels then sailed south again on December 23.

---

* The master of the *Prince of Saxe Coburg* was Matthew Brisbane, and she was owned by James Weddell, British naval officer and polar explorer. In the years 1819 to 1824 Weddell had explored (and sealed) all through the southern ocean. His 1822–24 voyage in the brig *Jane* and the sixty-five-ton cutter *Beaufoy* (the latter under the command of Brisbane) was written up in 1827 as *A Voyage towards the South Pole* (see also p. 184).[1] Brisbane made a second sealing voyage in the *Beaufoy* in 1824–26, remaining in the region until his death in the Falkland Islands in 1834.

South Again

The *Adventure* and *Adelaide* set sail directly for the Strait of Magellan, while the *Beagle* was sent to Port Desire to make chronometric measurements. Again the *Adventure* had difficulty getting through the First Narrows, and the *Adelaide* lost her anchor, but eventually they were back in Gregory Bay with Maria and the Patagonian Indians. Once at Port Famine, the *Adventure* was unrigged and battened down for the long Tierra del Fuego winter while the *Adelaide* was prepared to take over the work.

Meanwhile, King was again worrying about the *Beagle*, now a whole month overdue. She finally turned up, and as a matter of fact, instead of simply making chronometric observations, Stokes had examined the whole coast from Port Desire to Cape Virgins. He had been held up a little at the Gallegos River, at the mouth of which (where the tides ran forty-five feet) he found the brig *Adaeona* (owned by a Mr. William Low) aground. In going over to assist her getting off, the *Beagle* touched bottom, but neither vessel was injured. While they were surveying Port San Julían, Lieutenant Scholl had died.

On March 1 King was surprised to see three men onshore; they turned out to be deserters from Low's seal-oil schooner *Uxbridge* who were coming to volunteer. Soon both the *Uxbridge* and *Adaeona* arrived, but Low generously allowed King to keep the three deserters and also another man. Low then left, only to return a short while later in a whaleboat to request assistance in repairing the rudder of the *Uxbridge*. King was happy to oblige.

The *Adventure, Adelaide,* and *Beagle* now remained together at Port Famine, setting up a base for the winter and settling down to the surveying work. There was still a major question to be solved concerning the San Sebastián Channel, which was thought to open up the Strait of Magellan from Cape Monmouth due eastward. If this were the case, it would be an extremely useful alternative to the usual entrance to the strait. It had been recorded by most of the early voyagers, but no one had properly explored it. King in the *Adelaide* proposed to do just that. Meanwhile, the *Beagle* was given her own task: to survey the western coast of South America between the strait and forty-seven degrees south.

This simple-sounding instruction meant that the *Beagle* had to make the passage westward again, right through the strait, and then to survey from the point at which she had previously left off—the dangerous westerly end of the strait—northward. Stokes had strict orders to return by July 24.

One can only wonder at the decision being made to send the *Beagle* all the way west again, and north to boot, all in four short months. The officers had already seen how difficult it was to work the *Beagle* against the westerly gales. Stokes and King seemed to have agreed that a fore-and-aft–rigged vessel was essential for coastal work in these regions. King himself was proposing to work from such a vessel, the *Adelaide*. But his instructions had to be obeyed, and on March 18, 1828, the *Beagle* set off westward once again.

After the *Beagle* had gone, King set about his survey of the region of Cape Monmouth and traced eastward until he discovered that the so-called San Sebastián Channel was nothing but a large blind bay with no opening to the ocean. The bay was named Useless Bay, following the spirit in which local place-names seem to have been bequeathed. Having done this, which took very little time, King worked the *Adelaide* to the west, surveying Port San Antonio, Port Gallant, Cape Holland, Woods Bay, and Point Tinguichisoquia. Again he and his party encountered really bad weather. The winter was setting in with strong winds and penetrating rain, sleet, and snow. All along they had frequent contacts with the Fuegian Indians and had constantly to be on the lookout against pilfering and even half-hearted attacks.

On April 30 King's party explored around Cayetano Island, but they returned on May 21, having had their whaleboat stolen. Mr. Low (who, with other sealers, was based nearby at Bougainville Harbour) could not lend them one, having lost his own spare boats in the same way. So they set out to make one. Meanwhile, the weather continued to be atrocious, and more ominously, scurvy set in. Three men died, and the growing air of despondency was increased when Low's body was brought in for burial (the cause of death is not given). King decided to raise the flagging spirits of the expedition by announcing that as soon as the *Beagle* returned, they all would head back to Montevideo.

This cheered the crew for a while, but at the beginning of June the sealers *Uxbridge, Adaeona,* and *Mercury* departed for England, leaving the *Adventure* and *Adelaide* very much alone. No fresh food could be gathered, and the Fuegian Indians were becoming distinctly more hostile. The number of scurvy victims, despite all the attentions of surgeons Tarn and Park, had risen to fourteen, so the *Adelaide* was sent off for fresh meat from Gregory Bay. On the twenty-fifth, taking a gamble, King gave the order "Prepare ships for sea," and the general enthusiasm turned to positive rejoicing when the *Beagle* was sighted on the twenty-seventh. But as soon as she came to anchor, the *Adventure* received word that Captain Stokes was seriously ill.

"The Soul of Man Dies in Him"

King wrote:

I . . . found Captain Stokes looking very ill, and in low spirits. He expressed himself much distressed by the hardships the officers and crew under him had suffered; and I was alarmed at the desponding tone of his conversation. He told me that the *Beagle* had been up the western coast as high as Cape Tres Montes, in latitude 47 south, had surveyed the Gulf of Peñas and other portions of the coast.

During the survey of the Gulf of Peñas, they had experienced very severe weather, both stormy and wet, during which the *Beagle*'s crew were incessantly employed, and had consequently suffered greatly. Captain Stokes appeared not to have spared himself. He appeared much gratified by my visiting him, and before we parted he was, for a time, restored to his more usual energy, detailing the circumstances of the voyage, and conversing upon the plan of our future operation with considerable animation.[2]

Three days later the *Adelaide* returned with a supply of fresh meat that helped relieve some of the immediate discomfort of *Beagle*'s crew. But strangely, Captain Stokes now was reluctant to return to Montevideo. He wanted to keep working toward the Pacific to reprovision at Chile or Valparaiso, "willing to renew the survey; which however, he himself seemed to dread, for he never mentioned the subject without a shudder. He was evidently much excited and suspicions arose in my mind that all was not quite right with him."[3]

The next day (the thirty-first) Stokes requisitioned provisions for his ship, but his officers, knowing "the diseased state of his mind," asked King to ignore him. Surgeon Bynoe of the *Beagle* was sent to talk to Surgeon Tarn about the situation. The next day "the surgeons were on board the *Adventure*, considering upon their report, which was, as I afterwards found, very unfavorable, when a boat came from the *Beagle*, with the dreadful intelligence that Captain Stokes in a momentary fit of despondency, had shot himself."

He lingered in a raging delirium for four days, during which time he went over the harrowing voyage detail by detail. Then he was better for three days. But he became worse again and in intense pain. He finally died on the morning of August 12 and was buried at Port Famine, in the small burial ground which had been set up for all those who had succumbed in that remote, godforsaken spot.

The official narrative assembled by King from Stokes's papers detailed the problems that Stokes and his men had encountered in their five months' absence to the west.[4] Each day "we resumed our daily struggle against the wind." They had rounded Cape Pillar and reached the Evangelists or Isles of Direction, then the Beagle Islands and on to Cape Santa Lucía, keeping well out to sea between capes Isabelle and Santa Lucía to avoid submerged rocks on which breakers could clearly be seen. Then, with good southerly winds, they pressed on to the island of Madre de Dios and examined the Trinidad Gulf.

On March 17 they reached the Cape of Tres Puntas and went on to Cape William, where they found an excellent harbor that they named Port Henry, and they stayed here for three days to survey. It was a dreary, misty landscape, and already Stokes was obviously overwhelmed by his responsibilities. Pushing on again, they ran into a stiff gale, which continued for four days "from the north, northwest and southwest with a confused mountainous sea. Our decks were constantly flooded . . . the little boat which we carried astern was washed away. . . ."

The winter weather had hit them earlier and harder than they had anticipated. When they tried to move again, they found themselves carried all the way north to Campana Island. The next day there was another gale, but this subsided quickly, allowing them to make land near Parallel Peak, "but could not close it." This continued on and off for two weeks. "The effect of this wet miserable weather, of which we have had so much since leaving Port Famine, was too manifest by the state of the sick list, on which were now many patients with catarrhal, pulmonary, and rheumatic complaints." One can just imagine the conditions on board the tiny ship with virtually no way of drying clothes; men constantly wet and, because of the awful weather, always up on deck working the sails, led by a captain sunken in despair.

They proceeded up the Gulf of Peñas and then surveyed the harbor of Santa Barbara, where they found a large oak beam, the only remains of HMS *Wager* of Lord Anson's squadron, wrecked there in 1741. "Nothing could be worse than the weather we have had during nine days' stay here. . . ." They put out toward the Cape Tres Montes and landed there, finding a nice harbor, which they called Port Otway after Sir Robert Otway, then commander in chief of the South American station.

All this time, despite the weather, they had doggedly kept up the survey, both from the *Beagle* herself and from her small boats; there could be no thought of neglecting or giving up the work. But at Port Otway the weather became so bad that the *Beagle* had to stop, and this gave Stokes's men some rest. Yet more storms came, and an ominous gap appears in Stokes's journal. Then, on May 9, he wrote that the *Beagle* moved to a new anchorage where there was ample water and fuel. But this new landfall was no bargain either: "[T]he shore on which we now stood was that of a horrid rock bound coast, lashed by the awful surf of a boundless ocean, impelled by almost unceasing west winds."

As they then slowly continued north into the Gulf of Estevan, they were delayed by more foul weather and now a new problem—ice. The crews working from the open boats were issued painted canvas to make waterproof trousers, but obviously little could be done to stave off the weather.

Stokes wrote again:

Nothing could be more dreary than the scene around us. The lofty, bleak and barren heights that surround the inhospitable shore of this inlet, were covered, even low down their sides, with dense clouds, upon which the fierce squalls that assailed us beat, without causing any change; they seemed as immovable as the mountains where they rested. . . . Around us, and some of them distant no more than two-thirds of a cable's length, were rocky islets, lashed by a tremendous surf; and, as if to complete the dreariness and utter desolation of the scene, even birds seemed to shun its neighborhood. The weather was that in which (as Thomson emphatically says) "the soul of man dies in him."[5]

In the course of our service since we left England, we have often been compelled to take up anchorage, exposed to great risk and danger. But the *Beagle*'s present situation I deemed by far the most perilous to which we had been exposed: her three anchors were down in twenty-three fathoms of water, on a bad bottom of sand, with patches of rocks. The squalls were terrifically violent, and astern of her, distant only half a cable's length, were rocks and low rocky islets, upon which a furious surf raged.

On leaving this place (June 10, 1828) the yawl was lost, smashed against the side of the *Beagle* as the men were trying to take her on board.

They tried to clear the Guaianeco Islands, but the storm drove them back, and considering the state of the vessel and the fact that their gigs and cutter were almost entirely useless (they had lost the yawl), they put back to Port Otway again for repairs. On June 15 the sick list was so bad that Surgeon Bynoe advised Stokes that the general situation was now critical. Stokes then curtailed any nonessential activity on board so that the men could gather shellfish, which helped in controlling the scurvy. The ship lay idle, her battered crew and officers recovering their strength and will.

On June 29 they were sufficiently recovered to head back to rendezvous with King, but Stokes shut himself in his cabin and began totally to neglect his duties. On the long way back to Port Famine, he insisted on stopping unnecessarily, even though they were desperately short of supplies. "At last, want of provisions obliged him to hasten to Port Famine; and the day on which he arrived every particle of food was expended."

After Stokes's burial at Port Famine, no one would stay a moment longer at the Strait of Magellan. Lieutenant Skyring was put in command of the *Beagle,* and on August 16 the three ships with their weary and ailing crews set off, in yet more gales, for Montevideo.

On the way back they stopped for more fresh meat. But even so, the men were not in good condition, and a man from the *Beagle* fell overboard one night and was drowned. Finally, as they entered the Río de la Plata, they fell foul of a Brazilian squadron that was blockading the port during a Brazilian-Argentine war. Their passage was impeded for a while, but they anchored the next day at Montevideo, where it turned out that all provisions were also in short supply. Luckily, however, a Senor Juanico supplied enough oranges finally to cure all the scurvy in the two crews.*

On October 13 King sailed for Rio de Janeiro to collect stores sent out from England and for the *Adventure* to be caulked and

---

* It was here also that they fell in with the *Beagle*'s sister ship HMS *Chanticleer* (Captain Henry Foster), then engaged in her pendulum voyage (Chapter 4).

refitted, while the *Beagle* remained in Montevideo. At Rio de Janeiro Sir Robert Otway arrived in his flagship, the *Ganges* (a second rate of eighty-four guns). King made his report to him, and Otway made some decisions.

First he appointed a new commander for the *Beagle:* his flag officer from the *Ganges*—Lieutenant Robert Fitzroy, whose name became as inseparably linked with the *Beagle* as Darwin's. It was certainly a little unfair that Lieutenant Skyring, who had been recommended for the command by King, was superseded. He had been Stokes's second-in-command during some extraordinarily difficult times and had surely earned the job. As King wrote, "Captain Fitzroy was considered qualified to command the *Beagle;* although I could not but feel much for the bitterness of Lieutenant Skyring's disappointment, I had no other cause for dissatisfaction."[6]

Kempe, mate of the *Beagle,* was promoted to lieutenant, and Mr. Matthew Murray, second master of the *Ganges,* was made master. Sir Robert also ordered the *Beagle* hove down so that her bottom could be examined and any necessary repairs made.

Fitzroy had transferred to the *Ganges* only four months previously, having previously served in the *Thetis* (fifth rate, forty-six guns), also on the South American station, where he had been close friends with Midshipman B. J. Sulivan. Sulivan later wrote that when the *Thetis* put into Rio, the first thing Fitzroy did "was to ask Captain Bingham [of the *Thetis*] whether he had any objection to transfer me to the *Beagle,* of course with the Admiral's consent, and in a very few days I joined her. I see by my log that I joined the *Beagle* on December 15th, 1828. . . ."[7] Thus began the long association of Fitzroy and Sulivan with the *Beagle.*

SEVEN

Fitzroy and the Beagle

ROBERT FITZROY WAS TWENTY-THREE YEARS OLD WHEN HE took command of the *Beagle*. Slender, elegant, and aristocratic, he was descended from the duke of Grafton, the illegitimate son of King Charles II and Barbara Villiers. His grandfather had been prime minister, and on his mother's side he was a nephew of a distinguished foreign secretary, Lord Castlereagh.

Like young Sulivan, who was five years his junior, Fitzroy had entered the navy the new way—via the Royal Naval College at Portsmouth. Up to about 1814 it had been the practice for an officer to begin his career as a first class volunteer or captain's servant. Such appointments were at the discretion of the captain, and to enter the service required this patronage. The system was unsatisfactory for a number of reasons. Apart from questions of fairness and efficiency in recruiting for the navy the best possible officers, it meant that recruiting was essentially out of the hands of the Admiralty. The new college was established for the education of fledgling officers under proper tutelage rather than at the hands of officers and men on the decks of a man-of-war.

Fitzroy did very well there and after only a year and eight months joined the *Owen Glendower* (October 18, 1819). On

September 7, 1824, at the age of nineteen, he was commissioned and joined HMS *Thetis,* soon followed by Sulivan. The two had not known each other at the college, where Fitzroy was frequently mentioned as having set an example to which all collegians should aspire. When Fitzroy took his examinations for lieutenant, for example, he got "full numbers," a notable feat.

On the *Thetis* the two young officers became fast friends, Fitzroy taking special pains to assist Sulivan where he could: "He advised me what to read, and encouraged me to turn to advantage what I had learned at college by taking every kind of observation that was useful in navigation. . . . He offered me use of his cabin and his books."[1]

Like many of the new breed of officers in the navy, but perhaps much more than most, Fitzroy was of a scientific turn of mind. He was a perfectionist and curious to learn everything he could. A creative scholar and innovator in meteorological science, he was also "one of the best practical seamen in the service." One cannot imagine anyone better suited to carry on the exacting standards of work set by surveyors such as Smyth who had set the foundation of modern hydrographic practice. Fitzroy's brilliance was not yet clouded by the mental troubles that were to shade his later career. He was elated to gain his first command and eager to test himself and his ideas.

His task with HMS *Beagle* was not an easy one: to take on a battered ship and a demoralized set of men and lead them straight back to the same desolate region where their previous captain had been driven to suicide. Life on board the *Beagle* was difficult in the first weeks of Fitzroy's command. His appointment and promotion to commander were generally resented, but the supplanted Skyring rose to the occasion, and King reports that he and Fitzroy came to work effectively side by side. Perhaps the officers and men of the *Beagle* also secretly welcomed a fresh face, especially a man who brought such boundless energy to this, his first command.

Fitzroy's job was made no easier by the persistent rumor among the men of the *Beagle* that the ghost of Captain Stokes walked the ship at night. This story was finally put to rest one evening when most of the officers and crew were ashore, bivouacked in tents. Around the fire the subject of the ghost came up, led by the carpenter Jonathan Mays, who swore up and down about the appalling things he had seen but could "never disclose to mortal man."[2] Later in the evening Sulivan, Lieutenant Kirke, and Midshipman Stokes were sent back on board with a number of men, but as the whaleboat came alongside, the watchman whispered: "Don't go aft, for the ghost is there." Sulivan scoffed at this and went on board. After a while, "retired to rest under the forecastle," they heard a noise from all the way aft and the poop cabin door began to slam. "Instantly there was a cry as to whose watch it was, 'Sulivan: go aft and shut the door. Take the lantern if you are afraid of the ghost.'" He set off aft, but the lantern blew out. He couldn't get the poop cabin door to latch properly in the dark, and so he wedged it open and groped his way back to the forecastle, where young Stokes announced, "I hear the sound as of someone breathing very loud ahead; you look after the starboard side and listen." Indeed, there was a dreadful labored breathing, and then footsteps, right over their heads. "The ghost! it is coming down. . . !" Sulivan got behind the companion, and sure enough, "there appeared first one naked foot on a step, then a second. I pushed my hands through the open ladder and seized both ankles, when a voice roared out, 'Oh! the ghost! it has got me!' It turned out to be one of the men, who having taken too much [to drink], had gone to sleep in the larboard head, and so missed the boat which took the other men ashore." After that there were no more ghost stories.

Fitzroy had more to do than raise the spirits of the crew. He had to weld them back into an efficient working team; there could be no letup in the work. When the damage to the *Beagle*'s keel was repaired, she would be on her way south again (and then Fitzroy himself would also be put to the test). The *Adventure* and *Adelaide* sailed from Rio on December 27, leaving Fitzroy to put the finishing touches to the *Beagle*. They arranged to meet up again off the mouth of the Río de la Plata.

No sooner had the *Beagle* set off to follow them than the test began. There had been a long period of very hot and humid weather, and on January 30 this culminated in a fierce storm of the type known as a pampero, the worst for twenty years. The first characteristic of a pampero is a rapidly falling barometer, then a very powerful squall, settling down to a steady south-westerly gale. It is the squall, coming almost unannounced, especially if one has not had an eye open for the barometer, that does the damage. Fitzroy's name is now firmly associated with the science of weather forecasting, and he, more than any-one, pioneered the practice of using the barometer to anticipate changes in the weather. But that came later. On this occasion, working his vessel carefully south, testing her, finding all her special characteristics and the strengths and foibles of his offi-cers and men, he was taken by surprise.

The *Beagle* was passing just inside Loboff Island, and the men could actually see the tips of the spars of the *Adventure* ahead in Maldonado Bay when the storm hit. The barometer suddenly fell to 28.50. When the first squall came, failing to get her bow into the wind, the *Beagle* was tossed around like a piece of driftwood. Sulivan, who was in his bunk in the poop cabin with a case of dysentery, gives the most vivid account of the storm.

The *Beagle* was on her beam-ends several times . . . and at length the water was nearly up to the bottom of my cot, the port side, and I was told that two men whose names I well knew had fallen from the yards into the sea. I thought I might have a chance for my life as well as the others. I managed to draw a pair of trou-sers on and crawl from my cot. The force of the wind was such as to crush in the weather-quarter boat where she pressed against the davits. I went up the starboard poop-ladder, and then I saw from the mizzen-mast on which I was standing, the Commander standing on one of the uprights of the poop-rail, and holding on by another upright. She was so much over that the top-sail yards blew up to the mast's head, with one man upon each yard arm clinging to the lift, the one on the lee yard arm with the help of the brace-block strop, while the one upon the weather yard arm managed to crawl in, and he was seen on the cap, where he was heard to say, "Thank God I have got in out of that!" I, from my standing place, the mizzen-mast, saw that she was standing direct for the rocks and breakers on Loboff Island, and I reported it to the Commander. He replied, saying, "so she is" and immediately ordered both anchors to be let go. The water was so shallow that she touched the small bower-anchor when passing over it; but the two anchors bought her up, and saved her running on Lobos.[3]

Fitzroy had been caught flat-footed and was saved only by a desperate measure. If the anchor cables had parted, the *Beagle* would have been destroyed.

Even in the relatively sheltered anchorage of Maldonado Bay, the storm had laid the *Adventure* over on her side but did no damage except to tents and a boat onshore. The storm settled down to a steady southwest gale through the night, allowing the *Beagle* to limp in next day, with both fore and main topmasts missing and many spars lost or damaged. While the men set to repairing the damage, another storm hit, destroying one of the *Beagle*'s boats.

On February 9 they moved up to Montevideo, and later, upriver, the *Adventure* grounded. It took them a long time to get back downriver, and then another gale struck. At one time the *Adventure* had 110 fathoms of cable out, and the *Beagle* 150. The *Adventure*'s windlass was damaged, and her jolly boat was washed away, so they had already lost four of the small boats that were essential to all their inshore work. The *Adelaide* had lost a topmast, her boom, and part of the bowsprit.

When they left Montevideo again, another gale separated the ships almost immediately. The men of the *Beagle* must have been wondering what gods they had offended, to be continually so at odds with the weather. On their way to rendezvous with the other ships at Port Desire, the *Beagle* had another boat carried away, and they lost all contact with *Adelaide*.

They met up first with the *Adventure*. Then the *Adelaide* eventually turned up, much to their relief, and they proceeded south together in fair weather. The *Adelaide* was then given six months' provisions, and the vessels separated again. The

Adventure headed along the eastern coast of Tierra del Fuego to Staten Island. It was here that by prior arrangement, the *Adventure* was to provision HMS *Chanticleer* to save her from having to return voyage to Rio de Janeiro for supplies. King was already late for the meeting. The *Beagle* and the *Adelaide* were to pass through the Strait of Magellan yet again, the *Beagle* to survey the southern shore of the strait and Jerome Channel and the *Adelaide* to survey the Magdalen and Barbara channels. Then all three vessels were to meet up again at San Carlos, Chile.

In other words, Fitzroy had to finish off the work that Stokes had started, despite the unsuitability of the vessel and the harrowing experiences of the crew not many months before. By contrast, King in the *Adventure* was not setting a very ambitious program for himself. Perhaps he had simply decided that the *Adventure* was too large and clumsy for the work. Whatever the case, King's active part in the surveying work appreciably diminished from this point onward.

At New Year's Harbour, Staten Island, the *Adventure* found only a note from Captain Foster of the *Chanticleer*, setting a new rendezvous at St. Martins Cape near Cape Horn, where the two ships met on April 16. As noted previously, although the *Adventure* carried all the spare stores, her crew was as badly affected by scurvy as that of the hard-pressed *Chanticleer*.

King made a survey of the Bay of St. Francis and helped Foster with some of his special measurements and observations. Then, delayed for some weeks by the weather, he set off around Cape Horn for Valparaiso: "On the 24th the *Chanticleer* sailed, and in two hours after we also left this dismal cove." The *Adventure* arrived in Valparaiso Bay on June 22, to wait for the others.

Taking Charge

Upon leaving King, the *Beagle* and *Adelaide* started the turn to the west, and now Fitzroy had his first chance to see the narrows guarding the Strait of Magellan. It was April Fool's Day,

1829, hardly propitious, but by now it was clear that Fitzroy would not let events dictate to him; he would make his own luck. They had the usual difficulty at the entrance to the First Narrows and, with darkness falling, tried to anchor, only to have the cable part. They had two alternative courses of action: to turn back or keep going. With the tidal current to help him, Fitzroy boldly ran the narrows successfully in pitch-darkness. From this point the voyages of the *Beagle* (the present one and the two to follow) came under control and never again did the elements get the upper hand.

The *Adelaide* got through, too, and they were both past the Second Narrows on the fourth. Fitzroy started a survey of the northeast coast of the strait. Here Kempe, Bynoe, and a boy set off on a shooting trip but failed to return by midnight. They turned up next day, having had nothing but a scare; things were going right! Then they continued the survey southward on to Port Famine, where the *Adelaide* was waiting. On the way Fitzroy the scientist had an intriguing first contact with the Fuegian Indians. He immediately started a study of their language, noting down their vocabulary as he deciphered it. He also began a series of remarkable sketches of the Fuegians, several of which survive and show considerable skill with a pen; he even persuaded the Fuegians to wash their faces so that he could draw their features correctly.

Fitzroy was more impressed with the majesty of the scenery than were other visitors to the Strait of Magellan: "I cannot help here remarking, that the scenery this day appeared to me magnificent. Many ranges of mountains, besides Mount Sarmiento, were distinctly visible, and the continual change occurring in the views of the land, as clouds passed over the sun, with such a variety of tints of every color. . . ." Then again: "the night was one of the most beautiful I have ever seen: nearly calm, the sky clear of clouds, excepting a few large white masses, which at times passed over the bright moon, whose lights striking the snow-covered summits of the mountains by which we were surrounded, contrasted strongly with their dark gloomy bases, and gave an effect to the scene which I shall never forget."[4]

One cannot help noticing the contrast between Fitzroy's exhilaration and Stokes's depressed diary notes. Stokes had obviously been sick for a long time. A combination of ill health, constant anxiety, and terrible working conditions finally broke him. Fitzroy also was given to depression, the more so as he grew older, but at the beginning of this first command there was little sight of it. He was now assured and vigorous, his legendary temper already evident as he could never suffer fools gladly, but he got the men to work for and with him.

They continued the survey work as they moved west, using parties from small boats wherever necessary. Fitzroy had to be especially careful because his first officer, Skyring, was away on the *Adelaide* (no doubt he *did* need to get away from the man who supplanted him), so there was no senior officer on board who had been in the strait before. More than once sudden squalls drove the *Beagle* toward the rocks, but she always escaped.

At Port Gallant Fitzroy started systematically varying the men's diet. Instead of constant salt beef rations he put them whenever possible on an alternating regimen: three days of beef, three days relying on fresh-caught foods: fresh mussels, limpets, wild celery, and pressed meat. They had brought a pig from Montevideo, and they ate that. All this was very successful in keeping them fit and free from scurvy. Fitzroy tried every way to keep the men as comfortable as possible, for example setting up painted canvas awnings to provide a dry working space on the deck.

On May 7 Fitzroy, with John Lort Stokes and a party of sailors, took a cutter and a whale boat to explore the Jerome Channel. The task was to see if it connected to any other part of the strait and, if so, to discover what possible shortcuts and / or escapes from bad weather it would provide. They took a month's provisions, and "each man had his clothes covered with canvas, or duck, well painted; and instead of a hat, everyone had a southwester (like a coal-heaver's cap)." For nighttime there were sleeping bags of blankets. Even so, it was a cold and unpleasant little jaunt, notwithstanding the adventure of getting up the narrow regions of the channel into "the mysterious Indian Sound." The first night they nearly overturned the cutter, and some of the instruments and gear were spoiled in the seawater.

On the fourteenth Captain Fitzroy noted "so mild was the weather that I bathed this morning and did not find the water colder than I have felt in the autumn on the English coast."[5] In fact, Fitzroy's log for that day records an air temperature of 39°F, and the water was 42°F. Evidently Fitzroy was a hardy soul when it came to sea bathing.

As they moved north through the channel, they discovered that it led into a huge body of water that they called Otway Water. The chances seemed good that it would connect back somewhere with the strait. They worked along the eastern shore of Otway Water and found a narrow channel at its northern tip through which a good current passed, hinting at the connection they sought. Here they named a small cove Donkin Cove after the brand of preserved meat. They found that the channel (later named Fitzroy Channel) was roomy and easily navigable and led into another very large sea lake (to be named Skyring Water). However, faced with strong contrary winds and running short of time, Fitzroy decided they could not investigate it fully. Instead they surveyed the narrow strip of land separating Donkin Cove and the Strait of Magellan to the southeast. Fitzroy climbed some low hills and got a good view of the Gregory Range. Then they started the return trip, but back on Otway Water the next day the wind began to get up. Fitzroy in the whaleboat had to get in the sails and use the oars, ordering Stokes in the cutter, if he could, to stand out away from the shore for safety. They became separated.

The weather was too rough for Fitzroy to attempt a landing, and soon the short Fuegian day was over. "After dark, finding we could not well be worse off as to risk, I bore up, and pulled with the sea rather than abaft the beam, twisting the boat end-on to each wave as it came, hoping to get into smooth water to the westward." They were actually only a mile or so from the shore but in desperate danger of being swamped. "Shortly after bearing up, a heavy sea broke over my back, and half filled the boat; we were baling away, expecting its successor, and had little thought of the boat living, when—quite suddenly—the sea fell, and soon after the wind became moderate." The men had been rowing the heavy whaleboat for more than five hours and had to jettison some precious firewood. But they quickly rowed to shore and in ten minutes were back in Donkin Cove. Fitzroy reported, "No men could have behaved better than that boat's crew: not a word was uttered by one of them; nor did an oar flag at any time, although they acknowledged, after landing, that they had never expected to see the shore again."[6] The next morning Fitzroy allowed them all to sleep until ten. Happily the cutter survived the sudden storm, too, and they were able to work back south again into the Jerome Channel. On May 30 Stokes took the cutter back to the *Beagle,* but Fitzroy continued his work, evidently enjoying it, vigorous though it was.

So far Fitzroy and his men had excellent relations with the Fuegians. At one point Fitzroy exchanged some tobacco for a Fuegian puppy, but the owner was so dismayed to see what he had done that Fitzroy took pity on him and gave it back.

On June 8, after they had been away one month, a following wind carried them back into Port Gallant, and the *relatively* civilized amenities of the *Beagle* were more than welcome. "I never was fully aware of the comfort of a bed until this night. Not even a frost-bitten foot could prevent me from sleeping soundly for the first time in many nights."[7] The next day the *Adelaide* turned up safe and sound, having successfully and safely surveyed the Magdalen Channel all the way to the open ocean.

Things went so well that, instead of proceeding directly to Chile as instructed, Fitzroy decided to keep the work here going. This would be a good opportunity for the smaller and handier *Adelaide* to explore for a possible opening into the large sea lake they had just discovered (generously named Skyring Water by Fitzroy). So he wrote orders to this effect. The *Adelaide,* with Skyring in command, would work her way toward the Trinidad Gulf, exploring all channels possibly leading back eastward as she went and also tracing a safe "inshore" passage up to the north. Graves generously volunteered. The party, supplied with the *Beagle*'s whaleboat, spare anchors and cables, and extra clothing, set off toward Cape Tamar. In the meantime, the *Beagle* laid course directly to Chile for the appointed meeting with King. They fairly swept out of the Strait of Magellan and scudded north with a stiff following wind, reaching San Carlos on July 9, 1829. Unfortunately they lost another boat on the way and immediately started on a major refit, the ravages of wear being taken care of and new boats being built by the ever-capable Jonathan May, the carpenter.

Fitzroy was surprised to find no sign of the *Adventure* either here or at Valparaiso, where they sent off for stores. In fact, King had just arrived at Valparaiso and was busy having the chronometers cleaned and repaired and the *Adventure* refitted and reprovisioned. He also had to engage in a diplomatic mission. There were rumors everywhere that these British warships were planning to invade Chiloé Island. King had to travel inland to Santiago to meet General Pinto and put his mind at rest before heading south again to join up with the *Beagle*.

By the time the *Adventure* reached San Carlos (August 26) the *Adelaide* still had not arrived. However, King was content to settle in at San Carlos and wait. He wrote: "The *Adventure* was made snug, and, by way of relaxation, such of the officers as could be spared . . . resided in turn at the town, where also the ship's company had frequently permission to amuse themselves."[8] King had also sent word to the Admiralty requesting permission to omit the final part of the voyage (requiring him to go right around the world, via Australia and the Cape of Good Hope) and go straight home instead. Eventually the packet giving this permission arrived.

The *Adelaide* turned up, but Skyring had not been able to find a connecting channel from the Pacific side into Skyring Water.* Now she needed a refit, and despite the rumors about the British ship's hidden mission, they were allowed to use the

* In fact, Skyring Water does have a narrow connection to the strait, but it was not discovered until much later. Skyring and Kirke also climbed to the top of what is now Mount Skyring and left some mementos under a cairn. In 1981 a party from the Chilean survey ship *Piloto Pardo* recovered from the site some coins and medals and other objects.[9]

town's fine flagpole as a new mast. King gave his new orders: to the *Beagle* on November 18 and the *Adelaide* on December 7. Fitzroy was ordered to "survey the southwestern coast of Tierra del Fuego. The rendezvous would be at Port Famine on April 1 or Rio de Janeiro on June 1. The *Adelaide,* continuing with the very successful combination of Skyring and Graves, was "to trace the mainland from the Peninsula of Tres Montes to the southward," thence keeping to the coast all the way to the Strait of Magellan. They were to attempt again to get through to Skyring and Otway waters and the Jerome Channel, with the same final rendezvous as the *Beagle*.

Trouble with the Fuegians

After the *Beagle* and *Adelaide* had set off, King also finally departed, first spending nine days at Valparaiso, then heading for the Strait of Magellan. On April 5 or 6, 1830, he reached Fortescue Bay, and since the *Adelaide* was evidently not ahead of them, the men decided to make chronometric measurements from Port Gallant to Port Famine. But now they fell in with a new group of Fuegian Indians, equipped with oared canoes. By April 11 some eighty Indians had gathered at the *Adventure*'s anchorage and trouble was brewing. A major incident came when one of the ship's officers cut a lock of hair from a Fuegian woman. The Indians became very disturbed, "and one of them taking it away, threw half into the fire, and, rolling up the other portion between his hands, swallowed it. Immediately afterwards, placing his hands to the fire, as if to warm them, and looking upwards, he uttered a few words, apparently of invocation: then, looking at us, pointed upwards, and exclaimed with a tone and gestures of explanation, 'Pecheray, Pecheray.' "[10] This was repeated with locks of hair from the officers. King was inclined to make light of the incident, but his officers thought it more serious.

The ship moved to Port Famine to wait for the *Adelaide,* but a week or so later nine canoes of Indians arrived and set up an encampment. Relationships quickly became distinctly unpleasant; King's men frequently had to fire their muskets over the Fuegians' heads to keep them away. The Indians armed themselves, and a confrontation developed: stones against guns. The next day the ship fired off one of her 6-pounders, and that drove the Fuegians off.

On May 3 the *Adelaide* joined them, and King, very glad finally to be free of the attentions of the Fuegians, set off for Rio.

Meanwhile, Fitzroy had reached the western entrance of the Strait of Magellan on November 24, and he began to work his way along the southwest coast of South Desolation Island. A party of men that he sent to the eastern shore of the Landfall Islands ran out of supplies and was attacked by Fuegians. Their rescue made for an eventful Christmas.

The men continued to land onshore to survey, with others sent off in small boats sounding the shallower waters. In this way they worked around to the southern entrance of the Barbara Channel to connect up with the survey previously made by Lieutenant Skyring. On the twenty-eighth they anchored off the Brecknock Peninsula, and on the twenty-ninth Matthew Murray was sent off with several men in the new whaleboat that had been built at San Carlos to visit Cape Desolation ("which well deserves the name"). Another gale now struck, and Fitzroy soon began to worry for Murray's safety. Then, on the fifth early in the morning, "I was called up to hear that the whale-boat was lost—stolen by the natives." Fitzroy told the full story in a subsequent letter to King.

I sent Mr. Matthew Murray (Master) with six men, in a whale-boat to Cape Desolation; the projecting part of a small, but high and rugged island.... Mr. Murray reached the place, and secured his party and the boat in a cave near the cape; during a very dark night, some Fuegians, whose vicinity was not at all suspected, approached with the dexterous cunning peculiar to savages and stole the boat.

Thus deprived of the means of returning to the *Beagle,* and unable to make their situation known, Mr. Murray and his party formed a sort of canoe, or rather basket, with the branches

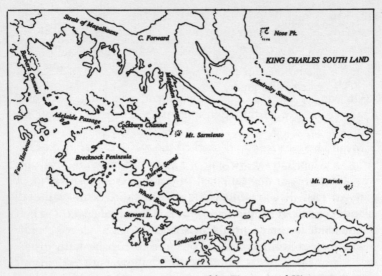

Southwest Tierra del Fuego, as mapped by Fitzroy and King, 1835; see note 46; original spelling.

of trees and part of their canvas tent, and in this machine three men made their way back to the *Beagle,* by his directions: yet, although favored by the only fine day that occurred during the three weeks that the *Beagle* passed in Townsend Harbor, this basket was twenty hours on its passage.

Assistance was immediately given to the Master and the other men, and a chase for our lost boat was begun, which lasted many days, but was unsuccessful in its object, although much of the lost boat's gear [including the chronometer, theodolite, and other instruments] was found, and the women and the children of the families from who it was recovered, were brought on board as hostages. The men, excepting one of them, escaped from us, or were absent in our missing boat.[11]

Fitzroy continued on the lookout for evidence of his boat.

At the end of February the *Beagle* anchored in Christmas Sound, but before this time all our prisoners had escaped, except for three little girls, two of whom were restored to their own tribe, near "Whale-Boat Sound," and the other is now on board. She seemed so happy and healthy that I determined to detain her as a hostage for the stolen boat, and try to teach her English.

From the first canoe seen in Christmas Sound, one man was taken as a hostage for the recovery of our boat, and to become an interpreter and guide. He came to us with little reluctance and appeared unconcerned. I resolved to take the youngest man on board, as he, in all probability, had less strong ties to bind him to his people than others who were older, and might have families: Reflecting that by getting one of these natives on board, there would be a chance of his learning enough English to be an interpreter, and that by this means we might recover our lost boat. The girl was christened Fuegia Basket [after the improvised boat] and the young man York Minster [after the nearby promontory named by Captain Cook]. Fuegia, cleaned and dressed, was much improved in appearance: She was already a pet on the lower deck, and appeared quite contented. York Minster was solemn at first, yet his appetite did not fail. . . .[12]

The indefatigable Mr. May made a new boat out of boards sawn from a thick spar salvaged at San Carlos. When exploring around the promontory of York Minster, the *Beagle* broke her best bower anchor in yet another gale. More Fuegians, mostly men, were sighted, and skirmishing began that lasted on and off for several days.

Life was becoming nerve-racking and frustrating. The loss of the new whaleboat was no small matter, for the work depended on the boats. After endless previous trouble with the boats, losing them either to the Fuegians or to the weather, this incident was the last straw. The Fuegians were too slick for them. Probably the whaleboat was sunk quietly out of view. The equipment and stores were not so easily hidden and were recaptured as the men from the *Beagle* hustled from place to place, trying to keep up with the Fuegians, who clearly were past masters of deception and light-fingeredness.

"A few days afterwards, traces of our boat were found at some wigwams on an island in Christmas Sound, and from the families inhabiting the wigwams I took another young man, for the same purpose as that above-mentioned. No useful information respecting our lost boat was, however, gained from them, before we were obliged to leave that coast, and she remained the prize of their companions." This young man was given the name Boat Memory.[13]

It must have seemed a good idea to take hostages at first, but it quickly became clear that the Fuegians did not prize their children as highly as Europeans did. Not only had Fitzroy lost the boat, but he now had his Fuegians to take care of. And once he had lost contact with their families, he was hard put to return them.

There seemed no point in continuing the fruitless search in foul weather or in mounting some kind of punitive exploit; that would only make matters worse. So, the Fuegians having gained the advantage over them, Fitzroy decided to give up and leave. And perhaps scarcely knowing why, he took the hostages with him.

The *Beagle* left Christmas Sound and sailed for the Ildefonsos, hoping to locate the elusive Diego Ramírez Islands, but they were forced back toward the Hermite Islands, having to take refuge eventually in Nassau Bay. Here they found a safe quiet anchorage and better weather, much to the relief of the hard-pressed crew. The surrounding land "looked much more cheerful than the high dismal mountains under which we had last anchored. Wood and water were plentiful, and easily obtained. Wild fowl were numerous, and our people brought on board a serviceable supply, enough for all the sick, and for most of those who were in health."[14] More Fuegians materialized, but they were of a different tribe (Yapoos), and the three Fuegians on board, who could not understand their language, were extremely scared of them.

On April 16 they sailed again and just cleared the west cape in light winds. At Cape Horn they left a memorial in a stone jar and collected geological samples. They also tried to get at least a good fix by sight of the position of the Diego Ramírez Islands. A whaleboat, again with Mr. Murray in charge, set off to survey the coast as far as Cape Good Success while Fitzroy went

Fuegian Wigwams at Hope Harbor (Magdalen Channel), from Fitzroy and King's *Narrative;* see note 46.

Robert Fitzroy's sketches of Fuegia Basket (left), Jemmy Button (center), and York Minster (right) in their city clothes (1833); see note 46.

inland. Stokes, in another boat, surveyed the easterly parts of Nassau Bay, and Kempe was left to continue refitting and watering the ship.

While exploring a promising-looking new east-west passage that he later called Beagle Channel, Fitzroy and a small party "were stopped . . . by three canoes full of natives, anxious for barter. We gave them a few beads and buttons, for some fish; and without any previous intention, I told one of the boys in a canoe to come into our boat, and gave the man with him a large shining mother-of-pearl button."[15] This boy, christened Jemmy Button, also remained with the *Beagle,* and now four Fuegians were on board.

When the decision was made to return to Rio de Janeiro, Fitzroy "made up [his] mind to carry the Fuegians . . . to England." Certainly time was running short. There was now no opportunity to return Fuegia Basket, Boat Memory, and York Minster to their own regions, and it was equally impossible to leave them with the extremely hostile Indians at the eastern end of Tierra del Fuego.

Fitzroy was greatly intrigued by the Fuegians. He had observed them carefully all through these last months, and now he had a chance to observe some at close hand, being particularly struck by the differences between the various tribes. A mixture of his missionary Christian feelings and his scientific interest in anthropology led him to attempt to civilize his captives. His aim became that after having been educated in England and taught the values of husbandry, industry, and thrift, his four charges would return to their native land. There they would both educate and civilize their fellows and be a valuable source of information about the ways and habits of the Fuegians.

I . . . hold myself responsible for their comfort while away from, and for their safe return to their own country: and I have now to request that, as senior officer of the expedition, you will consider the possibility of some public advantage being derived from this circumstance. . . . Should not His Majesty's Government direct otherwise, I shall procure for these people a suitable education, and, after two or three years, shall send or take them back to their own country, with as large a stock as I can collect of those articles most useful to them, and most likely to improve the condition of their countrymen, who are scarcely superior to the brute condition [letter to King, written at sea, September 12, 1830].[16]

With the survey along Cape Good Success complete, they were down to three weeks' worth of provisions, and only a few days were left before their appointed rendezvous at Rio de Janeiro. Taking the four Fuegians with them, they set off north to Montevideo. The *Adventure* and *Adelaide* had already come and gone, so they continued to Rio de Janeiro, where the expedition was reunited on August 2, 1830. King was delighted to learn that the *Beagle* did not need to stay in harbor for refitting, having been put in very good condition by Kempe during the last months. So no time was lost in preparing to leave for home. Four days later the *Adventure* and *Beagle* sailed, leaving their trusty tender *Adelaide* in the service of the flagship at Rio de Janeiro.

On October 14, 1830, after a "most tedious voyage" (the last leg of a homeward voyage is always tedious, but considering the circumstances and length of their absence, each hour of this one must have dragged interminably), they once more put into Plymouth Sound.

The expedition had accomplished a great deal. Long stretches of the coast of South America and particularly the region of the Strait of Magellan, had been surveyed, and at least two alternate routes of exit from the strait that could be used by vessels boxed in by northwest gales had been accurately charted and described. The men had also picked out a useful route from the westerly end of the strait to the Gulf of Peñas, fixed the position of the Diego Ramírez Islands, and finally established that there was no entrance to the strait at the eastern end through Useless Bay. They had discovered the two large sea lakes (Otway and Skyring waters) although unfortunately these seemed not to provide an alternate passage out of the strait. The Beagle Channel, which they discovered right at the end of the voyage, seemed, however, to afford another valuable "escape route" bypassing Cape Horn. But despite a lot of extremely hard work in dreadful conditions, there was still an enormous amount of work to be done in that region and on the western coast of South America before even a good first survey could be called complete. As they arrived in England, they must have felt reasonably sure that another expedition would be sent south to continue the work. Many of the officers hoped to serve on such an expedition; Fitzroy expected to be leading them.

EIGHT

Second Rebuilding:
Preparation for the
"Darwin Voyage"

BACK IN ENGLAND, THE FOUR FUEGIANS WERE A PROBLEM. The Admiralty received Fitzroy's letter of explanation to King, written while at sea. In a guarded reply their lordships seemed to agree that while they would not undertake any of the expenses of maintaining the four hostages—now guests—they would arrange for their passage home. Meanwhile, the Fuegians were lodged at a quiet farmhouse near Plymouth while Fitzroy tried to get the Church Missionary Society interested in sponsoring them. They were vaccinated (vaccinations at Montevideo apparently did not take), but soon they all had to be admitted to the Royal Navy Hospital at Plymouth suffering from smallpox. Boat Memory had a very bad case, and despite all the careful attentions of a number of doctors, he died.

The Church Missionary Society helped Fitzroy arrange for the other three to be moved to London under the auspices of the splendidly named National Society for Providing Education of the Poor in the Principles of the Established Church. Matthew Murray accompanied them on the stagecoach journey to London, where they were lodged at an infants' school in Walthamstow, London, under the care of the rector at Walthamstow, the Reverend William Wilson.

Fitzroy was already up in London, taking care of many of the official duties remaining in connection with the voyage. He and King had to supervise the final drafting of hundreds of charts and plans. Meanwhile, the *Beagle*'s crew dispersed, much to the regret of Fitzroy, who recognized the value of an efficiently working group of men and the difficulty of retraining another. At Devonport the *Beagle* was stripped and cleaned and once again lay in ordinary. (And the *Adventure* at Woolwich.) News came that King and Skyring had been promoted.

York, Jemmy, and Fuegia sank into a taciturn, almost totally withdrawn state. Nothing seemed to excite or interest them, but eventually Fuegia and Jemmy began to learn a little English and to pick up at least a patina of civilized habits. York Minster continued stubborn and recalcitrant. One can scarcely imagine how either they or the other children at the school viewed the bizarre situation: in a small genteel classroom, three husky dark-skinned Fuegian "savages" sitting down to lessons with five- and six-year-old pale and skinny London children.

Life settled down to a routine, but they were plagued with visitors and well-wishers, for Fitzroy's savages were a matter of news in the whole country. They even made an appearance at court. King William IV (the "Sailor King") talked interestedly with Fitzroy about his adventures while the three Fuegians, dressed in English finery, were quizzed by Queen Adelaide. Fuegia took Her Majesty's fancy, and she was given one of the royal bonnets, a ring, and a purse of money.

Eventually, despite some modest success in educating the Fuegians and considerable public interest in their fate, Fitzroy was neither satisfied with the Fuegians' situation nor content to see it continue. Although at first he planned to keep them in England for two or three years, he began a campaign for their early return. The existence of the Fuegians became a useful lever in getting another surveying voyage authorized; the Fuegians were now hostages to another cause. The Admiralty had agreed to return them; the best way to do it would be as part of another surveying expedition with Fitzroy as its head.

By late spring 1831 Fitzroy's responsibilities with respect to the last voyage were over. He was restive to be active again. Captain King (now retired) assured him that a follow-up voy-

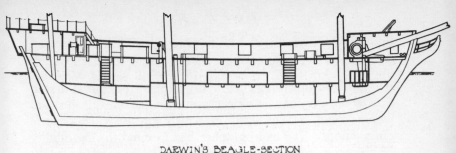

DARWIN'S BEAGLE-SECTION

HMS *Beagle* as a bark for the Darwin voyage, elevation; based on Admiralty drawings of sister ships.

age was planned and wrote an elaborate testimonial to Fitzroy's abilities. If any voyage to South America was to be mounted, Fitzroy was an obvious choice to lead it. The Admiralty, however, changed its mind and was in no immediate hurry to send ships south again.

Frustrated, Fitzroy requested a year's leave of absence from the service so that he could charter a vessel and return his three charges to Tierra del Fuego himself. A vessel from London (the brig *John*) was hired (June 8, 1831), and Fitzroy assembled a large store of supplies and equipment with which to set up the nucleus of a Christian colony in Tierra del Fuego.[1] There the three "educated" Fuegians would begin to civilize their compatriots. Of course, Fitzroy's zeal for this missionary venture had totally outstripped his common sense. Three young people could scarcely accomplish such a task with only a few months' exposure to the concepts that Fitzroy wanted them to espouse, especially since they had been educated to these virtues totally against their will.

While preparing to set off on his own, Fitzroy continued to keep pressure on the government for the commissioning of a full surveying voyage. Suddenly, through the good offices of "a kind uncle"[2] (probably Lord Londonderry), the Admiralty reversed itself and approved an expedition with Fitzroy in command.

There were in fact many valid reasons for another voyage south, quite apart from the matter of the Admiralty's half promise to return Fitzroy's Fuegians. The northeastern coast of Tierra del Fuego, the southeastern coast of South America, and much of the southwestern coast remained to be surveyed. Furthermore, Beaufort, the chief hydrographer, recognized that in Fitzroy the navy had an officer with a unique scientific bent, to whom could be entrusted extremely precise chronometric observations.[3] The hydrographer had in mind the desirability of making a complete circumnavigation of the world to establish a full chain of meridian distances by chronometric measurement. By such a means it would be possible to get a really accurate fix of the relative positions of known points on the surface of the globe. It would be a complement to the Pendulum Voyage of Foster in the *Chanticleer*. A large number of isolated chronometric observations existed, from different previous sources, but no one had ever attempted to make the complete chain of measurements right around the twenty-four-hour / 360-degree circle to put everything into a single frame of reference. To do this required instruments of great accuracy; meticulous attention would have to be paid to the effect of weather (especially temperature) on the chronometers' rates. The precise and scientific Fitzroy had impressed Captain Beaufort; he would be an excellent person to pursue such a mission.

Probably we will never know just how much the second surveying voyage was due to political pressure on behalf of Fitzroy, to his own ambitions, or to his responsibilities to the Fuegians and how much stemmed directly from the needs of hydrographic survey. In any case, once the decision was made, events moved quickly. On June 27, 1831, Fitzroy was reappointed to the *Beagle* for her second and most famous voyage.

Curiously enough, HMS *Chanticleer,* the *Beagle*'s sister ship (now lying in ordinary at Woolwich), was the Admiralty's first choice for the new voyage. But a survey showed her to be unfit. The only other surveying vessel available was the recently returned *Beagle*. Unfortunately for the lords commissioners (and the taxpayer) the Admiralty found itself in for considerable expense nonetheless. The *Beagle* was in poor enough condition that a major rebuilding had to be started.

Second Rebuilding

The refit of the *Beagle* at Devonport Dockyard took a long time and considerably delayed the start of the voyage, so much so, in fact, that the Admiralty became restive and demanded to know the reasons. It soon became obvious: Fitzroy was personally supervising the refit, "resolved to spare neither expense nor trouble in making our little Expedition as complete with respect to material and preparation, as my means and exertion would allow, when supported by the considerate and satisfactory arrangements of the Admiralty."[4] For Fitzroy, nothing but the best would suffice, and he had many ideas on how the *Beagle* might be improved.

According to the "Admiralty Progress Book," the total bill for the *Beagle*'s refit was £7,583—only £220 less than her original cost. The ship ("almost completely rotten") was stripped right down to her timbers and carefully rebuilt. In the process, by Fitzroy's request, the upper deck was raised by eight inches aft and twelve inches forward, increasing the headroom below-decks to about six feet. This "proved to be of greatest advantage to her as a sea boat, besides adding so materially to the comfort of all on board."[5] Interestingly Fitzroy did not have the bulwarks raised commensurately. Up to this point the tendency had been to *raise* the bulwarks on these brigs, increasing their deep-waistedness. However, by raising the lower deck and not raising the bulwarks, Fitzroy states, "she will be much dryer on deck;—Her waist will be less deep. . ."[6]

Since raising the deck by a foot meant lowering the height of the bulwarks from fifty-two to forty inches (top of the rail to the deck), it seems odd at first that this could be done without making problems for the gunports. However, as Fitzroy noted, "The *Beagle* is ordered to carry only two six-pound guns,—therefore raising the deck will not be of consequence as respect the guns and their ports."[7] (In fact, Fitzroy ended up carrying nine guns, all still small.) It will also be remembered that the original design for the *Beagle* called for the gunwale to be raised

DARWIN'S BEAGLE-DARWIN'S CABIN

0   10   20   30 FT.

1 BINACLE COMPASSES	4 FLAG LOCKER	7 TABLE	10 WASH STAND
2 SHIP'S WHEEL	5 WATER CLOSET	8 MIZZEN MAST	11 INSTRUMENT CABINET
3 CABIN	6 BOOK CASES	9 CHEST of DRAWERS	12 STOKE'S CABIN

HMS *Beagle* as a bark for the Darwin voyage, plan of the poop cabin; based on the Cambridge University Library drawing.

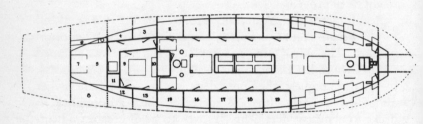

DARWIN'S BEAGLE-LOWER DECK PLAN

0   10   20   30 FT.

1 STORES or CABINS	7 FITZROY'S TABLE	13 BYNOE'S CABIN	19 BOS'N'S CABIN
2 ARTIST'S CABIN	8 FITZROY'S BED	14 STEWARD'S STORES	
3 CHAFFER'S CABIN	9 GUN ROOM	15 ROWLETT'S CABIN	OTHERWISE SEE
4 WICKHAM'S CABIN	10 SIDEBOARD	16 MATE'S CABIN	"PACKET-LOWER DECK"
5 FITZROY'S CABIN	11 CHRONOMETER ROOM	17 CARPENTER'S CABIN	
6 FITZROY'S SOFA	12 SULLIVAN'S CABIN	18 GUNNER'S CABIN	

HMS *Beagle* as a bark for the Darwin voyage, lower deck plan; based on the P. G. King drawings made for the 1890 edition of *The Voyage of the Beagle* and Admiralty drawings of sister ships.

beyond the original specifications for the 10-gun brig: four inches aft and six inches forward. This had increased the height of her gunports from thirty-two to thirty-six inches. Now the gunports would have to be cut down to twenty-seven inches, leaving a nine-inch sill—the size of the bow port of the original 10-gun brig. In all, these changes brought the bulwarks of the *Beagle* closer in line with normal dimensions for a small brig than the original very deep-waisted design.

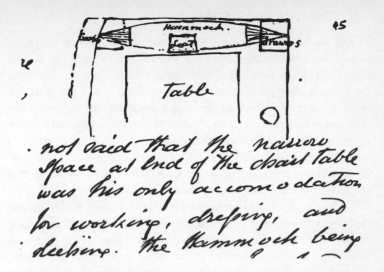

Hammock.

foot

Table

*. not said that the narrow
space at End of the chart Table
was his only accomodation
for working, dressing, and
sleeping. The Hammock being*

HMS *Beagle,* sketch of portion of the poop cabin showing Darwin's hammock; detail from a letter by B. J. Sulivan, by permission of the Syndics of Cambridge University Library (DAR.107).

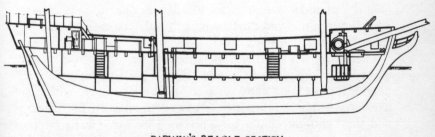

DARWIN'S BEAGLE-SECTION

HMS *Beagle* as a bark for the Darwin voyage, midships section; based on Admiralty drawings for HMS *Barracouta* and P. G. King drawings for the 1890 edition of *The Voyage of the Beagle.*

Raising the deck meant that the forecastle and poop decks also had to be raised, and the stern completely rebuilt. While there was some doubt about the extent of the break of the forecastle and poop of the *Beagle* during her first voyage, with this new alteration, we can be reasonably confident in restoring them as shown in the figures. However, it is not clear what sort of rail enclosed the poop deck. Some sort of rail or handline would have been essential. King's drawings show a rail on the forward side; it would be surprising, considering the fact that the men made observations from this deck, if the rail had not been continuous, but there is no evidence of any massive wooden rail. Brenton in his *Naval History* gives us an answer to the puzzle. In discussing the redesign of frigates, he states: "I would lower [the poop] as much as possible, the barricade upon it should be invisible, a small iron rail with a netting; this should look snug and hold no wind. . . ."[8]

"While in dock, a sheathing of two-inch fir was nailed on the vessel's bottom, over which was a coating of felt, and then new copper. This sheathing added about fifteen tons to her displacement, and nearly seven to her actual measurement. Therefore, instead of 235 tons, she might be considered about 242 tons burthen."[9] These changes increased the draft of the *Beagle* by six inches to thirteen feet aft. As the draft forward increased by only an inch, Fitzroy had materially altered the trim, with the majority of added weight being aft. The *Beagle* now sat somewhat lower in the water than originally intended even when not extra-heavily laden with stores.

There were many other innovations. "The rudder was fitted according to the plan of Captain Lihou: a patent windlass supplied the place of a capstan: one of Frazer's stoves, with an oven attached, was taken instead of a common galley fire-place; and the lightning conductors, invented by Mr. Harris, were fixed in all the masts, the bowsprit, and even in the flying jibboom. The arrangements made in the fittings, both inside and outside, by the officers of the Dockyard, left nothing to be desired."[10]

These modifications show that Fitzroy was completely on top of the latest developments in seagoing gear. Frazer's patent stove had been experimented with on *Chanticleer*'s Pendulum Voyage. Its principal advantage over the open-galley fireplace that was standard equipment at the time was safety. The fire did not have to be put out in rough and dangerous weather. Thus, just at the times that hot meals were most needed, they could be provided. The new windlass also came from the *Chanticleer*.

William Snow Harris's lightning conductors are a story all of their own. Strange to relate, even in 1831 the exact nature of the hazards of lightning at sea and ways to avoid them were still not understood in the navy or indeed among the general populace. Although Benjamin Franklin and others had demonstrated the essential nature of the problem and how to deal with it, most naval personnel were deathly afraid of lightning and were still convinced that to put metal in the masts would not conduct the charge safely to "ground" but would in fact attract lightning to the ship.

Harris's lightning conductors were based upon the correct principle and were soon to be adopted by the navy. The technique employed was simple: a strip of copper let into the mast and grounded to the keel. Harris toured the country demonstrating a model ship in a tank. He exploded a pinch of gunpowder on the deck of the model by the spark touched to the mast. When the model ship was properly grounded from mast, to keel to water, the gunpowder failed to go off. But in 1831 it was only the scientist Fitzroy who dared (actually was eager) to test the conductors at sea. The experiment at sea turned out to be as complete a success as the model in a tank that impressed society ladies on Harris's tours. (See also Appendix E.)

The *Beagle* was rigged with extra-strong "squarer" crosstrees and heavier rigging "than is usual in a vessel of her tonnage. . . . Chains were used where found to answer and in no place was block or sheave allowed which did not admit the proper rope or chain freely. Our ropes, sails and spars, were the best that could be procured. . . ." In addition to the usual sail plan, Fitzroy added "large try-sails between the masts, made of stout canvas, with several reefs, and very useful we found them."[11]

On the main deck Fitzroy carried seven guns at first. These were as follows: "On the forecastle was a six-pound boat-carronade: before the chesstree were two brass six-pound guns . . . abaft the main mast were four brass guns, two nine-pound and two six-pound."[12] There was some trouble with the Admiralty about these. Although it wanted just two, not only did Fitzroy insist on carrying a pretty full armament, but he also insisted that the guns be brass so that they would not interfere with the compasses. In the end, faced with the refusal of the Admiralty to supply him with nine guns, Fitzroy provided two more nine-pounder long guns at his own expense, buying them at Rio de Janeiro.

This matter of armament gives us another insight into Fitzroy's character. So many guns were certainly unnecessary. The *Chanticleer* had been perfectly safe with only two guns; and the guns themselves, apart from adding unnecessary weight to the ship, must have been in the way of activities on the already crowded decks. But Fitzroy was running a complete naval expedition, even if it was a one-man show. Nothing was omitted, and if *Beagle* were a man-of-war, she would go fully armed.

Further cluttering up the decks, so much so that working during really bad weather must have been very difficult indeed, were the small boats. But no one could deny the importance of the small boats for the sort of work that the *Beagle* was to be doing. In the previous expedition they had been absolutely invaluable, so the *Beagle* carried a full complement. Amidships she carried two largish boats, built "on the diagonal principle," for extra strength: a yawl of about twenty-six feet and a slightly smaller cutter stowed inside it. These were built by William Johns of the Plymouth Naval Dockyard on his "diagonal" principle (later patented), using two sets of sheathing at right angles. This made the boats rather heavy but extremely durable and watertight. "Over the quarter deck, upon skids, [were] two whale boats, eight-and-twenty feet long"; these were Fitzroy's personal property. "[U]pon each quarter was a whale boat twenty-five feet in length, and astern was a dinghy."[13] Most of these boats had to be replaced during the voyage because losses and damage were heavy. The paraphernalia on the main deck was completed by the spare booms lashed to the gunwales on either side amidships.

An interesting note may be added in connection with the boats. In the navy of the day the term *dinghy* was not in general use. It is an Indian word used only on vessels of the East India Company. Fitzroy is generally credited with having introduced the term to the Royal Navy to replace *jolly boat*.[14] In this voyage he also introduced the word *port* in preference to *larboard* to the Royal Navy (again borrowing from long-accepted merchant practice), greatly reducing the possibility of confusion in shouted orders.[15]

Preparations on the scientific side were equally comprehensive. The hydrographer to the navy, Captain Beaufort, stated, "Few vessels will ever have left this country with a better set of chronometers."[16] In fact, Fitzroy took twenty-two chronometers with him, and three of them were still working perfectly when they returned.

The chronometers were so important because only by having exact time could longitude be determined with accuracy. Of the twenty-two chronometers that the *Beagle* carried, only eleven belonged to the government. Six were Fitzroy's own property, four were lent to the expedition by their makers, and one belonged to Lord Ashburnham. The chronometers were stowed very carefully in the little cabin set aside for them. Each was "suspended in gimbals, as usual, within a wooden box" and then "placed in sawdust, divided and retained by partitions, upon one of two wide shelves."[17] This kept them completely free from vibrations, even when the guns were fired.

It has to be admitted, however, that despite their looking very warlike, the guns of the *Beagle* were largely for show. Fitzroy fired them as infrequently as possible, in order to protect his chronometers. When a signal or salute had to be fired, one of the six-pounders was used, from a bow gunport. As for the gunports, a watercolor by Conrad Martens *(Christmas Day at Port Desire)* shows six ports on each side and is fuzzy in the area of a bow port.[18] Stanley's later watercolor *(The Beagle at Sydney Harbour, 1841)* shows no fewer than eight ports on the side and no bow port.[19] The most forward of these ports might be the bow port misplaced too far aft. However, the eighth port has to be either a mistake or a fake port painted in, probably the latter.

Belowdecks

From various available drawings we can describe the internal accommodations of the *Beagle* as finally revised by Fitzroy. Because of its importance to Darwin (who is about to enter the scene), we must describe the poop cabin first. The cabin was entered via a door on the starboard side (the banging door of the "ghost story") and inside measured less than eleven feet square. On the starboard and stern were cases housing the ship's library, an important collection of all the books that the officers would need to refer to for their work, as well as recreational reading of every sort. On the forward bulkhead were (from port to starboard) a chest of drawers, a cabinet for instruments, and a washstand. Between the table and the port bulkhead Darwin had a small "cabinet" with "my seat" immediately forward of this.

The cabin was dominated by the "great table"—the drafting table for the surveying officers and Darwin's worktable whenever he could get access to it. The mizzenmast stood straight through the cabin, and the great table was built over the steering gear. There was not much room. Midshipman King slung his hammock on the starboard side, and Darwin had the port side; each had just two feet of space between their faces and the deck above. As Darwin was well over six feet tall, in order to have room for his hammock, he had each night to take out the top drawer from the chest of drawers in the forward bulkhead, the hooks for attaching the hammock being inside. Despite the inconvenience, Darwin was so prone to seasickness that his hammock was "left hanging over this head when the sea was at all rough, that he might lay in it with a book in his hand when he could no longer sit at the table." Sulivan, in reporting this, also gives a little sketch (unpublished) of Darwin's cramped quarters: "his only accommodation for working, dressing and sleeping."[20] (This sketch incidentally confirms the drawing in the Cambridge Darwin archives [see Chapter 4] showing that the poop cabin extended only to a longitudinal bulkhead that was the starboard side of a passageway to the stern.) Given the fact that part of the poop cabin overhung the stern, every movement of the vessel must have been magnified, to the discomfort of poor Darwin, who suffered dreadfully throughout the voyage from his seasickness.

Apart from the poop cabin the only space that Darwin had at his disposal was a locker in the forecastle where he stored his specimens. When the *Beagle* was actively working in South American waters, several of the surveying officers would be away on the smaller vessels that Fitzroy hired or purchased and Darwin had more space in the poop cabin. When they returned, they all squeezed into the cramped quarters again; even at the best of times there was no privacy on HMS *Beagle*.

There was room for a small cabin under each of the poop deck companions. The one on the starboard side was occupied by J. L. Stokes. The port side one was a bit smaller, and we do not know who was in it. In one of his sketches King shows the foot of each companion standing on "flag lockers."

Among the drawings that Philip Gidley King made for the publisher John Murray in 1890 is a plan of the lower deck.[21] It is extremely diagrammatic, and unfortunately it does not match up perfectly with his other drawings. But we may combine it with the Admiralty plans of the *Barracouta* and *Cadmus* to fill in some of the missing details.

The captain's cabin was the largest after the poop cabin and had a skylight above, giving light from the main deck. There was a sofa on the port side with Fitzroy's bed opposite it. Two seats at the table accommodated Fitzroy and Darwin, and the captain also had a small writing desk. In the forward bulkhead of the cabin were a washstand and a door leading to the after companion. A locker where the chronometers were stored lay behind the companionway, with access through the gun room. At the foot of the companion was a hatch to the magazine, guarded by a marine sentry.

Smallish sleeping quarters, most of them far too small to be graced with the name cabin, were set off on either side of the lower deck as far forward as the main hatch to the hold. Naturally these were assigned in strict order of priority, the bigger cubicles nearer to the captain's being given to the more senior officers. The first lieutenant had his cabin on the port side, aft, and the second lieutenant had his on the starboard side, off the gun room.

The artist Conrad Martens described the cabin he occupied on the *Beagle* as being about six feet long by five feet wide and six feet high. The bunk took up one side of the cabin and had three drawers beneath it. There was just room for a small table and desk.[22]*

The gun room had a large skylight and a central table, with a separate sideboard or "buffet" against the forward bulkhead. A narrow passageway led past the port side of the gun room to the midshipmen's berths. The midshipmen stowed their chests forward of the main hatch, where the men's mess was.

There has been debate about the location of the galley. Stanbury, following one of King's drawings, believed that it was under the forecastle, while Darling more cogently argues that the most appropriate place for the galley was on the lower deck, with its chimney just aft of the foremast, as in all the other 10-gun brigs.[23]

There is similar difficulty about the companionways. Darling restores a companion at the fore hatch and one aft, in front of the captain's cabin, both running athwartship. King's drawings show companions at both the fore and main hatches, both oriented fore and aft, with the captain's companion athwartship. As King has gone to the pains of distinguishing the companions in this way, it might be reasonable to conclude that his drawing is accurate in this regard. But Darling believes there is no evidence for a companion at the main hatch at all and that the fore companion had to be athwartship in order for the sea-

---

* Unfortunately King's drawing of the lower deck does not locate Martens's cabin. Since King labels spaces for both the surgeon and an assistant surgeon (of whom there was none after Bynoe's promotion), perhaps Martens had the latter's space. An amusing item here is that in the final versions made for publication by Murray from King's sketches, the purser's cabin was labeled "*Parson* Rowlett."

men to have access under the stem of the yawl stowed on deck.*

King shows the sick bay right up under the starboard bow and "men's lockers" on the port side. Plans of the *Barracouta* as a packet service bark (National Maritime Museum, 4053) show a "Carpenter's Store Room" at the port bow, "Gunner's Store Room" amidships, and "Boatswain's Store Room" to starboard. More boatswain's and carpenter's stores are in the hold, reached by scuttles on either side of the foremast. In the *Barracouta* the coal store in the hold was reached via a scuttle on the port side just aft of the foremast. King showed the coal in the hold right under the forecastle. He also put the sail room in the hold, just aft of the foremast. The plans of the *Barracouta,* however, clearly show "pursers' stores" and "sail bin" on the lower deck.

King's drawing is consistent with the *Barracouta* plans in the position of the spirit room. However, he shows the bread room in the hold and "Captain's Stores" in the recess under the very stern. Since the poop cabin has a large fixed table just where otherwise there would be a scuttle to the normal bread room in the stern, King is probably correct in placing the bread room in the hold, where access would be easier.

Stores

Without exaggeration Fitzroy wrote: "[P]erhaps no vessel ever quitted her own country with a better or more ample supply (in proportion to her probable necessities) of every kind of useful provision and stores than the little ship. . . ." The provisions the *Beagle* carried included "various antiscorbutics—such as

---

*In her arguments concerning the galley and fore hatch, Darling[24] refers to Augustus Earle's famous drawing *Crossing the Equator* as if it showed men cavorting around the foremast. In fact, from the fact that Earle shows both a skylight (which must be the gun room skylight) instead of a hatch cover *and* another mast beyond, they are clearly holding Neptune's Court around the mainmast.

pickles, dried apples, and lemon juice—of the best quality, and in a great abundance as we could stow away; we also had on board a very large quantity of Kilner and Morsom's preserved meat, vegetable, and soap; and from the medical department we received an ample supply of antiseptics, and articles useful for preserving specimens of natural history"[25] (the latter, of course, specially increased for Charles Darwin's use). Having just returned from the regions to which they would be traveling, Fitzroy prepared the best possible inventory of foods and medicines, given the limitations of contemporary science for their needs. Also crammed somewhere in her hold lay the vast array of articles to be used to set up the colony on Tierra del Fuego.

One of His Majesty's Bathing Machines

There is plenty of evidence concerning the *Beagle*'s sailing characteristics after her modifications: from the King and Fitzroy official *Narrative,* Darwin's diary and letters, Sulivan's memoirs, Stokes's official narrative of the third voyage, and the diary of Benjamin Francis Helpman, mate for the third voyage.[26] In addition, there are brief references to the sailing of the *Barracouta* and *Chanticleer,* which, as we have seen, were rigged almost exactly like the *Beagle.*

Most of these accounts are full of praise for the handling characteristics and seaworthiness of the *Beagle.* No doubt these may in part be attributed to the loyal, even romantic prose that often overtakes these mid-nineteenth-century writers: "our stout little ship gallantly carried us through the waves," etc., etc. We may pick our way through all this and still see that the *Beagle* was uncomfortable, but not vicious, and generally behaved well, even in rough seas.

The forecastle and the raised upper deck improved her general performance in straightforward bad weather. She seems to have been able to cope with vast quantities of water shipped from directly ahead, as long as she maintained steerageway. Even with the addition of the forecastle, however, the major problem with the *Beagle* remained that in any sort of weather at all the decks were flooded, the basic defect common to all 10-gun brigs, however modified. Helpman, in his diary of the third voyage, constantly complained of there being several inches to a foot or more of water on the decks at all times and that it was difficult to keep the water from working its way to the main deck below. For comparison, the *Chanticleer* seems to have had as safe a record of service in foul weather as the *Beagle,* and Webster evidently wrote from both affection and the experience of many uncomfortable days when he describes "being perpetually soused in salt water in one of His Majesty's bathing-machines, viz. a 10-gun brig; but a hero's honor let a hero have, and as such the little *Chanticleer* deserves the meed of praise."[27]

All 10-gun brigs had an awkward quick and deep roll. Water came pouring in over the sides under most weather conditions. Under optimum conditions the *Beagle* was capable of making about nine knots, as the following typical diary entries by Helpman show. July 16, 1837: "Course SSW1/2W going nine knots nearly before the wind and taking water in both sides, rather much seas, wind NE . . . reefed mainsail, double reefed topsails, topglnt sails, jib." Tuesday, July 25, 1837: "Course SW. Middle watch, fine nights, fresh breeze "Wind NE, Going 9 knots; all studsls, royals, etc. . . ." Tuesday, October 24, 1837: "[Course SE by E] Wind steady from W.S.W. . . . under topglnt sails, single reefed topsails, courses, jib, wind S.W. 9 knots." Wednesday, November 1, 1837: "The wind freshened last night, and the seal getting up. We shipped immense quantities of water, sometimes a foot deep. Under double reefed topsails. Furled the main sail. Shipping green seas on both sides . . . wind N.W. by W. going 7 1/2 knots."

As one could easily predict, while the *Beagle* was difficult to handle and a wet ship when sailing heavily laden, she was also unpredictable and hard to manage when very light. Helpman, Tuesday, March 5, 1839: "Wind fresh from the east. Thick misty weather towards the afternoon. The craft being very light, she works dreadfully badly, making about 2 points leeway. . . ."[28]

As noted before, the deep-waisted 10-gun brigs were especially vulnerable when caught carrying too much sail in a squall. Like them, the *Beagle* could easily be pushed around, fail to answer the helm, and immediately be right abeam of the waves. Normally in stormy weather Fitzroy tried to keep a minimum sail of a main topsail and five reefs, and in especially high winds he would reluctantly reduce this to his specially made storm trysails and fore staysail (Appendix A).

In the storm encountered by the *Beagle* in January 1833, off Cape Horn that has already been mentioned (p. 96), the crew managed, by keeping the minimum sail up, to maintain the all-important steerageway until three extremely large waves hit the vessel in succession. The first one came head-on, and she shook it off fairly well, but in the process her forward motion was momentarily halted. At this instant the second huge wave hit her. She was immediately dead at the helm and thrown off the wind so that the third wave caught her broadsides on and nearly sank her from the enormous weight of water that surged over her. Her lee bulwark was two to three feet underwater. Luckily she just managed to roll up, and because of some prompt action by the crew (see below), the water trapped on her upper deck poured off her before another wave came. But a fourth wave like that would have laid her on her beam ends, never to recover.

That the way to deal with such emergencies was learned only by hard experience is seen in the fact that at this time of this storm Fitzroy still maintained his preference that the gunports should always be fixed shut. When they were hit without warning by those heavy seas, it was only the prompt action of the carpenter, who had been told by Sulivan to keep a handspike ready for just such emergencies, that saved the ship: "[O]n . . . reaching the deck from below, he [Sulivan] found the carpenter up to his waist in water, standing on the bulwark, driving a handspike against the port, which he eventually burst open."[29]

It is somewhat hackneyed, but perhaps an analogy with an unruly and awkward horse could be made. In order to ensure a safe ride, the rider has to exercise a very firm control at the rein. The record of safe performance compiled by Fitzroy in the second voyage and by Wickham and Stokes in the third voyage of the *Beagle* is a function not only of the vessel herself but of the strict care and attention devoted to her handling by officers who were among the most skillful of their generation. The performance of the *Beagle* cannot fairly be compared with that of the typical packet brig with a poor crew and less than superbly efficient and zealous officers. The *Beagle,* particularly under Fitzroy, sailing alone in uncharted and difficult waters where any mishap could develop into real disaster, was manned with the utmost efficiency and the greatest attention to detail.

Nonetheless, like any square-rigged ship, even with the conversion from brig to bark, the *Beagle* could not sail close-hauled into the wind. This made her difficult to handle in tight situations where there was little space to maneuver. We have already seen references to the *Beagle*'s having to remain under way overnight or in adverse conditions, when fore-and-aft–rigged vessels working with her were able to put safely into a sheltered anchorage.

Even in the worst conditions the crew needed to keep a basic minimum of sail to avoid falling beam-on to the weather. Again from Helpman's diary (Thursday, November 9, 1837): "At 10:00 A.M. blowing very hard. Laid to under close (reefed) fore topsail, treble reefed main topsail, fore staysail—laying very

HMS *Beagle* rounding the Cape of Good Hope, 1837, original drawing possibly by J. L. Stokes, courtesy of the National Maritime Museum; see note 198.

quiet . . . blowing a heavy gale from Southward, with heavy squalls. Took in the fore topsail, the first that has been taken in yet. . . ."

Some of Fitzroy's program for efficient handling was recorded by Sulivan and has been published recently by his grandson.[30] His first line of defense against being put in a dangerous situation consisted of his keeping a very careful eye on the barometer and the weather. Fitzroy made this a systematic science rather than an art. Extensive reliance on the evidence of the barometer was novel in the 1830s. For example, in the first volume of the official *Narrative* it is clear that King thought it a bit of a gadget and unreliable, whereas Fitzroy in the second volume is at pains to point out its usefulness at every opportunity.

NINE

Charles Darwin Joins the Beagle

TO SAY THAT THE *BEAGLE* WAS EXTREMELY CRAMPED, EVEN
given the expectations of the time, would be a supreme
understatement. The ship was, after all, no longer than the distance between bases on a baseball field. If you imagine both
baseball teams, plus umpires and trainers standing along the
base line, that would still be fewer than the number of people
on board.

The *Beagle* sailed from Plymouth with, in addition to
Fitzroy:

John Clements Wickham	Lieutenant
Bartholemew James Sulivan	Lieutenant
Edward Main Chaffers	Master
Robert McCormick	Surgeon
George Rowlett	Purser
Alexander Derbishire	Mate
Peter Benson Stewart	Mate
John Lort Stokes	Mate and Assistant surveyor
Benjamin Bynoe	Assistant surgeon
Arthur Mellersh	Midshipman
Philip Gidley King	Midshipman

Alexander Burns Usborne	Master's Assistant
Charles Musters	Volunteer First Class
Jonathan May	Carpenter
Edward H. Hellyer	Clerk

There was also a sergeant of marines and seven privates, an acting boatswain and thirty-four men and boys. Wickham, Sulivan, Bynoe, Stokes, Mellersh, King, Sorrell, May, the sergeant of marines, four of the marine privates, the coxswain, and some of the seamen ("these determined admirers of Tierra del Fuego") were veterans of the first voyage.

In addition, there were several supernumeraries. The Reverend Richard Matthews, who intended to act as a missionary among the Fuegians, was sponsored by a public subscription. He and the three Fuegians made up the missionary party. Fitzroy also took along Augustus Earle, a talented artist, to record the adventures of the expedition. George James Stebbing, the son of the instrument maker at Portsmouth, was taken along as "instrument maker." It was his responsibility to keep the chronometers and other instruments in first-class condition; he also doubled as librarian. Syms Covington, was originally shipped as "Fiddler and boy to the poop cabin" and later became Charles Darwin's servant and assistant. Darwin taught him to prepare specimens and came to rely heavily upon him for shooting specimens. (Covington stayed on as Darwin's assistant after the voyage, working for a couple of years before emigrating to Australia.) Last but not least there was Charles Robert Darwin.

Why Was Charles Darwin on Board?

That Charles Darwin sailed with the *Beagle* as naturalist is something that is as familiar to most readers as the name of the vessel itself. Just how he came to be chosen, however, is a fascinating and still controversial story.

Charles Darwin was born at Shrewsbury, England on February 12, 1809 (the very same day as Abraham Lincoln).[1] His father, Robert Waring Darwin, was a distinguished doctor and his grandfather Erasmus Darwin was a famous doctor, naturalist, and poet whose own theorizings about evolution are thought to have been influential not only with his grandson but also the well-known French biologist Jean Baptiste de Lamarck. Darwin's mother was the daughter of Josiah Wedgwood, founder of the famous pottery.

Darwin was the fifth of six children. His mother died when he was eight, and he grew up spoiled by his older sisters. From very early on he had a passion for natural science, particularly collecting minerals and insects, and he was a devoted outdoorsman for whom shooting was probably always more important than studying. He and his older brother, Erasmus, spent many hours at experiments in chemistry. At first his father intended him to become a doctor, and at age sixteen he enrolled at Edinburgh University.

At Edinburgh he studied with several of the greatest natural scientists of the day. One in particular influenced him for the rest of his life: Dr. Robert Grant (later professor at London University), who introduced him to marine biology and the study of microscopic forms such as larvae. Professor Robert Jameson, however, with his exceptionally boring lectures, almost put him off the study of geology for the rest of his life. Darwin learned a great deal at Edinburgh, especially through the Plinian Society, a society devoted to the study of natural science that he was invited to join in 1826. But he had no stomach for medicine. Observing operations performed on young children without anesthetic (yet to be invented) revolted him, and he left Edinburgh.

For a young man in his position, after medicine and the army, the only possibility for a career was the church, so Dr. Darwin sent his son to Cambridge University in February 1828. At Cambridge, where there was no program in science per se, he came under the influence of the Reverend John Stevens Henslow, a leading botanist, and under him he continued his natural history interests, together with much hunting and shooting. It would be easy to get the impression that he was something of a playboy. But he cared passionately about science, and with people like Henslow, the astronomer and philosopher John Herschel, and the zoologist Reverend Leonard Jenyns he learned informally far more than he did in the classroom. With them he was very serious indeed. Probably because of his experiences with Jameson, even though the great Professor Adam Sedgwick was at Cambridge, he took no formal training in geology. But he fell under the spell of the writings of the explorer Alexander von Humboldt and began to plan, with his friends, an expedition of his own.

While Darwin obviously grew up in a world of upper-middle-class prosperity, it was also a world deeply divided by social issues as well as new scientific ideas. Henslow was very active politically. To be a Whig, as Darwin and Henslow were, was not to side with traditional authority. In science it was a time of equal turmoil, focusing particularly on views of earth history: whether the present form of the earth was shaped by a series of great catastrophes (and not just the biblical flood) or more gradually over time by the same sorts of forces that we see acting today.

The old categorization still applies: By the 1830s astronomy and physics had fallen into place as scientific subjects in the sense that the underlying laws and principles were identified and quantifiable. The earth sciences were poised to be the next. After that would come biology with, eventually, Darwin as its Lyell and Newton.

It was a time to challenge and a time to resist. Darwin joined the challengers early on. His particular brilliance was to be able to harness the same fierce intellect both to a naturalist's eye for detailed observation and a feel for the fittedness of nature and to an analytical gift for distinguishing the general from the particular. There were wonderful opportunities for the sympathetic observer, and it would have been easy, as it still is, for observation to be enough. At least by the time he was at Cambridge, and for all we know much earlier, Darwin was an investigator and philosopher as well.

Darwin scraped through his studies with a reasonably respectable degree and that summer set off to fill in a gap in his training by assisting Sedgwick in an expedition to Wales; he had become deeply caught up in the question of scientific versus theological interpretations of the geological record.* Then he hoped to travel to Tenerife with some friends before settling down as a young curate somewhere in the country following, like Henslow or Gilbert White, the honorable tradition of the cleric-natural philosopher. But out of the blue came the invitation to join Fitzroy and the *Beagle*.

The letter came from his patron and mentor Henslow: "Captain Fitzroy is going out to survey . . . the vessel is fitted out expressly for scientific purposes, combined with the surveys: it will furnish therefore a rare opportunity for a naturalist and it would be a great misfortune that it should be lost: An offer has been made to me to recommend a proper person to go out as naturalist with this expedition: he will be treated with every consideration. . . "[3]

Here was a fantastic offer, for an adventure far greater than a trip to Tenerife to collect insects with his friends. It was exciting but, of course, out of the question. Five years on a tiny naval ship, with total strangers, for a man whose only experience abroad had been a quick trip over the Channel to France! Yet Darwin wanted very much to go if he could persuade his father. It would cost money. Of course, his father said no.

The Puzzle of the Offer

What kind of offer was this? We all are so familiar with the idea that Darwin was invited to sail with Fitzroy as the expedition's "naturalist" that it comes as a shock to learn that there are other, quite different views of the reasons for the appointment.

---

* In his memoirs Lord Sherbrooke recalls meeting Darwin during this expedition. "He was making a geological tour in Wales, and carried with him, in addition to his other burdens, a hammer of 14 lbs weight. I remember he was full of modesty, and was always lamenting his bad memory for languages and inability to quote. . . . I am proud to remember that . . . I saw a something in him which marked him out as superior to anyone I had ever met: the proof which I have of this was somewhat canine in nature, I followed him. I walked twenty-two miles with him. . . "[2]

Specifically the idea has been growing that Darwin was really invited only as Fitzroy's companion and that the title of naturalist was simply a cover.

One potentially confusing aspect of the situation has to be cleared up first. On any navy ship, particularly the exploring ships engaged in the Hydrographic Service, the surgeon was the *official* naturalist. It was part of his formal duties to collect specimens of animals, plants, and minerals and observe all aspects of natural history. The specimens that he brought back usually became part of the national collections. Among distinguished scientists who started their careers as ship's surgeon we can count none other than the great Thomas Henry Huxley (surgeon of HMS *Rattlesnake,* 1846–50 and later Darwin's great protagonist). Therefore, in a strict sense the official naturalist on board the *Beagle* would have been the appointed surgeon, a man named McCormick.

Robert McCormick (born in 1800) was older than either Darwin or Fitzroy and already a veteran of Parry's expedition to the Arctic. It is clear from his autobiography that he was an earnest, disdainful man, rather self-important and overbearingly ambitious. In 1830, lacking an appointment to a ship, he had gone to Edinburgh and taken classes in medicine. Ironically, it was Jameson's lectures in natural history that aroused in him a drive to make a name as a naturalist: "my object was to get employed in scientific voyages of discovery." But he aimed high, hoping to be posted to a "frigate or other desirable ship," being "wearied and tired out with the buffeting about in small craft, ofttimes very uncomfortable vessels, employed upon unhealthy stations. . . ."[4]

Some authors believe, therefore, that if McCormick was the naturalist, Darwin's intended function on board might have been something else.[5] From the time of Captain Cook and the botanist Joseph Banks, however, important voyages to new and unexplored lands had traditionally carried supernumeraries specifically brought along because of their particular expertise in natural history. The reason is not difficult to see. The surgeon might be both too busy with his first duty—the health of the ship's complement—and too inexperienced to do a truly first-class job as naturalist as well, beyond simple collecting as time allowed. So civilian "experts" were often carried along. When Philip Parker King explored northern Australia in the *Bathurst* (1817–22; see Chapter 13), he carried with him the botanist Allan Cunningham, already a veteran of exploration in Australia, who made many extremely distinguished contributions to the natural history of plants (he was murdered by some Aborigines in 1836). When F. P. Blackwood commanding the *Fly* and *Bramble* relieved the *Beagle* at the end of her career, again in Australian waters (1843), he carried with him as naturalists Joseph Beete Jukes and the geologist John MacGilivary employed by the earl of Derby, as well as an artist. Indeed, MacGilivary was later appointed by the Admiralty as a naturalist to the same voyage of HMS *Rattlesnake* in which, as previously noted, Huxley was the surgeon.

Any thorough expedition of exploration could therefore quite reasonably be expected to carry both an artist and a supernumerary naturalist. Fitzroy, who was accustomed always to doing things in a first-class manner, would naturally have wanted no less for his expedition.

We know that the request for a naturalist came from Fitzroy himself. Captain Beaufort approved the request, and Beaufort asked his friend the Reverend George Peacock at Cambridge to make a recommendation to him. But Fitzroy's motives in the matter have now been challenged, and what seemed very simple is now much more complicated. The suggestion that Fitzroy simply wanted a companion to accompany him on the voyage depends on the following argument.

First, it is argued that Fitzroy may have been only too aware of his hereditary disposition to mental disturbance and the family history of suicide. He had seen what a long voyage and the total loneliness of command (the traditional isolation of the naval captain) had done to Pringle Stokes. Possibly, therefore, he wanted to preserve his sanity by ensuring that there was someone on board with whom he could converse and be companionable. Such a person could not be another officer; the captain had to keep himself aloof. Someone like the aristocratic Fitzroy could mix socially only with someone of equal social standing. The artist or poor Reverend Matthews would not do as a companion. The conclusion follows that "What Robert Fitzroy wanted when he met Charles Darwin was a gentleman to help him bear the burdens of an arduous and isolated sea command, and the study of nature, in those far-off places he was sailing to, could provide an appropriate occupation for the Captain's guest. Darwin was on board the *Beagle* to give the Captain someone to relax with, someone talk to. . . ."[6]

The argument is also made that since Darwin was so young, he could not possibly have been invited on account of his expertise in natural history.

This is an appealing revision of a familiar story. It has many far-reaching implications, particularly in cutting Darwin down to mere mortal status if his appointment was not on merit but on social privilege. It opens the possibility that anyone who happened to have had the same wonderful chance so inappropriately dumped in his lap could have made the same discoveries.

To complicate matters further, we know that Fitzroy had in fact invited a friend to go with him before he asked Darwin, but that fell through. The only known references to this friend are in letters from Darwin to his sister Susan (September 5, 1831)—"it seems he had promised to take a friend with him, who is in office and cannot go"—and to Henslow (about the same date): "what has induced Capt. Fitzroy to take a better view of the case is; that Mr. Chester, who was going as a friend, cannot go; so that I shall have his place in every respect." This invitation to "Chester" probably does indicate that Fitzroy wanted some sort of companion on the voyage, and Chester's candidacy may in fact have been left over from the private voyage planned for the hired brig *John*. In any case, it does not solve the puzzle of why and how *Darwin* was invited.*

The question is not so simple as: Was Darwin chosen to go on the voyage for his naturalist's talents or simply as a companion? It is clear that Fitzroy wanted the "naturalist" to share his

---

* "Mr. Chester" was probably Harry Chester, then a clerk in the Privy Council office, later a novelist.[7]

cabin for meals. He would occupy, especially on that tiny ship, a very special position. To that extent, obviously, the positions of naturalist and companion were inseparable. We need to discover both what Fitzroy intended and what Darwin expected.

Of Fitzroy's private opinions, we have little firsthand evidence. We know that a special social position would be afforded to the naturalist as the captain's guest: "he offers me to mess with him" (Darwin's letter to Henslow, quoted above). At some point, either before or after the invitation to Chester, Fitzroy went to Beaufort and asked him to choose a naturalist. Did he ask for a companion who could double as a naturalist or someone who was chosen first for his ability as a naturalist and might double as a companion? In his own *Narrative,* Fitzroy states: "Anxious that no opportunity of collecting useful information, during the voyage, should be lost; I proposed to the Hydrographer that some well-educated and scientific person should be sought for who would willingly share such accommodation as I had to offer, in order to profit by the opportunity of visiting distant countries yet little known."

If the puzzle is to be solved, the key must lie in the letters exchanged among Beaufort, Peacock, Henslow, Darwin, and Fitzroy. They turn out to have been partially misunderstood.

What role did Darwin think was being offered to him? There are four letters that seem to address the question. The Reverend George Peacock's original letter to Henslow, quoted above, continues:

An offer has been made to me to recommend a proper person to go out as naturalist with this expedition: he will be treated with every consideration . . . if Leonard Jenyns could go, what treasures he might bring home with him . . . in the absence of so accomplished a naturalist, is there any person whom you could strongly recommend: he must be such a person as would do credit to your recommendation. . . . It would be a serious loss to the cause of natural science, if this fine opportunity were lost. . . .

Henslow then wrote to Darwin (August 24):

I have stated [to Peacock] that I consider you to be the best qualified person I know of who is likely to undertake such a situation—I state this not on the supposition of yr. being a finished naturalist, but as amply qualified for collecting, observing, & noting anything new to be noted in Natural History. Peacock has the appointment at his office, the opportunity will probably be lost. Capt. F. wants a man (I understand) more as a companion than a mere collector & would not take anyone however good a Naturalist who was not recommended to him likewise as a gentleman. . . .

In addition, Peacock wrote directly to Darwin (no date): "[T]he expedition is entirely for scientific purposes & the shop will generally await your leisure for researches in natural history, etc.; Captain Fitzroy is a public spirited & zealous officer, of delightful manners and greatly beloved by all his brother officers . . . you may be sure therefore of having a very pleasant companion. . . ."

These are the letters that have been interpreted as evidence that Fitzroy really was looking first and foremost for a companion. Yet I believe the evidence points in exactly the opposite direction.

Not only was the position first offered to the Reverend Leonard Jenyns, but Darwin states that Henslow wanted to go himself: "Mrs. Henslow most generously and without being asked gave her consent, but she looked so miserable that Henslow at once settled the point" (letter to Susan, September 4, 1831). Jenyns's position seems to have been equivocal. Darwin states to Susan (same letter) that "Jenyns . . . was so near accepting it that he packed up his clothes." Jenyns later recalled, however: "[Henslow] and Peacock pressed me to go. . . . I took a day to consider it;—at the end of which I was quite determined against going. . . ."

Fitzroy would hardly have given the choice of a pure companion to his superior Beaufort to pass off among the latter's friends at Cambridge. Beaufort himself evidently had no thought of the appointment's being "more as a companion." It is out of the question that the reverends Jenyns or Henslow would have seriously considered the position of "companion" to a ship's captain at least twenty years their junior.

Finally, on September 1, Beaufort reported to Fitzroy: "I believe my friend Mr. Peacock has succeeded in getting a 'Savant' for you . . . a Mr. Darwin."[8]

The most difficult phrase in all the letters is Henslow's: "more as a companion than as a mere collector." This does indeed seem to be a straightforward indictment. But Henslow was merely rephrasing Peacock's letter. Both letters by Peacock and Beaufort's letter to Fitzroy stress the scientific nature of the quest.

I believe the puzzle can be very simply resolved. The confusion stems from a basic misunderstanding of the social and scientific contexts of the invitation. We must acknowledge that Fitzroy did indeed realize that a companion of some sort would be a definite asset on a five-year voyage. But equally, he evidently intended that his little expedition would be as complete as possible, given that he had only one small vessel at his disposal. We also know that Fitzroy was something of a scientist in his own right. How natural that he would want to take along a naturalist. And how obvious that he should attempt to ensure that the right sort of naturalist would be chosen so that he could also be a useful companion.

The crux of the matter, which has hitherto been overlooked, is that in the state of society and natural science at that date there were basically two classes of person who might have been attracted to and qualified for the post of naturalist. The first was the working "collector," of whom there were many in the first half of the century, employed for the great patrons of science, to enhance their "cabinets." But these collectors (like Cunningham or McGilivary) had no social status and would not have served Fitzroy's other requirement. They would have been no better than the sort of person exemplified by McCormick himself. The other class was exemplified by gentleman naturalists like Peacock, Jenyns, Henslow, Darwin, and many others—also a common enough species at that time. But would such a refined person be the slightest interested in sailing for five years on a tiny rough-and-ready naval vessel? The answer is an obvious no. To find a naturalist who was also socially acceptable (someone "more of a companion than a mere collector"), Fitzroy needed the help of Beaufort and Peacock, hence the key phrase (Peacock's) "someone who would do credit to our recommendation."

Thus the language in Peacock's and Henslow's letters is explained. They are not going out of their way to explain to the innocent Darwin that he would be expected to be a companion first and a naturalist on the side. They are, on the contrary, trying to reassure the wellborn Darwin (and his even more socially conscious father) that as an independent naturalist he would be treated fully as a gentleman. Without this social understanding Darwin would have been mad (and in any case forbidden by his father) to have dashed off to spend five years on a British man-of-war.

Commentators anxious to devalue the accomplishments of Charles Darwin have also overlooked the extent of his prior qualifications. After his studies in Edinburgh with Grant and his years at Cambridge with Henslow, he was actually an extraordinarily well-trained natural scientist. He had spent the preceding summer learning geology with Professor Adam Sedgwick. He had written to Henslow (July 11, 1831) before they set off: "I suspect the first expedition I take, clinometer & hammer in hand, will send me back very little wiser & [a] good deal more puzzled than when I started.—As yet I have only indulged in hypotheses; but they are such powerful ones, that I suppose, if they were put into action but for one day, the world would come to an end." And when the suggestion of the *Beagle* voyage came, he was already planning his own modest scientific expedition.

How broad *was* Darwin's interest in science? The man who wrote to his sister in preparation for the voyage: "[L]ook in bedroom over the Edinburgh Journal of Science or some such title and see whether the following papers are in it: three by Humboldt on 'Isothermal Lines,' two by Coldstream and Fioggo on 'Meteorology,' one by Leslie on 'Meteorological Observations' . . ." sounds like someone who already knew his subjects rather than an aimless and amiable amateur. And from the first weeks on board HMS *Beagle,* he functioned with extraordinary skill. With the learning he brought in his head and the few books on board, he began not only a series of unique scientific observations but also theoretical speculations from geology to (eventually) evolution.

Darwin, at least, was under no illusions about his role. He thought of himself solely as the naturalist. He saw it as a superb scientific opportunity. He was so sure of the importance of his collections that he insisted that he should have the rights to their distribution, rather than their automatically passing to the government. Not until Beaufort satisfied him on this point and also confirmed that the voyage would go to all the promised places of interest (particularly the South Seas) did he finally commit himself to taking part.

The "puzzle" then turns out only to be a misreading of the evidence, but it is a useful means of understanding the complex social spectrum of life on board a ship and Darwin's unique position on the *Beagle*. In the end Fitzroy got his naturalist, more of a scientist than Beaufort, Peacock, or Henslow guessed. And despite their many disagreements, each had a stimulating companion for the voyage.

There is no doubt that Darwin was lucky—lucky enough in Edinburgh to salvage the best (Grant) before Jameson and medicine sent him away empty-handed. He was lucky in his association with Henslow; it might have been very different, for example, if his mentor had been the worthy but less imaginative Leonard Jenyns. He was lucky to be well enough provided for financially to be independent but not so rich as to lack ambitions. But luck is always earned—if only intuitively. He sought out Grant, Henslow, Sedgwick, and Herschel, so the *Beagle* offer was not luck at all.

However, Darwin did not get to sign on without quite a different battle. His father was against the venture. Among other objections he thought it would be "disreputable to my character as a Clergyman hereafter." But at least he was open to persuasion. Darwin's "Uncle Jos" Wedgwood, on the other hand, thought it was a marvelous opportunity, and with his help the good doctor's permission was given.

Darwin's peace of mind can scarcely have been increased by the fact that soon after everything was settled concerning his joining the expedition, Fitzroy started to show his erratic side. Quite apart from the fact that he was Tory and Darwin a Whig (these were the days of debate over repeal of the repressive Corn Laws), Fitzroy believed in physiognomy and thought the shape of Darwin's nose was all wrong!* After agreeing that Darwin could come, Fitzroy changed his mind (hence Darwin's early September letter to Henslow, quoted above, in which the subject of Mr. Chester comes up). Similarly (to Susan, September 9, 1831): "Capt. Fitzroy first wished to have [a] naturalist, and then he seems to have taken a sudden horror of the chances of having somebody he should not like on board the Vessel. . . ." Then he relented, and all was settled.

At times Fitzroy was Darwin's "beau ideal of a Captain." But when Fitzroy behaved very badly toward a shopkeeper at Plymouth, Darwin was revolted. In this way their lives began to be intertwined and opposed.

Orders from the Admiralty

Instructions from the Admiralty were written on November 11, 1831.[9]

> You are hereby required and directed to put to sea, in the vessel you command, as soon as she shall be in every respect ready, and to proceed in her, with all convenient expedition, successively to Madeira or Teneriffe; the Cape de Verde Islands; Fernando Noronha; and the South American station; to perform the operations, and execute the surveys, pointed out in the accompanying memorandum, which has been drawn up under our direction by the Hydrographer of this office; observing and following, in the prosecution of the said surveys, and in your other operations, the directions and suggestions contained in the said memorandum.

---

* Remarkably, when Darwin returned home after five years' voyage with Fitzroy, his father observed: "[T]he shape of your head has changed"!

You are to consider yourself under the command of Rear-Admiral Sir Thomas Baker, Commander-in-chief of his Majesty's ships on the South American station, whilst you are within the limits of that station, in execution of the services above-mentioned; and in addition to the directions conveyed to you in the memorandum, or the subject of your supplies of provisions, we have signified to the Rear-Admiral our desire that, whenever the occasion offers, you should receive from him and the officers of his squadron, any assistance, in stores and provisions, of which you may stand in need.

But during the whole time of your continuing on the above duties, you are (notwithstanding the 16th article of the 4th section of the 6th chapter, page 78, of the General Printed instructions) to send reports, by every opportunity, to our Secretary, of your proceedings, and of the progress you make.

Having completed the surveys which you are directed to execute on the South American station, you are to proceed to perform the several further operations set forth in the Hydrographer's memorandum, in the course therein pointed out; and having done so, you are to return, in the vessel you command, to Spithead, and report your arrival to our Secretary, for our information and further directions.

In the event of any unfortunate accident happening to yourself, the officer on whom the command of the *Beagle* may in consequence devolve, is hereby required and directed to complete, as far as in him lies, that part of the survey on which the vessel may be then engaged, but not to proceed to a new step in the voyage; as, for instance, if at that time carrying on the coast survey on the western side of South America, he is not to cross the Pacific, but to return to England by Rio de Janeiro and the Atlantic.

Given under our hands, the 11th of November 1831.

(Signed) T. M. Hardy,
G. Barrington.

To Robert Fitz-Roy, Esq.,
Commander of his Majesty's surveying vessel
 "Beagle," at Plymouth.
 By command of their Lordships,

Geo. Elliot

Captain Beaufort, the hydrographer, sent an accompanying memorandum to Fitzroy. The first major task would be to determine the exact longitude of Rio de Janeiro. It had been decided that in the future this would be the point from which all meridian distances in South America would be measured, but there was a considerable difference between the longitudes stated for Rio by Captains King, Beechey, and Foster, compared with Captain Owen, and those given by the French navigator Baron Roussin and the Portuguese. In making his chain of meridian distances, Fitzroy was to attempt to have more or less equal intervals between points. Therefore, he was to proceed first to Madeira (the position of which was agreed upon by everyone) and then to Porta Praya in the Cape Verde Islands and Fernando de Noronha on the way to Rio. He was also to fix the position of the Abrolhos Banks en route.

Because the French were actively surveying the coast between St. Catherine's and the Río de la Plata, he was to proceed from Rio de Janeiro direct to Montevideo and there rate the chronometers at exactly the spot where King had previously. The work of surveying would start with the coast from Cape San Antonio to Cape St. Georges, most of which was apparently incorrectly placed in previous maps. Then the ship was to survey the northeastern coast of Tierra del Fuego, the Beagle Channel, and Whale-Boat Sound and thus finish the survey of this region. After that the expedition was to head for the Falkland Islands and give a complete report on the territory, which was in dispute between Britain and Argentina. They were to survey from Cape Pillar to Cape Forward in greater detail than had been done previously (Pringle Stokes's fateful voyage) and also examine Admiralty Sound and Cape Orange. Moving northward, they were to study the seaward side of the Queen Adelaide Archipelago and up to the Guayaquil River. They were to visit Concepción and other points along the western coast of South America, before heading westward to start the rest of their circle around the world. Their destination would be the Galápagos Islands, Tahiti (visiting the point fixed by Captain Cook), and then Port Jackson, Australia. They would return home via the Cape of Good Hope, St. Helena, and the

Ascension Islands. During the latter part of the voyage they would not be engaged in much coastal surveying but would concentrate on their scientific observations pertaining to the fixing of chronometric distances.

Beaufort's accompanying memorandum was evidently meant for more eyes than Fitzroy's. It is a general statement on the whole art and purposes of the hydrographic survey. It contained detailed instructions on every aspect of the daily routine of meteorology and astronomy. It concludes with a warning about the natives of the Pacific who were known to be armed, cautioning against provoking any possible hostilities that could mar the voyage. Added at the end he included a code or classification of notations to be used to indicate the state of the weather and also the force of the wind. This was the famous Beaufort Scale still in use.[10]

TEN

The Second Surveying Voyage

My notions of the inside of a ship were about as indefinite as those of some men on the inside of a man, viz. a large cavity containing air, water & food mingled in hopeless confusion.

Charles Darwin,
Diary, November 23, 1831

THE EAGER YOUNG DARWIN, AGED TWENTY-TWO AND A half, arrived at Plymouth in late October 1831. His diary and letters soon give us a landsman's view of the hectic preparation of the *Beagle,* from her painting to the stowing of the chronometers and stores. Although work had been in progress on the *Beagle* since July 11, the ship was still "without her masts or bulkheads and looked more like a wreck, than a vessel commissioned to go around the world." Soon, however, the slightly euphoric Darwin was writing to his mentor, Professor Henslow (November 15, 1831): "She looks most beautiful, even a landsman must admire her. We all think her the most perfect vessel ever turned out by the Dockyard. One thing is certain, no vessel has been fitted out so expensively, and with so much care.

Everything that can be made so is of mahogany, and nothing can exceed the neatness and beauty of her accommodations."[1]

While the ship was being prepared, and before they all could move on board, Fitzroy and his officers, accompanied by the ever-interested Darwin, set about making the necessary observations to establish the precise point from which all their comparative measurements would be made. They went "to the breakwater, where we staid for more than an hour. Capt. Fitzroy was employed in taking angles, so as to connect a particular stone, from which Capt. King commenced for the last voyage his longitudes, to the quay at Clarence Baths, where the true time is now taken."[2]

Captain King came to visit them, accompanying his son Philip Gidley King, who was to be midshipman on this voyage. They also visited several times with Mr. Harris, who was in Plymouth to supervise the installation of his new lightning conductors. Later they "went to Athenaeum & heard a popular lecture from Mr. Harris" (see Appendix E).

The *Beagle* was now really taking shape, and Darwin was getting to learn everything about her, all the time very concerned about the minuscule space available to him. "I have just room to turn round and that is all." The space assigned to him was "the narrow space at the end of the chart table . . . for working, dressing and sleeping . . . his only stowage for clothes being several small drawers in the corner . . . for specimens he had a very small cabin under the forecastle."

By November 14 the paint was dry, and Fitzroy started stowing the chronometers and the library. On the twenty-third the *Beagle* was moved from the dockyard to Barnet Pool; "there remains very little to be done to make all ready for sailing. All the stores are completed and yesterday between 5 & 6 thousands of canisters of preserved meat were stowed away. Not one inch of room is lost, the hold would contain scarcely another bag of bread."[3]

Fitzroy gave a shipwarming party on the twenty-eighth, and on December 3 Darwin spent his first night on board, experiencing "a most ludicrous difficulty" in getting into his hammock. "In the morning the ship rolled a good deal, but I did not feel uncomfortable; this gives me great hopes of escaping sea-sickness. I find others trust in the same weak support. May we not be confounded."[4] But like many others before and since, they *were* confounded, and on the next day he wrote, "It has however blown a heavy gale from the South ever since midday, and perhaps we shall not be able to leave harbour. The vessel had a good deal of motion and I was as nearly as possible made sick."[5]

All they needed was a favorable wind. This was not forthcoming; for five days southerly gales kept them in harbor. Darwin occupied himself by fussing with the rearrangement of the poop cabin, stowing everything in the neatest possible way. Then it seemed to clear, and Fitzroy gave orders that they would sail the next day (December 9). "Accordingly at 9:00 o'clock we weighted anchors, and a little after 10:00 sailed. . . . I was soon made rather sick." But the barometer fell, and a heavy southwest gale came on. "The sea ran dreadfully high and the vessel pitched bows under. I suffered most dreadfully; such a night I never passed, on every side nothing but misery; such a whistling of wind and roar of the sea, the hoarse screams of the officers and shouts of the men, made a concert that I shall not forget."[6] Unable to make any progress to windward, they put back next day to Plymouth.

On the seventeenth a brig that had left Plymouth three weeks previously was driven back into port, so they waited it out until the twenty-first, when "the morning was calm and the sun shone red through the mist; everything gave up hopes of a steady N.E. wind, and a prosperous voyage." The ship sailed at 11:00 A.M. but struck a rock near Drake's Island, still in Plymouth Sound. Here they stuck fast for about half an hour until by making the crew run from side to side of the ship, they managed to get the *Beagle* swinging, and she slid off, apparently with no damage. Heading for the open sea, they were only about eleven miles from The Lizard when another southwest gale came on, and they put back to Plymouth once again.

Christmas Day found everyone despondent at being so delayed while Darwin was hoping that this gradual exposure to the open seas would help him become accustomed to sea-sickness. The men of the *Beagle* celebrated Christmas in a traditional way: by getting thoroughly drunk. Boxing Day (December 26) turned out to be a beautiful day for sailing, but the crew was not up to it; "the opportunity has been lost owing to the drunkenness and absence of nearly the whole crew. The ship has been all day in a state of anarchy."[7] Fitzroy started punishments by putting some of the men in chains.

The twenty-seventh was another beautiful day, and in the bright December sunshine an easterly breeze "filled every sail." They were finally on their way. Darwin went to his hammock with a calm stomach, his last for many weeks.

The favorable winds increased and drove them "onwards into the Atlantic as fast as a heavily laden vessel, with her scuppers in the water, could be forced."[8] On the second day out Fitzroy had the worst offenders from the Christmas disorderliness flogged.

Charles Darwin and Robert Fitzroy

The officers and crew of the *Beagle* soon found that their captain was a changed man from the Fitzroy of the first voyage. On the first voyage the excitement and challenge of his first command kept Fitzroy from sinking too deeply into introspection and depression. On the second voyage the responsibility brought out both the worst and the best in him. Fitzroy was determined that his ship would run on the most efficient lines. In his daily rounds of the ship with First Officer John Clement Wickham he endlessly checked every little detail of seamanship. Fitzroy would tolerate no mistakes and no sloppiness. The code word *hot coffee* soon came into use to signal the captain's temper. On a bad morning nothing pleased him, and his displeasure descended first upon poor Wickham and thence to the others. Every officer and crew member would try to make themselves invisible on a morning when a lot of "hot coffee" had been served. On other days, unpredictably, he would be relaxed and pleasant.

Fitzroy set out elaborate and extremely efficient guidelines for the handling of the ship: He drilled his men until they became polished and skilled in their duties. As the voyage went on, the advantages of Fitzroy's systems, especially his extensive reliance on the barometer, became evident. For example, in his diary for January 5, 1835, Darwin noted: "The barometer says we shall have fine weather; and although we have at present a foul wind and plenty of rain, we stand out to sea." Then the next day: "The captain's faith is rewarded by a beautiful day and a southerly wind. . . ."[9]

Fitzroy had a scientist's interest in the weather and eventually made a predictive science out of meteorology whereas others had been stubbornly empirical at the very best and for them meteorology was the collection of statistics. Eventually, of course, Fitzroy was credited with having been one of the founders of weather forecasting.

During the whole second voyage the *Beagle* suffered no major damage to masts, spares, or rigging as the result of storms. The crew lost no member in any accident in handling the ship.

Fitzroy was a firm believer in the importance of truly disciplined training. His men had to perform all possible duties as a matter of simple routine. Only in that way would they be able to respond quickly and safely to all emergencies. Although it was strictly not necessary, he also drilled his men in a number of "fancy" maneuvers and competed with other ships he met in the belief, frequently justified, that he could instill in his crew pride in their ship and in themselves. On the South American station later Darwin was to be impressed with their "showing off" the skills of the *Beagle*'s crew. "We have beat all the ships in maneuvering. . . . It was glorious today how we beat the *Samarang* in furling sails. It is quite a new thing for a 'sounding ship' to beat a regular man of war, and yet the *Beagle* is not a particular ship." Again, "we came, in the first style, alongside the Admiral's ship, and we, to their astonishment, took in every inch of canvas, and then set it immediately again. A sounding ship doing such a perfect maneuver with such certainty and rapidly is an event hitherto unknown in that class. It is a great satisfaction to know that we are in such beautiful order and discipline."[10]

They had no shortage of opportunities to test their discipline in real situations. Arthur Mellersh later recalled an incident that shows perfectly the importance of Fitzroy's training:

> We were near the western entrance of the Straits of Magellan, in mid-winter, going westward; it was blowing hard; treble-reefed topsails and reefed courses; the main sail hauled up but not furled; wind from the westward. I [then a mate] was officer of the middle watch [midnight to 4:00 A.M.]. The Captain directed [Sulivan] to keep with me. The night was inky dark, when about 1 am the lookout man called out "Rocks close on the starboard beam." As we were land-locked the water was smooth. [Sulivan] gave the order "Lower main sail" and the watch ran the main tack on board, and hauled after the main-sheet so quickly that, though so close to the perpendicular rocks, the lee clew of the main sail nearly touched the wall-like cliff. The ship sprang off like an arrow from a blow. A moment's indecision would have been fatal; but there was none, and the ship was saved.[11]

Fitzroy's mental state fluctuated badly during the second voyage. As far as can be judged in hindsight, he was becoming more manic-depressive with time and with the press of his responsibilities. He alternated between periods of blank, silent despair and other times of boundless energy and enthusiasm. One of Darwin's first impressions of Fitzroy is probably as telling as any:

> The Captain continues steadily very kind and does everything in his power to assist me. . . . I never met a man who could endure nearly so great a share of fatigue. He works incessantly, and when apparently not employed, he is thinking. If he does not kill himself, he will, during this voyage, do a wonderful quality of work. His greatest fault as a companion is his austere silence, produced from excessive thinking: his many good qualities are great & numerous; altogether he is the strongest character I ever fell in with.[12]

Fitzroy soon came to have an equally high opinion of Darwin: "Darwin is a very sensible hard-working man, and a very pleasant mess-mate. I never saw a 'shore-going fellow' come into the ways of a ship so soon and so thoroughly as Darwin."[13]

The captain, of course, was a staunch Tory, and Darwin an equally earnest Whig. ". . . we get on very well—but I thank my better fortune he has not made me a renegade to Whig principles: I would not be a Tory, if it was merely on account of their cold hearts about that scandal to Christian Nations slavery" (Darwin to Henslow, a really determined Whig).[14]

As soon as he could, Darwin started collecting everything he could both on land and, with nets and lines, from the sea. As Wickham was responsible to the captain for the condition of the ship, Darwin soon became a great trial to him. Wickham frequently but good-naturedly cursed the "flycatcher philosopher" for his "damned beastly bedevilment" of the litter of specimens in barrels and crates on his neat decks. "If I were skipper, I would soon have you and all your damned mess out of the place."[15] Darwin and Wickham became good friends; to Darwin, Wickham was "by far the most conversible person on board. I do not mean talks most for in that respect, Sulivan quite bears away the pawn."[16] Soon Darwin was stuck with the nickname Philos.

The personal relationship between Fitzroy and Darwin has been discussed by many authors, usually emphasizing their many differences. But despite the fact that the two men argued often and fiercely, they became very fast friends. I believe that the differences in outlook between the two men and the philosophical divergence concerning evolution and biblical truth (much of which developed over later years) have been overestimated by biographers and have been allowed to divert attention from the remarkable bond that grew up between them on the voyage. Although Darwin spent all the time he could onshore, when on board he ate every meal with Fitzroy. They had to make the best of each other, and the best was very good indeed. The few surviving letters between them, like that quoted in the previous chapter, are full of an intense, almost schoolboyish affection and camaraderie. Intellectually they differed on many issues, but they both *were* intellectuals.

A word must also be added here concerning Darwin's health. He seems to have been a normally healthy young man, with bad skin and a slightly nervous stomach. None of his ailments during the voyage, from palpitations and faintness before the voyage started to possible Chagas' disease from a bug bite, were out of the ordinary. The famous ill health of his later years, with the water cures and enemas, miraculously cleared up once he stopped publishing controversial books on evolution and returned to other aspects of natural history. No doubt this later ill health was psychosomatic. While it was no less debilitating than, say, ulcers or diverticulitis, it also became a sustaining way of life. In fact, that Darwin went from youthful adventurer to Victorian careful old man is far less surprising than if he had continued his reckless adventuring of South American days into late middle age like some sort of improbable Conan Doyle hero.

The dashing Fitzroy was much more the sort of man whom we might nowadays expect to become a television "personality." His life, like Darwin's, was one of conflicts. It was the rare naval officer who could combine the best of a traditional-bound service with the openly inquiring and testing mind of the mid-century, pressed everywhere by change: in science, in the complexities of world politics, and in the technology of the ships themselves. A life cannot easily cope with everything changing at once. Darwin's fixed point became the security of home and family. Fitzroy's became the simple authority of the established church. Both men were intensely ambitious, but on this voyage they both needed the security of a collegial friendship. Ninety feet of ship plus ninety men and boys, against the whole sea, are indeed a lonely place.

To South America

As the *Beagle* left the English Channel and forged southwest across the Bay of Biscay, the officers were surprised to find no more gales, but she still rolled extremely disagreeably, as the suffering Darwin could testify. Fitzroy, naturally, was anxious to observe the handling of the *Beagle* now that she had been modified.

"In her previous voyage the *Beagle* was as easy a sea-boat as could be desired; but, having raised her upper deck, altered her stowage and trim, loaded her more heavily, and sheathed her with two-inch plank . . . I had abundant cause to feel anxious until the practical effects of such changes were ascertained." They were soon judged a great improvement. However, "a little alteration was required near the compasses, for owing to some ill-placed iron-work, they did not quite agree; but, after the change was made, we were gratified by finding four first-rate compasses, three fixed for steering, and one for bearings, agree precisely." They were not affected by local attraction owing to "her having only brass guns; and to some very large iron davits for the quarter boats, which were placed rather closely abaft and above the compasses, and perhaps counteracted the effect of iron in the hold. . . ."[17]

They searched briefly for some rocks called the Eight Stones that really didn't exist and on January 4 reached Porta Santo in the Madeiras but could not enter port because of unfavorable tides. They pushed on to Tenerife but, to Darwin's bitter disappointment, the authorities prevented them from landing because of a cholera scare in England. Perhaps it was symbolic that they passed so quickly by the island that had been the focus of Darwin's undergraduate dreams.

On the sixteenth the *Beagle* reached St. Paul Rocks, and here Darwin was able to make his first geological explorations. What kinds of islands were these? Oceanic islands like this should usually be either coralline or volcanic. We now know they are part of the Mid-Atlantic Ridge system caused by the splitting open, beginning one hundred million years ago, of the Atlantic basin. It showed Darwin how many opportunities there would be to make a significant scientific contribution on this voyage.

That same evening the ship crossed the equator, which provided a much-needed opportunity for the crew to let off some steam. They had been worked very hard in these early weeks, and the traditional visit by King Neptune was the excuse for elaborate high jinks. Some flavor of the events is given in Earle's drawing.[18] Darwin was terrified by the spectacularly garbed seamen (he had been primed in advance by many lurid tales of such ceremonies). The neophytes, including Darwin, were "imprisoned below" and then brought up to face Neptune's Court. "Before coming up the constable blindfolded me and thus led along, buckets of water were thundered all around: I was then placed on a plank, which could easily be tilted into a large bath of water. They then lathered my face and mouth with pitch and paint and scraped some of it off with a piece of roughened iron hoop; a signal being given I was tilted head over heels into the water . . . most of the others were treated much worse."[19] He then was allowed to sit next to the captain, and the youngest ship's boy crept up on them and doused them both with a bucket of water.

They put in first at Bahia (Salvador; Bahia de Todos os Santos), Brazil, to rate the chronometers and get water. Then they sailed past Cabo Frio, where the *Lightning* (paddle sloop, three guns) and *Algerine* (another 10-gun brig) were engaged in the salvage of a vast amount of bullion from Fitzroy and Sulivan's old ship *Thetis*, which had unaccountably wrecked there a little while before. On April 3 they entered the harbor of Rio de Janeiro to find that Sir Thomas Baker (flag commander of the South American station) had put his whole squadron on military alert because of a mutiny of Brazilian troops and anarchy in the town. They were not prevented from landing, and unfortunately several men caught a fever (presumably yellow fever) while camped ashore; a seamen named Morgan, a boy named Jones, and Midshipman Charles Musters (a special protégé of Captain Fitzroy's and the son of Lord Byron's friend Mary Chaworth Musters) all died.

Fitzroy at once discovered a difference of more than four miles longitude from Bahia and Rio, between the *Beagle*'s determinations and those of the earlier French expedition under Baron Roussin. So although it was not in his orders, he set off back to Bahia and then returned to Rio de Janeiro. He thereby got three separate readings, all of which agreed precisely and showed the French survey to have been wrong.

Once the *Beagle* was back in Rio de Janeiro, boat races were organized against crews from the *Warspite* and *Seringapatan*. Here also Darwin started what was to be his general practice: Whenever the ship was in port, he explored far and wide inland, usually on horseback. And what he saw amazed and delighted him, for no book, even Humboldt's, can quite do justice to the amazing spectacle of the tropics, the abundance of animal and plant life. Not only was everything completely different from the fauna and flora of the cold north temperate zone, but the diversity was almost overwhelming. "The delight one experiences in such times bewilders the mind; if the eye attempts to follow the flight of a gaudy butter-fly, it is arrested by some strange tree or fruit; if watching an insect one forgets it in the stranger flower it is crawling over ... the mind is a chaos of delight, out of which a world of future & more quiet pleasure will arise...."[20]

Here Darwin also encountered something that completely horrified him: slavery and the abuses by slaveowners in South America. He had been expecting to be appalled, but it was beyond anything he had imagined, and the experience affected him permanently. There was an immediate problem, too. When back on board the *Beagle*, Fitzroy and Darwin got into a terrible row about slavery, dreadful evidences of which were all around them. It ended with Darwin's stalking out of Fitzroy's cabin as the latter shouted that he would no longer share his table with him. The shaken but sympathetic officers reassured Darwin that he could mess with them, but Fitzroy soon calmed down and sent Wickham to Darwin with an apology. Fitzroy's diversion back to Bahia to recheck the positions gave Darwin the chance for another shore exploration and also for the argument to be forgotten.

At Rio they made several small changes to the *Beagle*'s rigging, as a result of experiences gained on the voyage out, and obtained the two extra guns mentioned before. There were also changes in the ship's company. The most significant one is referred to by Darwin in his diary as follows: "During my absence several political changes have taken place in our little world. Mr. McCormick has been invalided, and goes to England by the Tyne. . . ."[21]

The departure of McCormick was not mourned by anyone. He had been bitterly jealous of the social position afforded Darwin as the captain's guest and the fact that Darwin was able to do all the collecting he wished, with Fitzroy's willing assistance. McCormick saw that any hopes he had of establishing a position as expedition naturalist would be doomed. It is a pity that there is no contemporary record of Darwin's and McCormick's interaction during this first part of the voyage. Darwin, obviously not a disinterested party, wrote in a letter home that McCormick was "disagreeable to the Captain and Wickham. He is no loss." To Henslow, he had written dismissively from Plymouth on October 31, 1831: "My friend the Doctor is an ass, but we jog on very amicably; at present he is in great tribulation, whether his cabin shall be painted French Gray or a dead white. . . ."[22] Now he wrote: "He was a philosopher of rather an antient date; at St. Jago by his own account he made *general* remarks during the first fortnight & collected particular facts during the last."[23]

Despite lofty ambitions and considerable opportunities, McCormick never made a mark as a naturalist in his later career. When he followed Darwin's path to the Falklands and Tierra del Fuego, he merely engaged in collecting of the most routine kind, as he had in the first weeks of the Darwin voyage itself. His writings show no skill as an observer of nature, and he clearly had no interest in the swirling ferment of ideas in Edinburgh and Cambridge. McCormick gives the impression of someone who liked his world tidy, comfortable, and convenient. Creativity usually demands the opposite.

In his autobiography McCormick does not mention the names *Beagle*, Fitzroy, and Darwin. Instead he refers to two postings on "small miserable craft," the first of which was to a "small surveying ten-gun brig fitting out at Plymouth." His bitterness still shows as writing fifty years later, he implicitly dismisses Fitzroy with the following: "[S]ix months had been dawdled away in fitting a small ten-gun brig for sea. . . ."

Of his leaving the *Beagle,* McCormick simply wrote that he obtained permission to return home, "[h]aving found myself in a false position on board a small and very uncomfortable vessel, and very much disappointed in my expectations of carrying out my natural history pursuits, every obstacle having been placed in the way of my getting ashore and making collections. . . ."[24]

After his brief experience on the *Beagle,* McCormick served on James Clark Ross's 1836–38 voyage to the Antarctic, following in the track of the *Beagle* to the Falklands and Tierra del Fuego. While in Tasmania, he met Sir John and Lady Franklin (see Chapter 15). When Franklin was later lost in the Arctic, McCormick called on her and eventually joined in the search efforts in 1852, exploring Wellington Strait in a whaleboat, aptly named *Forlorn Hope,* manned with volunteers from HMS *North Star;* like all the others, he failed.

The positive side of McCormick's departure was that Bynoe was promoted from assistant surgeon to surgeon. The importance of Bynoe in the expedition can hardly be overestimated, as Darwin well recognized when he paid special tribute to him in the preface to *The Voyage of the Beagle.* Other minor changes in the officers and crew were to be expected, after personalities had been tested in the shakedown part of the voyage. In fact, a large number of the crew deserted at Rio.

A New Kind of Voyage

The three voyages of HMS *Beagle* were totally different in character. The first was a voyage of old-fashioned exploration, one that could easily have been undertaken a century earlier with few differences in the ships, the techniques of surveying, or the conditions of naval service. The third and last voyage (to Australia) was a typically Victorian venture concerned with colonial investment, harbors and railways, and world trade. The second (Darwin) voyage was something of a transition between these two. It was conducted in a context of developing nationalistic politics—a new South America, where, for Great Britain, show of force needed to be carefully balanced with diplomacy. The expedition soon found just how things were changing.

The *Beagle* sailed south on the fifth, urged on her lonely mission by three cheers from the men of the *Warspite,* a rather unusual salutation to a 10-gun brig. On July 22 the crew was off the Río de la Plata and keeping a close eye on the barometer for warning of the infamous pamperos of this region—*el infierno de los marineros.* None came, but it took them four days to beat up into Montevideo, where the usual observations were taken.

Fitzroy started to make a visit to Buenos Aires, for some modest diplomatic consultation with the governor and to study some Spanish maps held there. "However, we did not remain an hour, for the misconduct of a Buenos Aires officer on board a vessel under their colors, and a vexatious regulation with respect to quarantine, decided my returning forthwith."[25] Fitzroy reported back to Captain Hamilton commanding the *Druid,* and Hamilton set out at once in the *Druid* to demand full apology.

What happened is explained in Darwin's diary. Fitzroy had sailed boldly into the port, past a guard ship which fired blanks and then a live shot to try to stop them. A boat came out to inform the *Beagle* that port regulations required her to have her bill of health inspected before she could enter the port. Fitzroy refused, turned the *Beagle* around, "loaded and pointed all the guns on one broadside, and ran down close to the guardship. Hailed her, and said, that when we again entered the port, we would be prepared as at present and if she dared fire a shot we would send our own broadside into her rotten hulk."[26] The British flag could not so easily be insulted in Buenos Aires.

Fitzroy's actions, albeit while making a retreat, seem somewhat high-handed. The expedition had, after all, already been refused permission to land at Tenerife because of the scare of cholera in England. But it turned out that Fitzroy's grasp of the need for firm action was fully vindicated when, back at Montevideo, a military revolution that had been brewing when they first arrived broke out in earnest. The governor, chief of police, and the British consul general immediately enlisted Fitzroy's help in preserving order in the town and protecting British lives and property.

The revolution was very minor, and such disturbances had been extremely common in recent years. However, on this occasion the party that had wrested control had seized British properties while some black troops loyal to the ousted regime were mutinying and had regained control of the citadel. "The politicks of the place agree quite unintellible."[27]

Fitzroy landed a party of "50 well-armed men" and garrisoned the principal fort. The dashing Fitzroy and somewhat bemused Darwin paraded through the streets of Montevideo with men armed with pistols and cutlasses. The arrival of the bluejackets produced a stalemate, and the next day armed citizens, together with some government reinforcements, surrounded the mutineers and Fitzroy withdrew his men.

The skirmishing and backing and filling by various groups of partisans continued for several days and prevented Darwin and the others from exploring on land for another week. Finally, just before they were setting off to start their survey work, HMS *Druid,* which had missed the fun and games by having to go off to Buenos Aires, returned with a satisfying apology from the government over the guard ship incident. The *Beagle* sailed on the nineteenth, avoiding a wreck in the harbor by some smart seamanship.

The Survey

The men worked their way south, stopping occasionally to fix the ship's position. Fitzroy preferred, when possible, to work both from on board the ship and from high points on the coast itself. The *Beagle* would make soundings in the deeper water of the approaches to the coast, and the small boats would be sent out to work making transects with the lead line in shallow water. At most stations they would set up a small observatory, made to be assembled and knocked down easily. The most important duty was first to rate the chronometers, to make sure that the voyage from the last station, and local vagaries of climate, had not affected their running.

In the *Beagle*'s measurements of meridian distances, time was invariably obtained by a series of equal, or corresponding altitudes of the sun; obtained by one and the same person with the same sextant, and the same artificial horizon, in the same manner, both before and after noon. Latitudes were obtained by other sextants, and by circles . . . it sometimes happened that there were six observers seated on the ground, with as many different instruments and horizons, taking the sun's circummeridian altitudes, or observing stars at night. Where so many were working against each other, errors were soon detected. . . ."[28]

Fitzroy discovered that Stokes was by far the most accurate observer and soon gave him major responsibilities for the work.

Off Port Belgrano (near Bahía Blanca) they had a great deal of trouble working the *Beagle* in the confined shallow inland waters. Luckily they fell in with an English trading schooner, owned by a Mr. Harris, who was able to pilot them.

While working in this region, Darwin made his most important discovery so far. At a low series of bars of shingle and gravel at Punta Alta he found an exposure of huge fossil bones belonging to extinct and archaic mammals, including the giant sloths *Megatherium* and *Megalonyx* and the ungulate *Toxodon*. These finds were extremely important. The bones were crated up and shipped back to England, and by the time Darwin returned home in 1836, he was already famous as their discoverer. Darwin had immediately realized their importance. Many of the specimens represented species closely related to living animals, but they were different species and much bigger than their living counterparts. What were their origin and history? What had caused them all to become extinct? Darwin later made still more discoveries of giant mammal fossils, and debate raged both in his head and over the table with Fitzroy and the other officers. For example, could the biblical Ark have carried so many different types of animals? Were these fossils evidence of the Great Flood, or were they hundreds of thousands of years old? These discoveries reinforced Darwin's growing questioning of the accepted view of origins and relationships among living organisms and began to provide the evidence pertaining to what otherwise seemed wild and heretical hypotheses.

Just as the officers had discovered in the first voyage, the *Beagle* could not work effectively without smaller tenders, especially in the confined coastal waters along this whole section of the South American coast. So, acting on his own authority, Fitzroy hired two small schooners from Harris. Wickham, with Harris as pilot, took the larger, and Stokes, with Harris's friend Roberts, the smaller. All this was arranged on the spot, on Fitzroy's own authority and with his own money. But he had every expectation that the Admiralty would approve his plans and reimburse him. "I believe that their Lordships will approve of what I have done: but if I am wrong no inconvenience will result to the public service, since I am alone responsible for the agreement with the owner of the vessel and am able and willing to pay the stipulated sum."[29] In fact, the rent of the two vessels came to more than fifteen hundred pounds.

The two small vessels, typical small sealing schooners, were not exactly the romantic craft that one might have hoped.

The *Paz,* of about fifteen tons burthen, was as ugly and ill-built a craft as I ever saw, covered with dirt, and soaked with rancid oil. The *Liebre,* of about nine tons burthen, was a frigate's barge, raised and decked—oily like the other; but as both had done their owners good service in procuring seal and sea-elephant oil, I saw no reason to doubt our being able to make them answer our purpose. Yet the prospect for those who so handsomely volunteered to go in anything, with or without a deck, could not be otherwise than extremely unpleasant; for they did not then foresee how soon a thorough cleansing and complete outfit would be given to both vessels, and how different they would afterwards appear.[30]

The *Paz* and *Liebre,* "transformed . . . into smart little cock-boats," sailed from Port Belgrano with the *Beagle* on October 18 to work northward inshore while the *Beagle* went back to Buenos Aires for Fitzroy to consult with the government. The *Beagle* then returned to Montevideo, to be provisioned for at least eight months. She met up again with her two small tenders at the end of November.

> Mr. Wickham came on board. . . . Notwithstanding the protec-
> tion of a huge beard, every part of his face was so scorched and
> blistered by the sun that he could hardly speak, much less join-
> ing the irresistible laugh at his own expense. His companions
> were similarly sunburned though not to such a degree. They had
> been much occupied in sounding extensive banks and harbors,
> under a hot sun, and while a fresh wind kept them constantly
> wet with spray. But this inconvenience was trifling, one of the
> more important was excessive seasickness, in consequence of the
> short and violent movements of such small craft under sail
> among the tide races and eddies so numerous on that coast.[31]

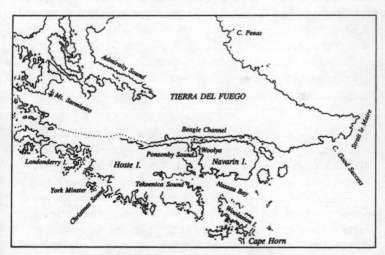

Southeast Tierra del Fuego, showing the Beagle Channel, as mapped by King in 1831 *(Journal of the Royal Geographical Society)*; original spell-ing, location of Woolya added from Fitzroy and King, 1835; see Chapter 5, note 16.

On the day they parted from the *Paz* and *Liebre* "suddenly myriads of white butterflies surrounded the ship, in such multitudes, that the men exclaimed 'it is snowing butterflies.' They were driven before a gust from the north-west, which soon increased to a double-reefed topsail breeze and were as numerous as flakes of snow in the thickest shower. The space they occupied could not have been less than two hundred yards in height, a mile in width, and several miles in length."[32]

The two schooners turned out to be a great asset, so Fitzroy "determined to give Mr. Wickham fresh orders enlarging considerably his share of surveying operations. He was desired to continue exploring the coast, even as far as Port Desire, until *Beagle*'s return from her visit to Tierra del Fuego and the Falkland Islands."[33] So it looked as though the experiment cruising with two small schooners were going to work out, although Fitzroy was a little concerned by the fact that Mr. Roberts, the pilot of the *Liebre,* was a very large man and that "his little vessel looked, by comparison, no bigger than a coffin." Wickham assured him that everything was all right except that one day Roberts had gone aloft on lookout and had broken the mast.

ELEVEN

The Fuegians Go Home

ON DECEMBER 4, 1832, LEAVING THE SMALLER SURVEYING parties behind, the *Beagle* headed south. At last the time had come to take the Fuegians home and to set up Matthews's missionary settlement. They sighted Tierra del Fuego on the fifteenth, with Jemmy, Fuegia, and York Minster delighted to see familiar scenery—until they saw the first Fuegians, watching them carefully from the shore. Jemmy Button "asked me to fire at them, saying they were "oens men—very bad men."[1] Sailing into Good Success Bay, they saw more natives, who set up signal fires and shouted to them. The next day Darwin, Hammond (who had joined the *Beagle* at Montevideo from HMS *Druid*), and Fitzroy took a small party ashore. This was Darwin's and Hammond's "first meeting with man in such a totally savage state." Darwin later wrote to Henslow:

The Fuegians are in a more miserable state of barbarism than I had expected ever to see a human being. In this inclement country they are absolutely naked, and their temporary houses are like what children make in summer with boughs of trees. I do not think any spectacle can be more interesting than the first sight of man in his primitive wilderness. It is an interest that cannot well be imagined until it is experienced. I shall never forget this when entering Good Success Bay—the yell with which a party received us. They were seated on a rocky point, surrounded by the dark forest of beech; as they threw their arms wildly round their heads, and their long hair streaming, they seemed the troubled spirits of another world.[2]

Leaving Cape Good Success, they found a good spot to spend a cheerful Christmas, "not withstanding violent squalls, and cold damp weather." On December 31, "tired and impatient at the delay caused by bad weather, we put to sea again. The first day there was hope of not being driven eastward; and during the fortnight we tried hard to work our way towards Christmas Sound to land York Minster and Fuegia Basket among their own people, near March Harbor, and return eastward through the *Beagle* Channel, landing Jemmy Button also with his tribe, the Tekeenica. Part of Whale-Boat Sound and the western arms of the *Beagle* Channel were to be surveyed; by this scheme I proposed to combine both objects."[3]

During the next few days the expedition had typical Tierra del Fuego weather. It was here, off the hazardous Diego Ramírez Islands, that they hit the gale mentioned on page 96. "Carrying a heavy press of sail, our good little ship weathered [the islands] cleverly, going from seven and a half to eight knots in an hour, under close-reefed top sails and double-reefed course—the top-gallant masts being on deck."[4] This lasted for several days until the thirteenth, with the mainmast bending and whipping in the wind under close-reefed storm trysails and the forestaysail. There was no chance of carrying the fully reefed (five reefs) main topsail that Fitzroy usually preferred in such situations. Three enormous rollers nearly swamped the boat, "taking her right a-beam, and turning her so far over that all the lee bulwark, from the cat-head to the stern davit, was two or three feet under water." For a moment it looked as though the *Beagle* were gone, but she gamely rolled back again. As it was, she lost the quarter boat on the lee side. Although it had been hoisted three feet higher than usual, it was buried under and smashed away. Darwin's collections in the poop cabin and forecastle were badly damaged by seawater.

On the fourteenth they got to shelter and decided to use small boats to survey the inner passages rather than try to get the *Beagle* farther westward. But even this proved difficult; eventually they were forced into the Goree Road, which was at least a spacious anchorage. "Here, to my surprise, York Minster told me that he would rather live with Jemmy Button in the Tekeenica Country than go to his own people."[5] Fitzroy accepted this plan, little suspecting what schemes York Minster had in mind and pleased that the three of them could settle together. So on January 18 Fitzroy set out with four boats (three whaleboats and the yawl) carrying Reverend Matthews and the Fuegians with all the paraphernalia that had been given to them in England. Darwin, Bynoe, Hammond, Stewart, and Johnson and twenty-four of the crew went with them. Fitzroy's plan was to go north around the western shores of Navarino Island and Murray Narrows, leaving the Fuegians and Matthews there, and then to continue westward to explore the western parts of the Beagle Channel and Whale-Boat Sound. They would then return to Matthews and see how things were working out.

Even with sails set, the heavily laden yawl had to be towed by the other boats, and for most of the trip they had to rely on the manpower alone. They saw some natives, but Jemmy Button did not want to land. "York laughed heartily at the first we saw, calling them large monkeys; and Jemmy assured us they were not at all like his people, who were very good and clean. Fuegia was shocked and ashamed; she hid herself, and would not look at them a second time." These apparently were "Yapoos"—"no better or worse than other Fuegians," Fitzroy wryly noted. On the twenty-second, in the evening, "we reached a cove near the Murray Narrows; and from a small party of Tekeenica natives, Jemmy's friends, whom we found there, he heard of his mother and brothers, but found that his father was dead."[6] (Strangely, this confirmed a dream that Jemmy had previously related to Fitzroy.) Jemmy and York Minster tried to speak with the natives, but Jemmy had almost forgotten his own language while York Minster, although he belonged to another tribe, was the better interpreter.

The next day excited Fuegians began to gather at the camp,

and canoes "began to appear in every direction, in each of which was a stentor hailing us at the top of his voice."[7] The party was on its guard, for eventually some thirty or forty canoes turned up. Fitzroy broke camp and moved on to a place called Woolya, where the party from the *Beagle* had plenty of time to set up a small camp before the canoes caught up with them. As usual the native women ran away and hid while the men first spoke to the white men. The presence of so many canoes made Fitzroy's party more nervous so they set up sentries and a boundary line, explaining to the Fuegians that they should not cross it. Eventually Jemmy Button heard a voice from a canoe that he was sure was that of his brother. Sure enough, there was a reunion among Jemmy, his mother, two sisters, and four brothers although they treated him with a good deal of suspicion. That night the three Fuegians slept with the local inhabitants in their wigwams and seemed to get along well together.

Woolya seemed a very favorable place to start Matthews's settlement. "Rising gently from the waterside, there are considerable spaces of clear pasture land, well-watered by brooks, and backed by hills of moderate height, where we afterwards found woods of the finest timber trees in the country. Rich grass and some beautiful flowers, which none of us had ever seen, pleased us when we landed, and augured well for the growth of our garden seeds."[8] Over the next week the party from the *Beagle* built a small outpost and finally unloaded all the incredible paraphernalia that had been sent from England by well-wishers, all the Victorian knickknackery that seemed so splendid in London but appeared ridiculously out of place at this remotest end of the world. A seemingly unending pile of soup tureens, chamber pots, wineglasses, and beaver hats was transferred from the boats, while more practical souls set about planting potatoes, beans, root vegetables, lettuce, and cabbage in the gardens.

Jemmy still was having great trouble communicating with his own people, and this made Fitzroy extremely uneasy even though the first interactions with the Fuegians were relatively untroubled, as long as they kept strictly to the correct side of the boundary trench that was dug. The situation steadily

The camp at Woolya, from a drawing by Conrad Martens; see Chapter 5, note 16.

became more tense, because of a lot of petty pilfering, probably spurred on by the fact that Jemmy had been handing out so many gifts. Then without warning, most of the natives disappeared with their canoes. Fitzroy, whose men were outnumbered at least ten to one, was sure that they were planning a sneak attack. Nonetheless, Matthews and the three Fuegians seemed willing to stay in the new camp.

Soon large numbers of Fuegians returned, stealing everything they could get their hands on (but, strangely, not yet from Fuegia Basket). Fitzroy made a couple of trials of the situation by setting off for a few hours and then coming back to make sure that everything was all right. As the situation did not worsen, he sent the yawl and one whaleboat back to the *Beagle* and set off in the other boat with Darwin and Hammond to explore the northwest arm of the Beagle Channel, as previously planned.

A couple of days later they were onshore at the foot of what were to be called the Darwin Mountains, admiring the view of the glaciers about two hundred yards away, when suddenly a massive ice face fell into the sea, setting off enormous rolling waves in the bay. Darwin was one of the first to realize the danger, and he and several of the men ran to the boats and just managed to secure them before they were washed away. His prompt action certainly saved the party because without the boats they would have been marooned. In his diary Darwin is extremely modest about his exploits, but the next day, when they entered a large new sound, Fitzroy promptly named it after Darwin.

In their small boats they went from Whale-Boat Sound to Stewart Island and back into the southwest arm of Beagle Channel where they met a large party of natives in full dress with paint, feathers, and goose down. They noticed one woman "far from ill-looking" who turned out to be wearing a piece of cloth that had been given to Fuegia Basket; "the sight of this piece of linen, several bits of ribbon, and some scraps of red cloth, apparently quite recently obtained, made me feel very anxious about Matthews and his party. . . . [There was] an air almost of defiance among the people. . . ."[9] So they hurried back to Woolya the next day.

As they went through Murray Narrows, they saw other parties of natives who were wearing tartan or white linen that they knew had come from the *Beagle* party. When they got ashore, "the natives came hallowing and jumping about us, and then, to my extreme relief, Matthews appeared, dressed and looking as usual. After him came Jemmy and York, also dressed and looking well; Fuegia, they said, was in a wigwam."[10] Fitzroy took Matthews into his boat and pushed off a little way to talk. It was a depressing story: Matthews felt completely unsafe; he had been threatened and harassed, and the stealing was endless. The garden had been trampled down. It was hard to see how the settlement could survive. In fact, it was a failure. Matthews begged passage to New Zealand, where his brother lived.

At the first opportunity they got the remnants of Matthews's property and a few things that had not yet been found by the Fuegians into the boats. As they abandoned the settlement, they distributed some axes, saws, nails, and so on and said good-bye to Jemmy and York, promising to see them again in a few days.

A week later Fitzroy set off again into Ponsonby Sound and to revisit Woolya. On returning to the encampment, he was relieved to find Jemmy, York, and Fuegia still safe, although most of Jemmy's things had been stolen. There had been at least one major fight with some strange natives of a different group. More or less reassured, Fitzroy left them again, this time to take the *Beagle* on a long run down to the Falkland Islands.

To the Falklands

When they arrived at the Falklands, they were surprised to find that in the previous month (February 1833) HMS *Clio* and HMS *Tyne* had visited the islands in some force and had hoisted British flags everywhere. The Argentine garrison at Port Louis had withdrawn, leaving the island under British authority. Thus was set in place another link in the chain of events that led eventually to war between Britain and Argentina, nearly 150 years later.*

Anchoring on the south side of Berkeley Sound, they saw a French flag signaling from ashore. Boats sent to investigate rescued the survivors of the wreck of the French whaling ship *Le Magellan*. Next, the sealer *Unicorn* (William Low, master—evidently a relative, perhaps son, of the William Low who helped the first voyage) arrived with survivors of a wrecked American sealer, the *Transport*. Now Matthew Brisbane turned up. Having been run off by the Argentine settlers in 1827, he had returned as the British resident in charge. (This was the same Matthew Brisbane who had sailed with Weddell in 1822. In 1824–26 he went south again, sealing in the *Beaufoy*. Then he became master of Weddell's *Prince of Saxe-Coburg* and was rescued from her wreck in Fury Harbor in 1827 by the *Beagle* on her previous voyage; see page 84.) To add to the general

---

*By this time Britain, France, Spain, and Argentina had each laid claim to the islands, probably first discovered by John Davis in 1592. In 1828 the Buenos Aires government (United Republics of Buenos Aires) gave rights to the islands to Mr. Vérnet in order to establish a colony. In 1831 he had confiscated some American sealing vessels, whereupon Captain Silas Duncan of the USS *Lexington* arrived in 1832 to punish the settlers. He destroyed all the buildings of the colony at Port Louis and banished the colonists. This created the vacuum of authority into which the British moved.

gloom, when Fitzroy returned from a visit to Port Louis, he found that Edward Hellyer, the ship's clerk, had been drowned on a shooting expedition while trying to recover a bird. At this point Fitzroy first showed signs of wavering in his resolve, allowing himself to doubt whether he could complete his appointed tasks. The "tedious, although not less useful, details of coast surveying" were taking so much time that he might not be able to complete the most important part of the voyage, which was to establish the chain of meridian distances around the globe.

He had been thinking of getting yet another tender to keep the work moving and had even negotiated to buy an American sealer. This deal had fallen through, but here at the Falklands was the schooner *Unicorn,* which would fit his purposes perfectly. She was a large, sturdy vessel of 170 tons, built of oak, and apparently an extremely good sea boat. Low was willing to sell because a bad sealing season had bankrupted him. Jonathan May, the carpenter, surveyed her, and Fitzroy decided to buy her for $6,000 (£1,300), payment to be made to Low's partners at Montevideo. Some of the crew of the *Unicorn* remained on the Falkland Islands, some left with the crew of the *Le Magellan,* and a few stayed on to work for Fitzroy. The vessel was renamed the *Adventure* (there is no small irony here), and Edward Main Chaffers, ship's master, was put in charge of her until he could be replaced by Wickham later.

Fitzroy was fortunate in being able to buy cables, anchors, and other salvaged stores from the masters of the wrecked *Transport* and *Le Magellan.* So not only was he able almost completely to fit out the *Adventure* in the otherwise barren Falkland Islands, but he did it at far below market price.

In all, the officers and men stayed a month at the Falkland Islands, during which time they were visited by the crews of several whaling or sealing vessels, and on several occasions Fitzroy found himself obliged to keep order. On April 6 they left the Falkland Islands, carrying with them the master and some of the officers and crew of the wrecked *Le Magellan.* They soon caught up with the *Adventure,* which had been sent off a couple of days earlier; three weeks later they anchored at Montevideo.

Now Fitzroy, full of energy again, borrowed a small decked boat that had just been built at Maldonado. He got it for two months in return for rigging it. This enabled him to send to Port San Antonio for Lieutenant Wickham. So the little *Constitución* sailed off on May 1 with master's assistant Alexander Usborne, Forsythe, and five men for the river Negro to assist Stokes and send Wickham back to take charge of the *Adventure*. Meanwhile, at Montevideo the fitting out of the *Adventure* continued, including coppering her bottom so that she would be sound for work in the Pacific. The *Constitución* soon returned with Lieutenant Wickham, who reported excellent results with the *Paz* and *Liebre*.

All the time they remained in the vicinity of Maldonado, working on the *Adventure* and refitting and repainting the *Beagle,* Darwin lived onshore, making extensive excursions to study the natural history of the region.

On July 24 the *Beagle* had finished with local survey work, and Fitzroy sailed down to Cape San Antonio, then along the coast of the river Negro to where the *Paz* and *Liebre* were working. Here Darwin set off to cross overland through Argentina to Buenos Aires, making an extensive inland survey of South America while the *Beagle* worked slowly back north.

There is a marvelous letter from Fitzroy to Darwin written about this time, one of the few to have survived. Considering what we have been led to believe about the differences between the two, it is almost shockingly intimate. Darwin is ashore exploring; Fitzroy writes from the ship (October 4, 1833): "But firstly of the first—my good Philos why have you told me nothing of your hairbreadth scapes & moving accidents? How many times did you flee from the Indians? How many precipices did you fall over? How many bogs did you fall into? How often were you carried away by the floods? and how many times were you kilt? That you were not kilt *dead* I have visible evidence. . . ." It continues in the same vein for several pages, finally ending in two postscripts, of which the last reads: "I do not rejoice at your extraordinary & outrageous peregrinations because I am envious, jealous, and extremely full of all uncharitableness. What will they think at home of 'Master Charles'? 'I do think he be gone mad.' Prithee be *careful. . . .*"[11]

By August the *Beagle* anchored off the river Negro finally to pay off the *Paz* and *Liebre*. Fitzroy owed a lot to Harris, not only for the generosity of the contract they had drawn up but also for the great care and attention that he and Roberts had devoted to the expedition. Without this arrangement the difficult inshore survey work could not have been done.

All their optimism was dashed, however, when word finally arrived from the Admiralty concerning the *Paz* and *Liebre*: "Their Lordships do not approve of hiring vessels for the service and therefore desire that they be discharged as soon as possible."[12] Fitzroy would have to bear the costs of the *Paz* and *Liebre* himself, while at the same time he had now taken on the *Adventure* (concerning which the Admiralty had only just been informed). As he owned the *Adventure,* he would have the opportunity to recoup some of his losses by resale, but Fitzroy was angry: "Captain King—with far less extensive orders—had *three* vessels upon this Station—The *Adventure,* the *Beagle* and the *Adelaide* tender, which was purchased at this place by the Government for *two thousand pounds sterling. . . .*"[13] He felt that he was being asked to do an impossible job without support.

But here was the *Adventure* all ready to go. Even though the Admiralty's letter clearly seemed to forbid all hiring of supplementary vessels, there was nothing to do but forge ahead.

On August 24 they reached Port Belgrano, where Darwin, who was nearby, heard of their arrival and rode to meet them. Then he went back inland to continue to Buenos Aires while the *Beagle* started the survey of the banks along the entrance to the Río de la Plata. Back in Montevideo on September 16 the crew had a chance to test their sailing prowess against the new HMS *Snake* (an experimental 16-gun brig, designed by Sir William Symmons and Captain Hayes).[14] Fitzroy was very pleasantly surprised to find that the *Beagle* could almost keep up with her.

With delays for fitting out the *Adventure,* shore leaves, and catching up with work on their charts and calculations, Darwin had plenty of time to work onshore. It was not until the beginning of December that the *Adventure* (with Wickham, Johnson, Forsythe, and Usborne and four of the precious chronometers) and the *Beagle* sailed south again together.

TWELVE

Making the Work Fly:
Chile, Galápagos, Home

T HE OFFICERS AND MEN OF THE *BEAGLE* HAD LONG SINCE
settled down into an efficient and cheerful group, with Fitzroy a hard but fair taskmaster. Frequent shore parties for making observations and collecting made a welcome counterpoint
to sea duty. For example, at Berkeley Sound in the Falklands:

We were fortunate to find plenty of wreck-wood on the beach
and we had a glorious fire, round which we sat singing till ten
o'clock at night, when a heavy hail shower drove us into the
tents. We all then crowded into one tent, and went on singing
till twelve, and I never under any circumstances saw a more
merry party. All the comic songs that anyone knew were mixed
up with yarns of English, Irish, Scotch, and Welsh; and as we
had about equal number of each country, it raised bits of laughter against them all in their turns: neither did the West country
escape.

And at the river Negro, September 1833:

We had among the men two or three excellent hands for keeping
everyone alive, and tonight they performed their part to perfection. Such hands are invaluable in a cruise of that kind, particu-

larly if the work is very hard, as they keep men's spirits up in a most surprising manner. I think I never in my life saw people more happy than all our party were: they were in roars of laughter from morning to night, and up to all kinds of amusements when on shore, except when I [Sulivan] brought them to an anchor occasionally to prevent their shaking the ground (near my instruments), and then they would find something amusing in that; and when men in those spirits are happy and comfortable, it is astonishing how they make the work fly.[1]

Fitzroy was a highly visible captain. Again Sulivan reports: "On one occasion, it being desired to find out the condition of the *Beagle*'s bottom after she had struck a rock, I dived down under the keel and having ascertained things were not very bad, came up the other side, bleeding from several scratches received from the jagged copper. Captain Fitzroy, wishing to make doubly sure, then performed the same action himself."[2]

One of Fitzroy's major contributions to the efficiency of the ship, once the basic routines of working had been set firmly in motion, was to keep the ship's company almost completely healthy. Relatively little of the debilitating respiratory illness that dogged the first voyage reappeared, and the old problem of scurvy was definitely under control.

On reaching the Strait of Magellan once again, they first put in at Port Desire, where they spent Christmas (Fitzroy entertained the crew by organizing "Olympic Games") and they left the *Adventure* for some alterations in rigging ("she is found not to sail well on a wind"). Leaving Port Desire, the *Beagle* hit a submerged rock. She slid over it with a crunch but did not start taking in water. Fitzroy was convinced that this was the very same rock that the *Beagle* had struck in 1829 but could not afterward find (see page 82).

The normal routine then continued, with the *Beagle* anchoring to make observations, parties being put onshore to take bearings, to explore inland, to climb any high ground to get better bearings, and, of course, always to get water and fresh food. The presence of Charles Darwin made these expeditions ashore especially interesting. His keenness and enthusiasm were transmitted to the officers, who all joined in the study and even competed with one another.

At the end of January they returned to Port Desire, "and our first employment was to look for the rock whose top (Mr. May assured me with a grave face) we had knocked off with our keel."[3] Then they were off again. Fitzroy sent the *Adventure* to the Falkland Islands with orders to meet the *Beagle* there in Berkeley Sound early in March. Failing this, they were to complete the survey in the Falkland Islands and meet the *Beagle* at Elizabeth Island on the first day of June. Fitzroy and the *Beagle* headed for Tierra del Fuego for the last time.

The *Beagle* passed through the First Narrows of the Strait of Magellan into Gregory Bay to a reunion with the Patagonian Indians, heading for Port Famine, where the men made chronometric observations for a week. Then they turned back through the First Narrows and around into the *Beagle* Channel.

On March 5 they visited Woolya again. A year had passed. They found the little encampment empty. All Fitzroy was able to salvage was some turnips and potatoes from the overgrown garden plot. Eventually three canoes were spotted.

> Looking through a glass I saw that two of the natives in them were washing their faces, while the rest were paddling with might and main; I was then sure that some of our acquaintances were there, and in a few minutes recognized Tommy Button, Jemmy's brother. In the other canoe was a face I knew yet could not name. 'It must be someone I have seen before,' said I,— when his sharp eye detected me, and a sudden movement of the hand to the head (as a sailor touches his hat) at once told me it was indeed Jemmy Button—but how altered. . . . He was naked, like his companions, except a bit of skin about his loins; his hair was long and matted just like theirs; he was wretchedly thin, and his eyes were affected by smoke.[4]

Jemmy told them that York and Fuegia had gone off together some months before to return to their own country, robbing Jemmy of all his clothes and tools. There had been a lot of trouble before they left, with the whole thing evidently carefully planned by York Minster. The settlement had also been attacked in large numbers by the "much-dreaded Oens-men."

Not only had the little settlement been wrecked, but Jemmy had lost all the signs of civilization so painstakingly bestowed upon the three Fuegians. With little more that could be done to help Jemmy Button, despite serious misgivings, they left— touched by the fact that Jemmy gave them a bow and quiver full of arrows for his old schoolmaster in Walthamstow.

"I cannot help still hoping that some benefit, however slight, may result from the intercourse of these people, Jemmy, York, and Fuegia, with other natives of Terra del Fuego. Perhaps ship-wrecked seaman may hereafter receive help and kind treatment from Jemmy Button's children; prompted, as they can hardly fail to be, by the traditions they would have heard of men of other lands; and by an idea, however faint, of their duty to God as well as their neighbor," wrote Fitzroy.[5]

The story of the three Fuegians does not end here, at least not for Jemmy Button. Others tried to pick up the missionary effort later, with even more disastrous results (see Appendix F).

Heading back to the Falkland Islands, Fitzroy found another scene of trouble. Occupation by British forces had done little to alter the running history of mutiny and murder in the settlement. When the *Clio* and *Tyne* departed, so did any vestige of law and order. A gang of three gauchos and five Indians murdered Matthew Brisbane, the storekeeper, and three others, plundering the houses and stealing all the cattle and horses. The rest of the settlers escaped to a small island until an English sealer, the *Hopeful,* found them. HMS *Challenger* (captained by an old friend of Fitzroy's, Michael Seymour) then arrived to try to restore law and order.

When their acquaintance William Low had returned to Port Louis, he found that his life was in danger because he had been a friend of Brisbane's. And so he escaped to Kidney Islet at the entrance of Berkeley Sound, also hoping to be rescued by a ship. By happy chance, the first vessel to pass by was the *Adventure.* He "immediately offered his services as a pilot." Wickham happily took him on, much to Fitzroy's later approval, hoping "that the Admiralty would approve of my so engaging a person who . . . could afford us more information than any other individual, without exception" about the Falkland Islands, Tierra del Fuego, Patagonia, and the Galápagos Islands.[6]

Meanwhile, the *Challenger*'s men had caught the bandits, and Fitzroy, when he arrived, was ordered to take Rivero, their leader, off the island. He was put on board the *Beagle* in chains and eventually returned to the mainland.

Leaving the *Adventure* to continue the work in the Falklands, the *Beagle* headed west to the river Santa Cruz, where the men beached the *Beagle* to examine her at low tide.* They needed to check what damage had been done when they struck the rock at Port Desire and make sure the copper sheathing was intact because they were soon to enter the Pacific, where boring worms would destroy unprotected planking. It was here on this beach, which they called Keel Point, that Conrad Martens (who had replaced Earle as artist at Montevideo) made the delightful drawing *The Beagle Laid Ashore, River Santa Cruz.*[9] They found merely that "a piece of false keel under the fore-foot had been rubbed off, and that a few sheets of copper were a good deal rubbed. By Mr. May's exertions all was repaired in one tide; and on the following day we were making preparations for an excursion up the river."[10]

This exploration of the river Santa Cruz was something that Pringle Stokes had tried on the first voyage, as had Weddell in 1824, but neither had got very far. Sulivan, Stewart, and King were left in charge of the ship, while Darwin, Chaffers, Stokes, Bynoe, Mellersh, and Martens, together with eighteen seamen and marines, accompanied Fitzroy up the river in three boats described as "whale-boats strengthened." It was a great adventure and another sharp contrast with the hazards and tedious work of coastal surveying from the ships. In fact, hauling the heavy boats upstream through shallows and round rapids was also desperately hard work in places. There were severe frosts

---

* It was not by chance that they beached the *Beagle* here. In the book on his sealing and exploring voyage in 1823–23, Weddell remarked: "The rise of the tide is so great in this river, being thirty-two feet, that the keel of the largest ship may be examined, by laying her on the ground. . . ."[7] A copy of Weddell's book is known to have been in the *Beagle*'s library.[8]

every night, and the men exhausted themselves. Darwin, however, was in his element. As they explored westward, they saw a great deal of wildlife. Eventually they reached a point with marvelous views of the Andes, only 60 miles from the Pacific Ocean, before they had to turn back. They were 140 miles in a straight line from the Santa Cruz estuary and traveled about 245 miles along the course of the river. Fitzroy guessed that the river might flow out of a lake, as it ran so clear. Indeed, it does: Lago Argentino. The lower part of the river valley—an arid plain covered with smooth pebbles—impressed them most. For Darwin, as he argued the matter with Fitzroy, this valley was clearly an exposed ancient seabed, while for Fitzroy it became evidence sine qua non of inundation of the region by the biblical Flood. The exploration of the Santa Cruz may well have marked a subtle parting of the ways between Darwin and Fitzroy, between the modern geologist and the strict biblical constructionist.

After loading more freshwater, the *Beagle* was ready to meet the *Adventure* coming up from the Falklands. The two vessels headed for Chile, sailing from Port Famine down the Magdalen Channel with excellent views of Mount Sarmiento, and on the tenth "beat to windward through the Cockburn Channel."

Only a small cove was available for anchoring that first night, so Fitzroy left that for the *Adventure*. It was the same old situation again, but now they were experts. The more maneuverable *Adventure* put into the cove and anchored quite safely, while Fitzroy had to keep the *Beagle* under way all night out in the bay.

Small rain nearly all the time, and squalls from the westward were frequent here. There were four square miles in which it was safe to sail to and from and for 14 hours we traversed that area in every direction. . . . It was necessary to keep under reasonable press of sail part of the time, to hold our ground against the lee tide . . . in a case of this kind a ship is so much more manageable while going through the water than she is while hove-to, and those on board in general so much more on the alert than when the vessel herself seems half asleep, that I have always been an advocate for short tacks under manageable sail, so as to keep as much as possible near the same place, in preference to heaving-to and drifting.[11]

On June 26 they got through to the west and turned north toward Chile, arriving at Valparaiso on July 22. They settled in to spend the winter months working on the tremendous arrears in computation and chart work. Fitzroy, Stokes, King, and Usborne moved to quarters onshore, while the remainder stayed on board to refit and reprovision the vessels. Wickham, who could speak Spanish, was sent to Santiago to make sure the Chilean authorities knew what the *Beagle* was doing and to make sure that there was no possibility of their work's being confused as a hostile act. Darwin was delighted to have time to explore the Andes.

Crisis, Earthquake, and Shipwreck

While they were in Valparaiso (September 1834), Fitzroy, already under great pressure from the work and the accumulated strain, received word from the Admiralty refusing authority to use the *Adventure* as a tender. "The mortification it caused frayed deeply, and the regret is still vivid . . . my own means had been taxed, even to involving myself in difficulties, and as the Lords Commissioners of the Admiralty did not think it proper to give me any assistance, I saw that all my cherished hopes of examining many groups of islands in the Pacific, besides making a complete survey of the Chilean and Peruvian shores, must utterly fail."[12]

So, with deep bitterness, Fitzroy had to discharge the crew of the *Adventure,* take her officers back into the *Beagle,* and sell the vessel. He fell into a deep depression and actually resigned, ordering Wickham to take over the ship and return straight to England via the Horn.

It was a bitter blow to all of them, much more than just a matter of Fitzroy's judgment being questioned and his pride hurt. They all were keen to complete the survey and knew they needed the *Adventure* for the west coast survey. Everyone, especially Darwin, had been looking forward to crossing the Pacific. Darwin's letters give a more personal view of the whole situation than Fitzroy's terse official account.

We have had some strange proceedings on board the *Beagle*. . . . Captain Fitzroy has for the last two months been working extremely hard, and at the same time constantly annoyed by interruptions from officers of other ships; the selling of the schooner and its consequences were very vexatious; the cold manner in which the Admiralty (solely I believe because he is a Tory) have treated him, and a thousand other etc., etc., has made him very thin and unwell. This was accompanied by a morbid depression of spirits and a loss of all decision and resolution. The Captain was afraid that his mind was becoming deranged (being aware of his hereditary predisposition), all that Bynoe could say, that it was merely the effect of bodily health and exhaustion after such application, would not do; he invalided and Wickham was appointed to the command. By the instructions Wickham could only finish the survey of the Southern part, and would then have been obliged to return direct to England. The grief on board the *Beagle* about the Captain's decision was universal and deeply felt. One great source of his annoyance was the feeling it impossible to fulfill the whole instructions. . . .

Wickham and Darwin set out to persuade Fitzroy to change his mind, pointing out that "from his state of mind it never occurred to him that the very instructions ordered him to do as much of the West coast as he has time for and then proceed across the Pacific. Wickham (very disinterestedly giving up his own promotion) urged this most strongly, stating that when he took command nothing should induce him to go to Tierra del Fuego again and then asked the Captain what would be gained by his resignation? Why not do the more useful part and return as commanded by the Pacific?"

It ended "capitally for all hands. . . . The Captain at last to everyone's joy, consented, and the resignation was withdrawn.

Hurrah! Hurrah! it is fixed the *Beagle* shall not go one mile South of Cape Tres Montes (about 200 miles South of Chiloé) and from that point to Valparaiso will be finished in about five months."[13]

Darwin also noted, "As soon as the Captain invalided, I at once determined to leave the *Beagle;* but it was quite absurd what a revolution in five minutes was effected in all my feelings." In the end the episode turned out rather well for Darwin. "I think we shall persuade him [i.e., Fitzroy] to finish the coast of Peru, where the climate is delightful, the country hideously sterile, but abounding with the highest interest to a geologist." Not only would they then go on to the Pacific after all, but less than three months later some of Darwin's most important scientific experiences were about to begin.

Interestingly, not only had Fitzroy been incapacitated by a major bout of depression, but at the same time as the crisis over the *Adventure* was unfolding, Darwin spent six weeks in bed with intestinal problems—his first real illness of the voyage, apart from periods of exhaustion and an infected knee.

Fitzroy got a pretty good price for the *Adventure* (fourteen hundred pounds) but was nevertheless the poorer by many hundreds of pounds. In the reduction of the expedition that followed, even Conrad Martens, the artist who had taken over from Augustus Earle, was released and left to fend for himself in Valparaiso.

By November they had finished drawing their charts of Patagonia, Tierra del Fuego, and the Falkland Islands, and these were shipped off to England. The *Beagle* was all ready to go to sea again on the second part of her voyage, with just a few loose ends to be cleared up. For example, when the *Beagle* had passed San Carlos on the way up to Valparaiso in July, Fitzroy had left Low, with his personal whaleboat and a crew of Chileans, to survey parts of the Chonos Archipelago. So, on leaving Valparaiso, Fitzroy first headed south to pick them up. When they arrived in San Carlos, other small expeditions were sent out. Sulivan took a party to survey "the east side of Chiloé and the islands in the Gulf of Ancud," while the *Beagle* worked along the western coast of Chiloé.

When they met up again, they spent another "sombre" Christmas, held down by foul weather. On December 28, while the *Beagle* was running for the shelter of Port San Esteban and "furling sails, some men were seen on a point of land near the ship, making signals to us in a very earnest manner." These turned out to be men from the American whaler *Frances Henrietta* (of New Bedford) who had deserted in a small boat that they had carelessly stowed in, marooning themselves on these islands. With their provisions exhausted they had survived for thirteen months on seals, shellfish, and the wild cherry. Yet "those five men, when received on board the *Beagle,* were in better health, as to healthy fleshiness, color, and actual health, than any five individuals belonging to our ship."[14]

With the survey of the Chonos Archipelago completed in mid-January, they started to work back north, Darwin all the while continuing to make expeditions inland. On February 8 they reached Valdivia, and then, on February 20, there occurred a great earthquake that ruined a vast part of the city of Concepción farther to the north, the ruins of which they saw when they reached there two weeks later. Earthquakes of varying severity were well known all along the coast, but this was a particularly severe one with a great deal of damage done by the accompanying tidal wave. Huge and irregular tides followed for many days all along the coast, together with some three hundred aftershocks.

In his recent explorations of the Andes Darwin had found evidence of quite recent marine sediments raised to thirteen hundred feet above sea level. This was a well-known phenomenon, but *proving* that such movements of the earth actually happened was another matter. At Concepción the expert surveyors of the *Beagle* confirmed the evidence of their eyes. The whole landscape was changed: The island of Santa María, for example, was raised up by an average of nine feet. The effect on Darwin cannot be overestimated. He had firsthand evidence of the way in which the earth's crust could be moved around, and eventually his observation of the earthquake became part of the jigsaw of evidences of the changing earth that was slowly accumulating and one day would be assembled in his geological writings and in his theory of evolution by natural selection. Darwin wrote home: "[I]t is one of the three most interesting spectacles I have beheld since leaving England. A Fuegian Savage;—Tropical Vegetation—and the ruins of Concepción. It is indeed most wonderful to witness such desolation produced in minutes of time."[15]

As a result of all the storms, the *Beagle* was down to her last anchor, so they had to put back to Valparaiso. They returned to the relief work at Concepción but a week later were back at Valparaiso, where, Fitzroy records, Darwin "came on board, and among other pieces of good news, told me of my promotion. I asked about Mr. Stokes and Lieutenant Wickham, especially the former, but nothing has been heard of their exertions having obtained any satisfactory notice at headquarters, which must diminish the gratification I might otherwise have felt on my own account."[16] Darwin, anxious to keep working at the geology of the Andes, at once set off again, arranging to meet the *Beagle* at Coquimbo.

At Valparaiso Fitzroy once again started to use an auxiliary schooner! Revived in spirit and undeterred by his rebuff from the Admiralty, he borrowed the thirty-five-ton *Constitución* and sent it, with Stokes, King, Stewart, and Forsythe, up the coast to Coquimbo to do a careful inshore survey. His instructions were that if all worked out well, they were to continue northward and meet Fitzroy and the *Beagle* at Callao. He had recovered his energy and was determined to continue the survey; if the Admiralty would not buy tenders for the expedition, he would improvise.

On June 14, 1835, just as Fitzroy prepared to leave Valparaiso for the last time, another adventure intervened. A letter to a local English merchant mentioned that HMS *Challenger,* long overdue for her arrival here, had been wrecked. There was no official word of this, but Fitzroy recalled that the captain of a recently arrived Swedish ship had mentioned seeing "an American brig" cast away near Mocha Island, south of Concepción. Fitzroy was convinced that this was the *Challenger* and confirmed this by pointing to the very similar HMS *Conway* nearby for comparison and the Swedes agreed. (The *Challenger*'s men had actually seen the Swedish ship and fired a signal gun.) Fitzroy had heard enough.

The next day he went down to meet the incoming mails and intercepted a packet addressed to the British vice-consul. The vice-consul's office was shut, but Fitzroy got someone to let him in. Inside were dispatches from the *Challenger* that he took down to HMS *Blonde,* the British flagship. These dispatches (from Lieutenant Collins of the *Challenger*) confirmed that she had been wrecked on the night of May 19 at the spot described by the Swedish captain. All but two of her crew had got ashore. (Fitzroy later speculated that the wreck had been caused by a change in current patterns following the recent earthquake, unknown to the *Challenger*.)

In his modest official narrative, Fitzroy merely reports that the *Blonde* prepared for sea and "also such assistance as I can render was accepted by the Commodore."[17] In fact, what happened was that Fitzroy had to work hard to persuade a very reluctant Commodore Mason to set off to Seymour's rescue on such a dangerous coast. Darwin, writing to his sister Caroline, could be more to the point than Fitzroy could be in the *Narrative:* "The old Commodore in the *Blonde* was very slack in his motions—in short, afraid of getting on that lee-shore in the winter; so that Captain Fitzroy had to bully him and at last offered to go as pilot ... the Captain and Commodore have had a tremendous quarrel; the former having hinted about a court-martial to the old Commodore for his slowness. We suspect that such a taut hand as the Captain is, has opened the eyes of everyone fore and aft in the *Blonde,* to a surprising degree."[18]

The *Blonde* set off south, calling in at Concepción, where there was more information. Seymour had sent two sets of messengers. First, the assistant surgeon (Lane) and clerk (Jagoe) had been sent to Concepción to find help while the crew of the *Challengér* set up camp onshore and salvaged stores from the wreck. The local British consul, Mr. Rouse, then set off with a party on horseback. (This is probably why, to Fitzroy's disgust, the consulate had been closed when Fitzroy arrived.) Seymour soon found that he needed to move to a safer camp. Large numbers of the local Araucanian Indians had gathered around the wreck site, and while they were mostly friendly (they might have been more aggressive if the *Challenger* had been a merchant ship rather than an armed naval ship with no cargo), Seymour worried that they might turn hostile. The shore was also not a good place for any rescue to be attempted by sea, so they set up a new camp in the estuary of the Leübu River. Lieutenant Collins was then sent back to Concepción to give this new information.

At Concepción, Collins found that because of the devastation from the earthquake, there was only one boat available—a schooner of dubious serviceability—and at an outrageous price. So Collins had sent off the request for help and returned to the camp.

Fitzroy at once took a horse and a guide and set off furiously overland to find Seymour's camp, some sixty miles away. When he got back to Concepción after a marathon ride, he found that the inept Mason had rented the same wretched schooner, the *Carmen,* that Collins had refused. Usborne, Biddlecombe (second master of the *Blonde*), three seamen, the boatswain from the *Beagle,* and the latter's whaleboat had been sent off with her to try to reach the shipwrecked party by sea. The *Carmen* had a local crew of ten tired men "almost no use as seamen."

Fitzroy insisted on the *Blonde*'s attempting the rescue (the row Darwin referred to), setting off on the twenty-seventh. Actually the *Carmen* had by this point passed by the river mouth where the wrecked men were. She had even been spotted from the shore but passed on, lost, and never did find the camp. By the fourth (some two months after the wreck) the *Blonde* was off the right coast but also had great difficulty in locating the river, an embarrassment to Fitzroy, acting as pilot, given that he had recently surveyed the region. Happily, on July 5 they spotted signal fires from the *Challenger*'s encampment, and three small boats were sent in immediately. They had a lot of difficulty getting the men off, but eventually all were on board the *Blonde,* along with Mr. Rouse, who sent his servants, horses, and mules back to Concepción by land.

On the way back to Concepción they had now to rescue the

schooner *Carmen*. The vessel was in ghastly condition; the foremast and the mainmast had been lost in a heavy swell, and for
a while the vessel had drifted as a complete wreck until they
managed to get up some temporary rigging, using a sail from
the *Beagle*'s boat. The men whom Mason had sent on board
the *Carmen* probably suffered as much as or more than the men
who had been shipwrecked in the *Challenger!* The two boats
were taken in tow by the *Blonde,* and they all finally returned
to Concepción.*

At the end of the month Sulivan turned up with the rented
Constitución. He spoke so highly of her and had made such an
efficient survey that Fitzroy, amazingly, decided to buy the vessel himself, which he did for about four hundred pounds. He
decided to leave the small boat to complete the survey of the
coast of Peru, while the *Beagle* set off on the homeward half of
the journey across the Pacific. He could not spare Sulivan, so
Usborne and Forsythe were put in charge of the *Constitución*
with Davis, who was master's assistant in the *Blonde,* seven
volunteer seamen, and a boy. "A stranger might well smile at
the idea of such a boat being started to survey, in eight or at
most ten months, the whole coast of Peru, from Paposo, near
Apacama, to the River Guayaquil; but the task was completed;
the charts are now engraved; and very soon seamen will be able
to test their accuracy."[20]

Usborne's small expedition sailed on September 6 with
instructions to return eventually to Callao, there to sell the vessel, and to get a passage back to England through the British
consul. The next day the *Beagle* sailed, too, finally leaving the
coast of South American en route for the Galápagos Islands,
which she reached on September 15, 1835.

Second Leg

The Galápagos Islands are forever associated with Darwin's
theory of evolution by natural selection. The islands are volca-

* An interesting firsthand account of the wreck is given in the anonymously written *A Diary of the Wreck of His Majesty's Ship Challenger* ... (1836).[19]

nic and of very recent geological age, covered with fresh and old lava flows. Several of the cones are still intermittently active. The present Galápagos are the successors of an earlier ridge of volcanic islands but still date back only a few million years. Even to the untutored eye the islands appear young and unfinished. While some of the islands are well covered with vegetation, everywhere there are lava flows that look as though they have just cooled—gray, black, and bare, sharp to the feet, and devoid of life.

Fitzroy's description of Narborough Island is typical: "[F]rom a height near Tagus Cove dismal indeed was the view, yet deeply interesting. To see such an extent of country overwhelmed by lava, to think of the possible effects of the seven dormant volcanoes then in sight, and to reflect that at some one period all this activity and dreadful combustion where we then witnessed only silent desolation, was very impressive."[21]

Desolate and barren, with virtually no freshwater except for rainwater collected in cisterns, at that time the islands grew almost nothing that would help a ship in need of supplies. There was a small settlement on the islands, and Charles Island was used as a penal colony by the republic of Ecuador. The islands were popular with the crews of American sealers, who killed the large Galápagos tortoises for their meat.

The islands are some six hundred miles from the South American coast and have been populated by a curious array of chance immigrant plants and animals, many of which, as we now know, evolved in this isolated spot into forms unique to the islands. In fact, in many cases each island has its own endemic species. Some of the most famous of these endemic groups of species are the finches (Darwin's finches), the land tortoises, the lava lizards, and many plant groups, including the peculiar tree-form species of *Opuntia* cactus (prickly pear). The Galápagos are now often referred to as a natural laboratory where one can see the results of evolution recently and presently in action, with the formation of new species adapted to particular local environments. It took Darwin's genius to realize this.

The sequence of events was particularly fortuitous for Darwin. He had only just left a scene of activity in the earth's crust that brought home to him most forcefully the way in which the surface of the earth and the biological environments it contains can be changed. In his studies of animals and plants in South America he had been struck by the way in which related species were geographically distributed. Now here was a set of islands, obviously much younger than the mainland, populated by strange forms related to those of the mainland. What was the manner of their origin?

"It would be impossible for any one accustomed to the birds of Chile and La Plata to be placed on these islands, and not feel convinced that he was, as far as the organic world was concerned, on American ground. This similarity in type, between distant islands and continents, while the species are distinct, has scarcely been sufficiently noticed."[22] The ancestors of the Galápagos species must have found their way here by chance *and changed here*. His collections were the evidence for this.

However, ironically, by this stage his zeal for collecting was flagging. Syms Covington, whom Fitzroy had assigned as Darwin's assistant, did most of the collecting of specimens, especially the shooting. It was not until Darwin had left the Galápagos that some of the pattern of distribution of species—each island with its own special forms—became clear, as he worked over his specimens with the aid of others such as the ornithologist Gould.

For Darwin the visit to the Galápagos was eventually to become a turning point in the "evolution" of his biological thinking, away from the traditional creationist view that he had started the voyage with toward a view that species were indeed transmutable. The observations, the evidence, the ideas all had been mounting. But now the part of the voyage where Darwin would make his most extensive collections and observations was over. The men would circle home, making their chronological observations and fixing positions, but spending less and less time on land. They were entering regions that had been much more fully explored, and with the long cruise home. Darwin had long hours to wrestle with the revolutionary, and rather frightening, ideas that began to take shape in his private notebooks.

At sunset on October 20, rounding the outlying islets of Wenman and Culpepper, they left the Galápagos assisted by easterly breezes and a current "that set for more than 60 miles to the west during the first 24 hours." On November 16 they saw Tahiti for the first time, a most impressive sight:

> grandly formed mountains: high, sharp, irregular peaks, and huge masses of rocks appeared between the mists, and again were hidden—deep valleys or glens showed darkly, and while the shadows passed, seemed to be denied the light of day. Strikingly different in appearance were the lower hills and dales, and the richly wooded land at the sea-side. There the bright sunshine heightened the vivid and ever-varying tints of a rich verdure. The beautiful alternation of light and shade, were each moment changing as the flitting shadows passed over every kind of green; the groves of graceful palm-trees; the dazzling white foam of the breakers on the coral reefs, contrasted by the deep blue of the sea, combined to form a most enchanting view.[23]

They had left the miseries of Cape Horn far behind. As they landed, Fitzroy and Darwin were surrounded by happy, smiling people led by Reverend Wilson, the community missionary. So many canoes approached the ship that Fitzroy had to have Wickham set up a small market to control their trading.

Fitzroy started making his observations on the very spot (Point Venus) where Captain Cook had had his observatory. Fitzroy and Darwin spent a long time exploring onshore in this novel version of a tropical paradise and were particularly interested in the activities of the missionaries vis-à-vis native customs. Later they published a short paper on the subject of the morals of natives in Tahiti and New Zealand. Fitzroy also had a series of discussions with Queen Pomare, acting as an official emissary to negotiate a touchy matter. In 1831 the merchant ship *Truro,* working in the Low Islands, had been captured and plundered. Queen Pomare had undertaken to pay the British government an indemnity of $2,835 by September 1835. Commodore Mason had instructed Fitzroy to see the queen and find out why it had not yet been forthcoming. After a little gentle diplomacy, Fitzroy got the queen to agree that the sum would be paid (in pearl oyster shell) to the next man-of-war that visited the islands.

The *Beagle* left the beauty of Tahiti and continued westward. On December 19 "we made the northerly hills of New Zealand ... we were all a good disappointed by the view ... after Otaheite, the northern part of New Zealand had, to our eyes, a very ordinary appearance."[24] The fledgling country of New Zealand was then in a slightly uncertain status with respect to British sovereignty, a question that was not fully cleared up for another ten years (see Chapter 16). At the time Fitzroy visited it, the only Europeans there were missionaries from England, visiting whalers and sealers who had set up shore bases, and a very few settlers. As soon as they put into the missionary station of Paihia to make observations, Fitzroy found himself acting as policeman between the Maoris and whaling factions. (Maoris working on the whaling boats were being treated badly; when they got back to land, where they were the majority, they made life uncomfortable for the whalers.) Fitzroy undertook these responsibilities with some reluctance, observing in his *Narrative* the importance, both here and in Tahiti, of the regular appearance of British men-of-war to keep order. Fitzroy was also fascinated by the giant war canoes and the discovery of not very old evidences of cannibalism.

After celebrating Christmas in a missionary church, where they were struck by the beauty of the singing of the Maoris, "on the last day of this year (1835) we passed the North Cape of New Zealand, and steered for Port Jackson," leaving Matthews behind. They arrived in Australia on January 11. "We saw the red, revolving light of Sydney Lighthouse" and were astonished to find that Sydney was a "well-built city."[25]

From this point in the voyage they were once again traveling relatively well-charted waters and visiting relatively well-trodden coasts. All that remained was to continue the chain of measurements of longitude at previously established points. They began to spend less and less time at each port of call, and perhaps because they were impressed by the turn of yet another year, their thoughts were turning more and more to the completion of the voyage. Having taken all their data at thriving Port Jackson by January 30, they moved on south to Hobart "on a blustery wet day. Fields of ripe corn, dotted, as it were, about the hilly woodlands . . ."[26] greeted their eyes. Here was a country good for settlers, and no doubt it reinforced their thoughts of home. On February 17 they set off around the south of Van Diemen's Land (as Tasmania was then called) and made the long leg westward to King George Sound, where the Aborigines treated them to a full-blown corroboree. On March 13 they sailed for the Keeling Islands (Cocos Islands) in the Indian Ocean.

Although they did not stop at the Cocos Islands for long, and neither Fitzroy nor Darwin gives them much mention in their narratives of the voyage, Darwin's observations of coral formations on the Cocos were crucial in the development of his theory of the origin of coral atolls. He began his career back in England as a geologist, and the study that first earned him a reputation as a theorist was a novel theory of how the puzzling ring-shaped coral atolls and associated phenomena were formed.Like his theory of evolution by natural selection, his theories on coral island formations have stood the tests of time.

A month later the *Beagle* was heading for Mauritius. "[O]ur passage was slow, but in smooth water. . . . The captain is daily becoming a happier man. He now looks forward with cheerfulness to the work which is before him. . . ."[27] After only a short stay, they rounded Madagascar and put into Simons Bay, Cape of Good Hope, on May 31, 1836. Then they were back at sea and off to St. Helena and Ascension islands. At last they were heading homeward up the great South Atlantic Ocean. But Darwin and the others, who were longing to set foot on British soil again, had forgotten something. Fitzroy steered off to the west again—to South America. The voyage could not be complete until the great circle of meridian distances was linked up at Bahia, Brazil: "a sore discomfiture and surprise to those on board who were most anxious to reach England."[28]

Finally, after further stops at Pernambuco, the Cape Verde Islands, and the Azores, "after a tolerably short passage, but with very heavy weather, we came to an anchor in Falmouth."

Darwin immediately jumped ship and set off by stage for Shrewsbury, leaving Fitzroy to take the *Beagle* on to Plymouth and then around into the Thames to the Greenwich Observatory. There he would rate the chronometers for the very last time. Three of them were still working, and when all the calculations were completed, they erred from making a perfect circle of longitude by only thirty-three seconds. It was a remarkable ending to a remarkable voyage, made especially satisfactory when "Mr. Usborne and his companions came on board. . . ." They had completed their work and even sold the *Constitución* for a small profit. Everyone was home, safe and sound.

THIRTEEN

Postscript to the Second Voyage and Preface to the Third

DARWIN HAD WASTED NO TIME IN QUITTING THE *BEAGLE* AS soon as she reached Falmouth. But leaving behind the others when they still had work to do felt awkward. It was not so easy to leave the men with whom he had lived for so long, and soon he wrote to Fitzroy a fascinating letter that, with Fitzroy's reply, confirms the ups and downs of a friendship that somehow withstood the trials and tribulations of five years at close quarters.

Four days after leaving the ship, Darwin wrote to Fitzroy apologizing for his hasty departure. "... I am thoroughly ashamed of myself in what a dead-and-half-alive state I spent the last few days on board; my only excuse is that certainly I was not well." After five years cooped up on the *Beagle*, he had been chafing to get home. The unexpected detour to Bahia may have been the last straw. But even the "new" experience of England was something best shared with a friend, just like the mountains of Tierra del Fuego: "The first day in the mail [coach] tired me, but as I drew nearer to Shrewsbury everything looked more beautiful and cheerful. In passing Gloucestershire and Worcestershire I wished much for you to admire the fields, woods and orchards. . . ."[1]

Darwin's letter continues with the hope that Fitzroy will

write back and that "your vexations and trouble with respect to our voyage, which we now know *has* an end, have come to a close. If you do not receive much satisfaction for all the mental and bodily energy you have expended in His Majesty's service, you will be most hardly treated."

Darwin also picks up the political theme: "I put my radical sisters into an uproar at some of the prudent (if they were not honest Whigs, I would say shabby) proceedings of our government. By the way, I must tell you for the honour and glory of the family that my father has a large engraving of King George IV put up in his sitting room. But I am now renegade, and by the time we meet my politics will be as firmly fixed and as wisely founded as ever they were."

Finally, we get a further taste of the almost giddy relationship between the two: "I thought when I began this letter I would convince you what a steady and sober frame of mind I was in. But I find I am writing most precious nonsense. . . . Goodbye. God bless you. I hope you are as happy, but much wiser, than your most sincere but unworthy Philos."

Fitzroy replied from Portsmouth on October 20 (by which time Darwin had already gone to London) with news of new problems he had been having with the Admiralty. But then he continues in a more personal mode:

> Fuller [presumably the steward from the *Beagle*], told me you looked very well and had on a *good* hat! I was delighted by your letter, the account of your family, and the joy tipsy style of the whole letter was very pleasing. Indeed, Charles Darwin, I have *also* been *very* happy—even at that horrid place Plymouth—for that horrid place contains a *treasure* to me which even you were ignorant of!! Now guess and think and guess again. Believe it or not,—the news is *true*—I am going to be *married!!!!!!* to Mary O'Brien. Now you may know that I had decided on this step, long, very long ago. All is settled and we shall be married in December.[2]

Fitzroy's immediate problem was almost the last straw in a load of petty vexations caused by the Admiralty. From Falmouth he had sent sheaves of charts and chronometric data to Beaufort in London. But Beaufort happened to be away, and there was confusion about what final observations should be taken. Obviously the *Beagle* needed to call back at Plymouth for the all-important final observations from the breakwater and then proceed to Greenwich. But the Admiralty had sent orders that Fitzroy should pay off the ship at Plymouth. Fitzroy at once traveled up to London and sorted matters out. In fact, one can imagine him storming from office to office, trying to get the Admiralty to see the necessity for ending the work properly. And he did persuade their Lordships. The *Beagle* called in at Plymouth to measure from stone 230 / 1 once again. And then they headed around to the Thames, where they anchored off Greenwich on October 26, 1836. With a set of observations at the prime meridian at Greenwich, the chronometric work of the *Beagle*'s expedition was ended.

The *Beagle* lay at anchor off Greenwich for several days, during which many visitors came to see the ship whose voyage was already famous. The press of visitors was such that Fitzroy gave orders that the accommodation ladder should be used only by "respectable-looking persons" and that others should be sent around to the gangway. The problem of deciding in which category "persons" should be placed fell to the lot of the sentry at the accommodation ladder. One day Sulivan, who was on watch, was surprised when a very pretty and stylishly dressed woman appeared, clambering over the gunwale. She had labored up the "gangway" (which consisted of nothing more than three-inch cleats fixed to the side of the ship and two ropes for handholds). As he rushed to help her onto the deck, there appeared, behind her, a "rather plain looking man, who asked for the captain." They were shown below to Fitzroy's cabin, and after a moment an embarrassed Fitzroy came up to ask just why the astronomer royal and his wife had been "treated with such scant ceremony." When confronted, the sentry replied: "Well, sir, he did not look respectable."[3]

The astronomer royal was no doubt attracted to the *Beagle* by the news of the expedition's remarkable scientific achievements. Beaufort, the hydrographer to the navy, would also have had good reason to go down to the *Beagle* and congratulate her officers on their stunning success in everything from seamanship to scientific results. Indeed, Fitzroy's and Darwin's fame were assured long before they returned to England. In 1832 alone Fitzroy had sent back seven charts of Tierra del Fuego and two plans of parts of the Gulf of Peñas; in 1834, nineteen charts and eight plans, together with forty views of the 1933 surveys; in 1835, eleven charts, two track charts, and twelve plans. In 1837 Fitzroy completed eighteen charts and thirty-four plans of the Chilean coasts, plus eleven charts and eleven plans of the whole coast of South America from the Chonos Archipelago to the Guayaquil River, six charts and eight plans of the Galápagos Islands, and four other charts and plans of Pacific islands—in the end, an impressive total of eighty-two coastal charts, eighty plans of harbors, and forty views.[4] Meanwhile, Darwin's scientific notes to Henslow were so interesting that they had been published by the Cambridge Philosophical Society.

After a while the *Beagle* passed down the river to Woolwich to be stripped and cleaned. On November 17, 1836, she was paid off, after (as Fitzroy recorded) "having completed the unusually long period of five years and one hundred and thirty six days" in commission and away from a home port.

With her officers and men all gone, the *Beagle* lay in ordinary back at the place where her career had started sixteen years before. She was still in excellent condition. It would not take much work to fit her out for work again. However, considering the service she had already given, it would not have been surprising if she had been sold or perhaps pensioned off to harbor duty.

Many of the officers and men of the *Beagle* went on to other duties, and we may note briefly the careers of those who had no further participation in the story of the *Beagle*.

Of the officers, Philip Gidley King left the service and eventually ended up in Australia, like his father and grandfather. Sulivan went on to a distinguished naval career. He returned to survey South America and the Falklands. He was made governor of the Falkland Islands and there developed geological interests, corresponding frequently with Darwin and remaining a very close friend. The Crimean War gave him a chance to shine in active duty, and he was knighted, promoted to admiral, considered (but passed over) for the position of hydrographer, and given the post of chief naval officer of the Board of Trade.

Peter Benson Stewart, after leaving the *Beagle,* was appointed to the *Alligator* (frigate 28) which was accompanied by the *Britomart* in an expedition to set up a new colony at Port Essington in northern Australia (to which further reference will be made below). After seeing active service in China, he was made captain of the *Royalist* (10) and later entered the Coast Guard Service as inspecting commander. Arthur Mellersh was soon appointed to a steam vessel—the *Phoenix*—and then to others. Eventually, after a long period of retirement from active service in the navy he reached the rank of admiral. George Johnson also reached the rank of admiral after a long and not particularly eventful career in the navy; he died within a few weeks of Darwin. Wickham, Stokes, Usborne, Forsythe, and Bynoe all served in the *Beagle* for one more voyage.

Darwin's subsequent career is well known. It is interesting, however, how little he and Fitzroy saw of each other over the following years apart from a few formal dinner parties with their wives. Their relationship steadily deteriorated over the years.

Not only was Fitzroy heading for marriage, but Sulivan very soon married to his long-standing sweetheart Miss Young. For Darwin, however, the subject of marriage was a more difficult problem, resolved eventually when he married his cousin Emma Wedgwood.

Fitzroy was not appointed to another surveying commission. He apparently became sick for quite a time while still heavily engaged in supervising the work on his charts for the Admiralty. After he finished his official reports, he started work on his "Sailing Directions" for South America and the great three-volume *Narrative* of the *Beagle*'s two surveying voyages (1826–30; 1831–36).[5]

On the long voyage back from Australia, Fitzroy and Darwin had discussed plans for a book or books. In a letter home in

April 1836 Darwin wrote that Fitzroy, "like myself, is busy all day writing, but instead of geology, it is the account of the voyage. I sometimes fear his 'Book' will be rather diffuse . . . he has asked me to join him in publishing the account; that is for him to have the disposal and arranging of my journal, and to mingle it with his own. Of course I have said I am perfectly willing. . . ."[6] Such an arrangement was, of course, quite impractical, and they eventually divided up the work.

During the voyage Darwin had filled eighteen pocket notebooks with daily observations. He also extended these into a series of scientific notebooks and at the same time kept a voluminous diary. It is not often sufficiently appreciated that Darwin at first considered himself to be principally a geologist. While on the voyage he planned to publish books from his geological observations and theories developed on the voyage, and he eventually completed works on coral reefs, volcanic islands, and the geology of South America. He started his career as an author, however, with his *Journal of Researches,* which appeared as the third volume of the official *Beagle* trilogy.

The *Narrative of the Surveying Voyages* . . . was published in 1839. The first volume (the first voyage) is largely Philip Parker King's work, but as he had lost interest, Fitzroy edited the final version. The second volume, which is Fitzroy's own, is presented with more verve although both are terribly verbose. Fitzroy added a companion volume of appendices containing many interesting snippets of information as well as the requisite tabular presentation of basic surveying and observational data. The third volume, Darwin's account of the natural history, immediately became very successful (1,337 copies were sold in the first three years—somewhat to Fitzroy's distress). In 1845 it was considerably revised and republished. As *The Voyage of the Beagle* it has remained in print continuously to this day.[7]

Not only was Darwin's volume a remarkably interesting book of natural history, but the four-volume *Narrative* forms perhaps the best of such narratives ever produced. The whole is not just an account of the two voyages. Fitzroy includes diverting information on the history of the places visited and fascinating observations on his favorite topics—anthropology and meteorology. Even Fitzroy's parenthetical pontifications are interesting. For example, the short essay "A Very Few Remarks with Reference to the Deluge" evidently grew out of his five years in the company of Darwin. As Darwin's views grew farther and farther away from biblical interpretation of the history of the earth (after all, Darwin began without having seriously questioned the basic tenets of the church whose ministry he planned to enter), Fitzroy's thinking had evidently progressed in the opposite direction: Fitzroy became convinced of the fact of the Flood.

Fitzroy's later career did not live up to its early promise. He became more and more entrenched in his fundamentalist views. He was elected Member of Parliament for Durham, but his victory was marred by a quarrel with a rival named William Sheppard that ended in a public brawl. He was appointed an elder of Trinity House and an acting conservator of the river Mersey. His parliamentary work included sponsoring a bill for the certification of merchant ship officers that eventually became the first Mercantile Marine Act (1850). In 1843 Fitzroy was appointed governor of New Zealand, the second governor in the young colony's history. But totally unsuited to the job, he was recalled on October 1, 1845, as a result of a petition from the settlers. He handled matters directly, according to his rigorous sense of duty, and naturally therefore lacked the flexibility and tact necessary to deal with the frequently conflicting interests of missionaries, Maoris, visiting whalers, settlers, and the home government.

Fitzroy recovered from this setback when he was recommended as the government's first official meteorologist in 1851 with the title Meteorological Statist in the Board of Trade. (Along with Lieutenant Matthew Maury in the United States, he founded meteorological science as we now know it.) He set up stations around Britain for recording and communicating information and set the science of weather forecasting (his word) firmly going.

Over the years Fitzroy saw little of Darwin, whose career went from success to success as he became progressively more reclusive. But in 1860 Fitzroy set off to Oxford for the annual meeting of the British Association for the Advancement of Science to give a talk about "wind diagrams." Most of the distinguished natural scientists of the day—Huxley, Owen, Hooker, Lubbock, Henslow, Daubeny, and Lyell—were present that year, and Darwin's new theory of evolution by natural selection was on everyone's mind, even though Darwin himself was characteristically absent. With the lines of battle already drawn, there was little doubt about the philosophical allegiances of most of those present. Among those highly visible at the meetings was the bishop of Oxford, Samuel Wilberforce, and the word was out that "Soapy Sam," perhaps one of the most forceful orators in Britain and an implacable foe of Darwin, intended to lead an attack on Darwin's theory.

The "Oxford Debate" became famous but changed no one's mind, and the level of debating now seems trivial. Wilberforce chose as the target of his assault a relatively innocuous-sounding paper to be delivered by Professor John William Draper of New York, a Darwinian and, incidentally, a great bore. Huxley had determined not to be drawn into the fuss, but the partly apocryphal legend has grown up that in his long peroration Wilberforce made the mistake of turning to Huxley and resorting to the crudely unsophisticated jibe of asking him whether he claimed descent from monkeys on his grandfather's or grandmother's side. Huxley is said to have whispered, "The Lord has delivered him into my hand." Darwin's old professor, the Reverend Henslow, was in the chair, and he called on Huxley, who reviewed the evidence for the Darwinian side. It was not sensational until he referred to the bishop's question. Huxley said he would not mind a monkey for an ancestor but would be "ashamed to be connected with a man who used great gifts to obscure the truth." Wild applause ensued from the audience that had only just finished lauding Wilberforce. Wilberforce did not continue the debate again that day, but it is said that a somewhat wild-eyed man brandishing a Bible stood up to assert that Darwin's views were totally unscientific. Few noticed, and fewer still recognized that it was Robert Fitzroy.[8]

As the years passed, Fitzroy became more and more unhappy and depressed. Whatever he did somehow managed to provoke ill will. He took every slight as a serious insult, every complaint as a hidden sneer. His health and his mind breaking down, he was passed over for the position at the Board of Trade that went to Sulivan. He was promoted to rear and to vice admiral. On April 30, 1865, he finished it all, by cutting his throat. Thus ended the brilliantly inventive, partly mad life of one of the most highly intellectual naval officers of the century.

Of all the tasks that remain with respect to the origins of "Darwinism," the most pressing is to discover more fully the nature, the mind, and the personality of Fitzroy. He remains a shadowy figure, despite all that is known about him. In 1831, as the officers and men excitedly set off in the *Beagle*, he had been the focus of all their lives. In order really to understand the impact of the voyage of the *Beagle* on Darwin and the world of Darwin's time, we need to understand Fitzroy better.

Australia Felix

With the end of the *Beagle*'s second voyage, a great deal of survey work in South America remained to be done. For example, Sulivan was sent for further surveying work on the Falkland Islands and the Río de la Plata from 1842 to 1845, in command of the *Philomel* (brig 8), and became involved in some exciting actions during a blockade of Montevideo. But in 1836 public attention was being concentrated on a new region of interest, Australia.

The eastern, southern, and western coasts of Australia were already the home of several thriving settlements, with agricultural ventures prospering, whole towns growing up, and fortunes were being made in land speculation at Sydney and elsewhere. The northern coast of Australia, however, was one of the regions about which speculation continued. It had been visited by William Dampier and Matthew Flinders, but most of the details were unknown. And nothing was known of the interior of the continent.

The elder Philip Parker King, before commanding the *Beagle–Adventure* expedition of 1826–30, had surveyed a part of the northern coast of Australia and had discovered a large harbor on the northern coast of the Cobourg Peninsula (of Arnhem Land, Northern Territory). He called it Port Essington (after Vice Admiral Sir William Essington) and in his report described the harbor in glowing terms: "As a harbour Port Essington is equal, if not superior, to any I ever saw; and from the proximity to the Moluccas and New Guinea, and its being in the direct line of communication between Port Jackson and India, as well as from its commanding situation with respect to the passage through Torres' Strait, it must, at no very distant period, become a place of great trade, and of very considerable importance."[9]

Various interests were at work in Britain promoting settlement of the barren northern coasts of Australia. Among others, Colonel George Windsor Earl, who had spent several years in the East Indies, thought that a thriving settlement in the north would find any lucrative markets for British manufactured goods in the Celebes and Moluccas and would rapidly become an important center of trade. The fleets of trepang fishers from Macassar might find a market in Australia rather than in Singapore. Further, it was urged upon the secretary of state for the colonies that a settlement in the north would be very useful as a refuge for the crews of ships wrecked in the Torres Strait. There seems even to have been a good deal of optimism that a settlement on the northern coast could be agriculturally self-sufficient.

In 1838, despite the fact that previous attempts to settle the Cobourg Peninsula had failed, a party set out under the command of Sir Gordon Bremer, with HMS *Alligator* and HMS *Britomart* (Captain Owen Stanley), to establish a settlement at Port Essington. The history of the *Beagle* became closely linked to this place over the next five years.

The optimism with which a new attempt at settlement in the north of Australia was launched flew in the face of experience, for none of the explorers of the northern and northwestern coasts—King, Flinders, Dampier—had discovered the one secret necessary to the opening up of this region of Australia to prosperous development—namely, water. The great enigma of

Australia was that such a vast continent should be so little habitable. Although, by 1836, several explorations of the barren central deserts had been attempted, there was still great hope for the existence of an inland fresh sea that would support a luxuriant flora that could be turned into an agricultural bonanza. Although all the rivers that flowed into the ocean on the eastern, western, and southern coasts had proved to be short coastal affairs, rumors (and hopes) persisted that one or more great continental rivers might flow north from the center and find their outlet to the sea in one or more of the embayments in the northwest, such as the Gulf of Carpentaria. With the discovery of this great river (or rivers), the way would be open for a great colonial development.

Careful exploration of the northern and northwestern coasts of Australia was therefore crucial to the orderly development of the country. In addition, the northern coast of Australia was of considerable importance to British seafaring interests. The route between Sydney and Singapore or other British colonial centers in the Indian Ocean passed through the Torres Strait, one of the more difficult and dangerous regions of the world, and not simply because of the natural hazards to navigation. The islanders of the Torres Strait were notoriously efficient shipwreckers. If settlements were to be successfully established along the northern coast, facilities for servicing ships, policing the area, and rescuing shipwrecked crews would be needed. For all these reasons it was important that the northern coast be surveyed and settled. Beaufort decided to send out a small expedition. A good surveying ship would in any case be extremely useful in preparing a good chart of the Bass Strait (between Australia and Tasmania), which, like the Torres Strait, was claiming more and more vessels as the merchant traffic to Sydney increased.

In early 1837 the obvious choice for such an expedition was the *Beagle,* just back from her circumnavigation and apparently in good condition. Many of her officers were available, and with their experience of both the work and the ship, success seemed assured.

Wickham was appointed to the command, with John Lort

Stokes as his first lieutenant. They must have felt themselves extremely fortunate to be off around the world again after only a few months onshore, instead of waiting for several years for another ship.

Once more the *Beagle* was back in a dockyard being fitted out for a voyage of several years' duration. This time she was at Woolwich, where she had been built, but Jonathan May, her faithful carpenter, was not on hand, having retired from his immense labors of the last ten years. A new carpenter, John Weeks, took over the care of the *Beagle*.

Commander Wickham supervised the refit. The *Beagle*'s rigging, sails, and cables all were replaced, she was cleaned and repaired wherever necessary, the copper was checked over carefully, and the small boats were prepared. The masts and principal yards were still in good shape, and Harris's copper lightning conductors in perfect condition. Where new spars were needed, new copper inserts were carefully put into place. All in all, the refitting of the *Beagle* for this voyage took less than a month, at a cost of only £2,384. Fitzroy had indeed kept her in good condition.

The full ship's complement, assembled at Woolwich in October 1837, was as follows:[10]

John Clements Wickham	Commander and Surveyor
James B. Emery	Lieutenant
Henry Eden	Lieutenant
John Lort Stokes	Lieutenant and Assistant Surveyor
Alexander B. Usborne	Master
Benjamin Bynoe	Surgeon
Thomas Tait	Assistant Surgeon
John E. Dring	Clerk in charge
Benjamin F. Helpman	Mate
Auchmuty T. Freeze	Mate
L. R. Fitzmaurice	Mate
Thomas T. Birch	Mate
William Tarrant	Master's Assistant
Charles Keys	Clerk

| Thomas Sorrell | Boatswain |
| John Weeks | Carpenter |

A corporal of marines
and seven privates,
with forty seamen and boys

The *Beagle* was ready for sea again, and all that remained was to receive the official instructions from the Admiralty, which contained one added duty: that of ferrying to Australia a small exploring expedition under the command of Lieutenant George Grey, who had persuaded the Royal Geographical Society to sponsor him in an attempt to be the first to find a way (on foot) into the great interior of the Australian continent. The *Beagle* was to take Grey and his party to the west coast of Australia and generally assist him in his exploring venture.

By the Commissioners for executing the office of Lord High Adral of the United Kingdom of Great Britain and Ireland, &c.

Whereas his Majesty's surveying vessel, *"Beagle,"* under your command, has been fitted out for the purpose of exploring certain parts of the northwest coast of New Holland, and of surveying the best channels in the straits of Bass and Torres, you are hereby required and directed, as soon as she shall be in all respects ready, to repair to Plymouth Sound, in order to obtain a chronometric departure from the west end of the breakwater, and then to proceed, with all convenient expedition, to Santa Cruz, in Teneriffe.

In the voyage there, you are to endeavour to pass over the reted site of the Eight Stones* within the limits pointed out by our Hydrographer; but keeping a strict look out for any appearance of discolored water, and getting a few deep casts of the lead.

At Teneriffe you are to remain three days, for the purpose of rating the chronometers when you are to make the best of your way to Bahia, in order to replenish your water, and from thence to Simon's Bay, at the Cape of Good Hope; where, having without loss of time obtained the necessary refreshments, you will proceed direct to Swan River; but as the severe gales which are

* They were still being looked for!

sometimes felt at that settlement may not have entirely ceased, you will approach that coast with due caution.

At Swan River, you are to land Lieutenants Grey and Lushington, as well as to refit and water with all convenient dispatch; and you are then to proceed immediately to the north-west coast of New Holland, making the coast in the vicinity of Dampier Land. The leading objects of your examination there will be, the extent of the two deep inlets connected with Roebuck Bay and Cygnet Bay, where the strength and elevation of the tides have led to the supposition that Dampier Land is an island, and that the above openings unite in the mouth of the river, or that they branch off from a wide and deep gulf. Moderate and regular soundings extend far out from Cape Villaret: you will, therefore, in the first instance, make that headland; and, keeping along the southern shore of Roebuck Bay, penetrate at once as far as the *"Beagle"* and her boats can find sufficient depth of water; but you must, however, take care not too precipitately to commit his Majesty's ship among these rapid tides, nor to entangle her among the numerous rocks with which all this part of the coast seems to abound; but by a cautious advance of your boats, for the double purpose of feeling your way, and at the same time surveying, you will establish her in a judicious series of stations, equally beneficial to the progress of the survey, and to the support of your detached people.

Prince Regent River appears to have been fully examined by Captain King up to its fresh water rapids, but as the adjacent ridges of rocky land which were seen on both sides of Collier Bay, were only laid down from their distant appearance, it is probably that they will resolve themselves into a collection of islands in the rear of Dampier Land: and it is possible that they may form avenues to some wide expanse of water, or to the mouth of some large river, the discovery of which would be highly interesting.

As this question, whether there are or are not any rivers of magnitude on the western coast is one of the principal objects of the expedition, you will leave no likely opening unexplored, nor desist from its examination till fully satisfied; but as no estimate can be formed of the time required for its solution, so no period can be here assigned at which you shall abandon it in order to obtain refreshments; when that necessity is felt, it must be left to your own judgment, whether to have recourse to the town Balli, in the strait of Allas, or to the Dutch settlement of Coepang [Kupang]; or even to the Arrou Islands, which have been described as places well adapted for that purpose; but on these points you will take pains to acquire all information which can be obtained from the residents at Swan River. . . .

The above objects having been accomplished, (in whatever order you may find most suitable to the service) you will return to the southern settlements for refreshments; and then proceed, during the summer months of fine weather and long days, to Bass Strait, in which so many fatal accidents have recently occurred, and of which you are to make a correct and effectual survey. . . .

The survey of Bass Strait should include, first, a verification of the two shores by which it is formed;—secondly, such a systematic representation of the depth and quality of the bottom as will ensure to any vessel, which chooses to sound by night or day, a correct knowledge of her position;—and, thirdly, a careful examination of the passages on either side of King Island, as well as through the chains of rocks and islands which stretch across from Wilson's Promontory to Cape Portland. This survey will, of course, comprehend the approach to Port Dalrymple, but the interior details of that extensive harbour may be left to the officers employed by the Lieutenant-Governor of Van Diemen's Land, provided you can ascertain that it is his intention to employ them there within any reasonable time. . . .

At Sydney you will find the stores which we have ordered to be deposited there for your use, and having carefully rated your chronometers, and taken a fresh departure from the Observatory near that port, and having re-equipped His Majesty's ship, and fully completed her provisions, you will proceed by the inner route to Torres Strait, where the most arduous of your duties are yet to be performed. The numerous reefs which block up that Strait; the difficulty of entering its intricate channels; the discordant result of many partial surveys which have from time to time been made there, and the rapidly increasing commerce of which it has become the thoroughfare, call for a full and satisfactory examination of the whole space between Cape York and the southern shore of New Guinea, and to this important service, therefore, you will devote the remaining period for which your supplies will last.

In this latter survey you will cautiously proceed from the known to the unknown; you will verify the safety of Endeavour Strait, and furnish sufficient remarks for avoiding its dangers; you will examine the three groups called York, Prince of Wales, and Banks' Islands; you will establish the facilities or determine the dangers of passing through those groups, and by a well-considered combination of all those results, you will clearly state the comparative advantages of the different channels, and finally determine on the best course for vessels to pursue which shall be going in either direction, or in opposite seasons. Though with this part of your operations Cook's Bank, Aurora Reef, and the other shoals in the vicinity will necessarily be connected, yet you are not to extend them to the 143rd degree of longitude, as the examination of the great field to the eastward of that meridian must be left to some future survey which shall include the barrier reefs and their ramified openings from the Pacific Ocean. You are, on the contrary, to proceed, if practicable, but most cautiously, in examining the complicated archipelago or rocks and islands which line the northern side of Torres Strait, till, at length, reaching New Guinea. . . .

Before your departure from Sydney you will have learnt that His Majesty's Government has established a new settlement at Port Essington, or somewhere on the North coast of New Holland; and before you finally abandon that district you will visit this new colony, and contribute by every means in your power to its resources and its stability. . . .

Given under our hands, the 8th of June, 1837.

Signed,

Char. Adam.
Geo. Elliot.

To J. C. Wickham, Esq.
Commander of Her Majesty's surveying
vessel *"Beagle,"* at Woolwich.
By command of their Lordships.
Signed,

John Barrow[11]

FOURTEEN

The Third
Surveying Voyage

IN MANY WAYS THE THIRD VOYAGE OF THE *BEAGLE* REPRE-
sents a continuation of the traditional exploration and surveying in the first two voyages. Wickham and his men were to
check old charts and follow up suggestions of previous explorers yet were free to strike out completely on their own. They
would make thousands of positional fixes and, above all,
explore and chart the coastlines, looking for new harbors and
rivers.

However, if the first two voyages belonged squarely to the
era of sailing ships, with the third voyage the *Beagle* entered
more fully into a new world. To be sure, most of the actual
surveying was in totally unexplored regions, but the expedition
worked from towns like Perth and Sydney and the newly developing Albany, Adelaide, Portsmouth, and Melbourne. The
modern age was rapidly developing. They anchored in company with steamships and worried about sites for possible coaling stations. When Stokes surveyed the port of Adelaide, one of
his first recommendations concerned the need for laying down
a railway line between port and town, in order to help carry the
new mineral exports of southern Australia. Many of the harbors to which they sailed had lighthouses.

None of the work was physically easier or less hazardous

than before. The explorations of the north and northwest of Australia were dangerous and difficult and completely new. But the days of new maritime exploration and the age of sailing ships were fast dwindling.

These changes did not come precipitously. But they had definitely been under way back in 1831, when Darwin and Fitzroy had made a passage together from London to Plymouth in a commercial steamer. Now, in 1837, a navy steam tug, the side-wheeler HMS *Boxer* (ex-*Ivanhoe*), recently acquired from the Post Office, towed the *Beagle* out into the Thames from her berth at Woolwich.

The *Beagle* arrived at Plymouth on June 20 and once again began the familiar set of meticulous procedures that had to precede any such voyage. For several days the officers tested the chronometers, balanced the compasses, and made the final series of fixes of position from the familiar point (stone 230 / 1) on the breakwater that had been the point from which Fitzroy and King had marked their departures.

On June 21 King William died, and Victoria ascended the throne. When the expedition left England on July 5, they carried with them, therefore, not only hopes for discovery in the young colonies but also the news of the beginning of a new era in the old country.

It is a strange fact that in a glorious period of service from 1826 to 1846, HMS *Beagle* only made three departures from a British port (if we discount the false starts in 1831). Whereas most of her sister ships had plied in and out of their home ports countless times for short patrols of the North Sea, the eastern Atlantic and the Mediterranean, HMS *Beagle,* her men and officers, essentially never saw home waters. Now, "running out of Plymouth Sound with a light northerly wind and hazy weather," the *Beagle* was off again.

Again she headed first for Tenerife and made the required search for the mythical Eight Stones. Then the fully loaded *Beagle,* "rolling very deep and taking water in fully both sides," headed for the equator, making good time, occasionally nine knots. In early August she arrived at Bahia to take on water and supplies and to compare chronometric measurements.

Stokes took an afternoon to visit the grave of Musters, but Bahia and South America had no great attractions on this trip, and soon the *Beagle* was away again, heading on a new course: south and east, for the Cape of Good Hope.

So far the voyage had been smooth and easy but just short of the cape the officers and men got a good taste of foul weather and were able to demonstrate to the landlubbers Grey and his party the awesome contrast between a 10-gun brig and a simple gale. "Wrapt in mute astonishment, they stood gazing with admiration and awe on the huge waves as they rolled past, occasionally immersing our little vessel in their white crests— and listening, with emotions not wholly devoid of fear, to the wild screams of the sea-birds. . . ."[1]

As at every port of call, the first task at Simons Bay, apart from watering and provisioning, was to take exact fixes of longitude. The men were pleased to discover that the chronometers gave a position within a few seconds of the fix made on the homeward journey of the *Beagle* in 1836. Having received ominous reports here of the state of supply at the Swan River settlement in Western Australia, Wickham crammed the *Beagle* with all the extra provisions he could obtain.

Some additional space was made available because Grey and his party decided to leave the *Beagle* at this point. Everyone here advised them that there would be no chance of hiring at Swan River the sort of schooner they would need to move up the western Australian coast to start their explorations. Possibly also impatient to be starting his own adventure, Grey hired a cape schooner, the *Lynher* (140 tons), and set off independently, arranging a rendezvous with the *Beagle* at Hanover Bay for the following April.

It was with some misgivings that the officers of the *Beagle* watched the novice Grey depart from the agreed plans so quickly. However, once fully provisioned, the *Beagle* moved on and, as soon as she left Simons Bay, hit very bad weather again. Immediately she began to show the old problem. She had needed to cram all possible supplies into her holds and onto her decks, but "owing to the deep state of our loaded little vessel, her decks were almost constantly flooded. For many days we had never less than an inch and a half of water on them all over; and this extra weight, in our already overburthened craft, did not, of course, add to her liveliness; however, she struggled on. . . ."[2]

After sighting Amsterdam Island, they sailed for three days under triple-reefed topsails, forestaysails, and trysails with "huge following seas" that sometimes ran "clear over us." A month later, on November 15 they made their first Australian landfall at Rottnest Island, off Swan River.

"There is nothing very particularly inviting in the first appearance of Western Australia; dull green-looking hills, backed by a slightly undulating range of hills, rising to nearly 2,000 feet are the chief natural features of the prospect. Fremantle, of which it was wittily said by quartermaster of one of His Majesty's ships who visited the place 'you might run it through an hour glass in a day,' is but a collection of low white houses scattered over the scarce whiter sand. . . ."[3]

The bustling little port and the settlement at Perth, just up the river, were, in fact, not so depressing on closer examination. The officers and men eagerly went ashore, each wanting to satisfy his own personal queries about what sort of place Australia was. They could tell immediately that it was not like places that they had been before. It was very hot and dry, and the edge of barren desert country lay very close to the settlement and opened up an untouched wilderness beyond. Many Aborigines worked in the settlement, and many more were imprisoned at Rottnest Island, learning the hard way the differences between the Englishmen's law and their own.

Everyone on board anxiously sought firsthand local opinion about the nature of the interior of the continent. What chance *was* there of the existence of a great inland sea? They found no shortage of rumors, but nothing very definite to go on. All their advisers agreed, however, that if they were going to work up along the northwestern and northern coasts, they had better make only relatively short trips and plan to return at short intervals. There were no safe landings, no water, and no food up there.

With so many of the officers and men already familiar with

one another and with the ship from previous voyages, the *Beagle* should have settled down quickly to a smoothly working team. As first lieutenant under Fitzroy, Wickham had needed an extraordinary grasp of every detail of the ship's management. He continued, as skipper, to be a martinet. Stokes worked well with him, but Wickham had a tendency to bad temper, and on a small ship like the *Beagle,* with such a small complement, the natural misunderstandings and arguments over little details could readily build into major "scenes."

A direct and personal account of life on board the *Beagle,* at least for the first part of the voyage, is provided by the diary of Benjamin Francis ("Frank") Helpman (now in the collections of the LaTrobe Library, Melbourne). Helpman was unhappy for most of his service in the *Beagle.* He had left behind a sweetheart of whose affections he was unsure. Every day in port he eagerly scanned incoming ships for a letter from home. He cannot have been a cheerful or cooperative shipmate. Very soon he and Thomas Tait, the assistant-surgeon, became frequent objects of the captain's displeasure, with Stokes and, of course, the indefatigable Bynoe, acting as peacemakers. But Helpman was also constantly at odds with Stokes. Birch and Freeze quarreled constantly as well.

These problems were only compounded when dysentery hit the ship. With Wickham debilitated, more and more of the work of the ship fell on Stokes's shoulders. All in all, however, the *Beagle* was an efficient ship. Although the work was hard and tedious and once again conducted in weather conditions for which the crew was abysmally unprepared (hot instead of cold), the fact that they could repair fairly frequently to the comfortable English confines of Swan River, Sydney, or Hobart made it all bearable. Both officers and men began to build up shoreside friendships and interests in a way that had not been possible on the two long South American voyages. Swan River and later Sydney, in particular, became their "home ports," where good friends would welcome them.

The whole ship's complement began to become wrapped up in the developing history of the continent, its exploration and settlement. They soon came to feel themselves part of a living process, the emergence of Australia. This was quite different from working in South America. The charts they were making and the information they obtained were put to immediate use by their new friends, military and settlers alike.

They planned to make their first explorations to the north, where there were no settlements of any kind. Along the whole coast from Swan River to the immediate vicinity of Port Essington, there was no house or military outpost—nothing except an enervating heat and, they soon discovered, an abundance of flies.

By late November all was ready to set off north to start the great adventure of discovering the northern rivers and the great inland sea. However, Wickham's dysentery was so severe that they were unable to leave until the New Year. Even then he did not fully recover his strength.

Forced to wait at Swan River, the officers of the *Beagle* set about charting the harbor and its rather dangerous approaches. The river itself, with its shifting banks and channels, needed attention, and there was plenty to keep them busy. They also had their first chance to meet the Australian Aborigines and hired one, named Miago or Megeo, to accompany them north as guide and interpreter.

The Fitzroy River

On January 4 the officers and men of the *Beagle* finally headed north into the heat, charting reefs and banks along the northwestern coast all the way to Roebuck Bay. The work was tedious and frustrating. From the sea, the shoreline was low and uninviting: a long series of mud flats, sandbars, and mangrove swamps with little clue to whether the banks and bars might conceal some major river beyond. Time and time again they would work their way in among the sandbars in small boats, but to no avail.

Roebuck Bay is named for Dampier's 1699 ship and had been partially explored by King. Of the whole of the northwestern (as opposed to the northern) coast, it seemed to offer the

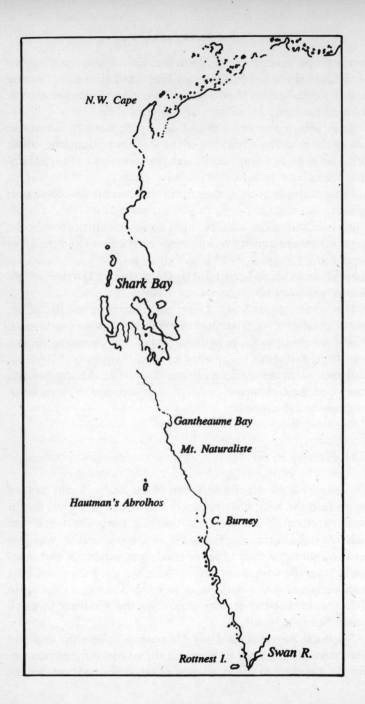

N.W. Cape

Shark Bay

Gantheaume Bay

Mt. Naturaliste

Hautman's Abrolhos

C. Burney

Rottnest I.   Swan R.

first hope for finding the outlet of a major river system. Survey of the bay showed nothing promising until Usborne returned from a sortie having "discovered a high water inlet in the south shore of the bay . . . having a dry bank of sand before it at low water."[4] This was interesting enough to check further. Usborne had also met up with a party of Aborigines who were unfriendly. Miago was nervous about them even though there were no overt acts of hostility.

The following day Usborne, a veteran of countless reconnoitering trips from the *Beagle* on the last voyage, set off in a small boat to examine the bank he had spotted. It turned out to be another disappointment. It had nothing but very shallow water beyond it.

Stokes also needed to find a better anchorage for the *Beagle* farther up the bay, and the next day Usborne took a small party in two boats off into the eastern part of the bay to explore. Stokes should have led this party, but like Wickham, he was ill. Indeed, many of the crew were suffering very badly in the hundred-degree weather.

Stokes waited eagerly for the return of the exploring party, but when the boats returned that evening, they bore an inert figure, that of Usborne, who had been accidentally shot by Helpman. The party had spotted some kangaroos, and Usborne wanted to shoot one. As they were creeping up through a thicket, a twig caught the trigger of Helpman's gun, and it went off. Usborne was shot in the side, just above the hip.

This all happened about ten in the morning, some twenty miles from the *Beagle,* and in his haste Helpman laid down his pistols and forgot them. It took until six in the evening to get Usborne back to the *Beagle,* against wind and tide, through the mudflats and channels of the bay. Usborne lived, nonetheless, and under Bynoe's care slowly recovered over the following months.

"Thus disastrously terminated our examination of Roebuck

The northeast coast of Australia as recorded by P. P. King in 1822 (Swan River is at the southernmost edge of the map), redrawn; see Chapter 5, note 17.

Bay, in which the cheering reports of former navigators, no less than the tenor of our hydro-graphical instructions had induced us to anticipate the discovery of some great water communication with the interior of this vast Continent. A most thorough and careful search . . . had clearly demonstrated that the hoped-for river must be sought elsewhere."[5]

When Usborne was well enough for the ship to put out to sea again, Wickham gave orders for the *Beagle* to stand away "to the north east." Stokes recorded one final thought about this first full-scale encounter with Australia and particularly its aboriginal peoples, a final paragraph that stands out to the modern reader as particularly sensitive and perceptive:

Our intercourse with the natives . . . when Usborne was well enough for the ship to put out to sea again . . . had been necessarily of the most limited character, hardly amounting to anything beyond indulging them with the sight of a new people, whose very existence, notwithstanding the apathetic indifference with which they regarded us, must have appeared a prodigy. What tradition may serve to hand down the memory of our visit to the third generation, should no newer arrival correct its gathering errors, and again restore some vestige of the truth, it is hardly possible to imagine; but should any misfortune follow their possession of Mr. Helpman's pistols, that in particular will be narrated as the motive for the visit of those white men who came flying upon the water, and left some of the secret fire upon the peaceful coast; and when again the white sails of the explorer glisten in the distant horizon, all the imaginary terrors . . . will be invoked to avert the coming of those who bring with them the unspeakable blessings of Christian civilization.[6]

Still full of optimism, the officers soon found another large inlet worth checking, but just a superficial examination showed it was not promising: "[T]he bar which locked its mouth, and over which the sea was breaking very heavily, rendered it impossible to take a boat across without evident risk, by which no real good would be obtained, the rise and fall of the tide, eighteen feet on this coast, was more than sufficient to account for the imposing, though deceptive appearance of this opening."[7] A final check from the main topgallant yard showed only level "boundless Plain." This was Dampier Land. The same exercise was to be repeated many times during the next months. They discovered a few good anchorages, but any inlets they found were barren. Most showed signs of occasional severe flooding, but no permanent waters flowed into the northwestern coast from the interior.

As they explored north and then northeast, a serious interest in the natural history of the continent on the part of many of the officers became apparent. No doubt as a result of the long years of association with Darwin, Stokes filled his diary with observations on geology, plants, and animals and not just with an eye to the eventual colonization and agricultural development of the land but with a real naturalist's gift for observation. His notes are full of the differences among the several groups of aborigines they met with—in dress, artifacts, language, habits—and are interspersed with conjectures about their relationship to one another and to their possible migrations and intermarriage.

Surgeon Bynoe was perhaps even more diligent and enthusiastic than Stokes.[8] As the official naturalist for the expedition (shades of McCormick) and an avid student of birds and mammals, he made many new discoveries.[9]

Despite Stokes's early forebodings, most of the time there was no real trouble with the Aborigines. Scarcity of freshwater was more centrally on their minds. And the heat and the flies were almost intolerable, particularly when they landed to dig wells (usually unsuccessfully). Occasional torrential downpours gave them some water for washing but then simply added to the humidity and discomfort.

At the end of January they got as far as King Sound and, following King's directions, moved south into the head of the bay, which was as yet unexplored. "It was reserved for us to take up the thread of discovery reluctantly abandoned by our enterprising and scientific predecessor ... nor can I describe with what delight, all minor annoyances forgotten, I prepared to enter upon the exciting task of exploring water unfurrowed by a preceding keel; and a shore on which the advancing steps of civilization had not yet thrown the shadows of her advent. . . ."[10]

Stokes took a party that landed first at Valentines Islands, a series of points and bars. They climbed to the highest point to survey the terrain inland. "We gazed with indescribable delight upon a wide expanse of water which lay before us in that direction, and already anticipating the discovery of some vast inlet. . . ." During the next days, as they picked their way through a series of creeks and channels, "several circumstances concurred to satisfy me that we were at the mouth of a considerable river; large trees drifted past us with the ebbing tide, while each cast of the lead proved that we were gradually, though nearing land, deepening the water."[11] Soon they landed for the night at a place that they could only name Point Torment.

Whenever they came near shore in this region, flies tormented them in the daytime—the flies for which Australia early became famous—Dampier had noted how bothersome they were, and even the Aborigines suffered dreadfully. "Their eyelids are always half closed, to keep the flies out of their eyes, they being so troublesome here, that no fanning will keep them from coming to one's face; and without the assistance of both hands to keep them off, they will creep into one's nostrils, and mouth too, if the lips are not shut very close. . . ."[12] However, Point Torment was named not so much for the flies as for the mosquitoes. "No sooner do [the flies] from sheer exhaustion, or the loss of daylight, give up the attack, than they are relieved by the mosquitoes . . . it may seem absurd to my readers to dwell upon such a subject; but those, who, like myself, have been half blinded, and to boot, almost stung to death, will not wonder that even at this distance of time and place I refer with disgust to the recollection."[13]

Camping ashore, the men, already exhausted from the day's work, were completely unable to sleep. Several took to the extreme expedient of covering themselves in their blanket sleeping bags, although the temperatures were in the eighties and nineties. Others half suffocated themselves in the smoke of fires, to keep the mosquitoes off. Eventually the only thing that made their shore explorations bearable was Helpman's discovery that the mosquitoes always remained close to the ground. By climbing trees and propping themselves in the branches, they could get a halfway decent night's sleep. But then, while they slept, their eyes, swollen and irritated by the flies of the day before, would discharge large volumes of mucus and become stuck shut.

For two more days they worked their way among the bars and points, still optimistic, but without finding a single main channel. "The bed of the river assumed the aspect of an extensive flat of mud, interested with small rivulets or streams that served to drain it."[14] They could go no farther by boat, so Stokes took Helpman and Seaman Ash to reconnoiter on foot across the mud flat, creeks, and stands of mangrove. Eventually they became cut off by the tide, but Stokes managed to wade back to within gunshot of the boat, and they were rescued in the nick of time. The terrified Ash, who could not swim, was not reached until the water had topped his shoulders. They reported back to the *Beagle,* and immediately a larger party was set up to explore further the newly christened Fitzroy River.

During the next five days they pushed some twenty-two miles inland but without reward. It was not navigable. No sooner would they find a short reach in which the water ran deep and clear between well-defined banks than they would turn a corner and find themselves in a shallow mud flat or mangrove swamp. All along they found many evidences of huge floods, but there was no regular flow of water. Finally, they had to conclude, in Stokes's somewhat despairing words, that the Fitzroy had "all the more distinctive features of an Australian river: deep reaches, connected by shallows, and probably forming, during the droughts which characterize Australia, an unlinked chain of ponds or lagoons; and in places, leaving no other indication of its former existence than the waterworn banks and deep holes, thirsty and desolate as a desert plain."[15] Clearly the Fitzroy did not flow from some permanent inland lake. It was a large but seasonally intermittent river.

For the next two months they surveyed all along the shores of King Sound, Collier Bay, and Camden Sound, finding nothing to give them new hopes. The first event to break the routine was their meeting up with Grey's party at the entrance of the Prince Regent River in Brunswick Bay. Grey was overdue.

Grey's adventures (which have been written up at greater length than they deserve) were an exercise in futility. At the time they were presented as the very stuff of heroism. For who can tell, except with the blessing of hindsight, whether a trek into the unknown will be a useless circuit through a barren, hostile country of which only the fringe can be tested and then at great risk, or indeed, whether over the next hill will be a shining river, grassy plains, inviting hills and forests? In fact, Grey's party suffered great hardships, largely through their own foolhardiness, and discovered nothing.

One might excuse the notable failure of Grey's expedition because after all, there was (as we now know) no major discovery to be made. There is, however, more than a faint smell of amateurism and rank stupidity about Grey's party, and Stokes reflects this when he describes Grey's appearance as he was relieved at last by the *Beagle:* "[B]adly wounded and half starved, he did indeed, present a melancholy contrast to the vigorous and determined enthusiast we had parted from a few months before at the Cape to whom danger seemed to have a charm, distinct from success."[16]

Grey and his party, having landed at Hanover Bay, had in fact only succeeded in trekking some sixty miles inland into the Macdonnell Ranges. They "found" a minor river, the Glenelg, that the *Beagle* had already charted and were as far from exploration toward the interior as they could be.

The desperate condition of Grey's expedition is perhaps best shown in Helpman's candid diary entry (April 16, 1838):

[T]he Captain, with the Yawl, went round into Prince Regent's River, when, in passing across Hanover Bay, they saw Grey's Schooner "Lynher." 'Twas very odd that they should have returned this very day, and what an awful state they would be in, the vessel was to have left on the 2nd May at the latest, and then they must have perished. They have had dreadful fatigues. On first reaching this place they formed a Tent ashore, and

Lushington took the schooner to Coepang, Island of Timor, and purchased 24 horses, besides several sheep, dogs, and goats. On returning they commenced their Inland trip, and could not get above 5 miles a day. The day they first made this place, Grey, the Corporal of Sappers, and two men, with three dogs, landed at a point to walk round to meet the vessel, but without fancying they had such difficulties to contend with. They left at 9:00 A.M. without any fresh water, and did not reach the ship until 2:00 next morning, more dead than alive. The men laid down, declaring they could not move another inch from want of water, and they preferred dying where they were. Grey, himself, deliberated whether it would not be best to blow his brains out than die such a death. The dogs, two laid down and were found dead on the spot next day; the other went mad into the woods. Grey was obliged to use stratagem to get the men on; he told them he would go ahead and fire if he saw the vessel. When reaching about 500 yards he would fire, they walked to this. He kept further ahead and fired again. To quench their thirst they laid in the salt water—how horrible. They in all reached only 60 miles, and fell in with the very stream of water I found. . . ."[17]

The master of the *Lynher,* his charter having long since expired, had continued waiting for Grey simply out of human concern. On May 9 the two vessels quitted the northern coast and headed back together to Swan River, where they arrived on May 25.

After a "light refit" and her crew having taken advantage of the annual horse races at Perth for a little relaxation, on June 20 the *Beagle* nosed out of the Swan River again, but this time she turned south for the long haul past Cape Naturaliste and eastward across the Great Australian Bight to New South Wales. With the aid of a westerly gale they bowled along toward the Bass Strait accompanied "in solemn silence" by many albatrosses, but bad weather prevented them from entering the western opening of the strait, and instead they rounded Tasmania to the south. After narrowly avoiding being run onto a lee shore, and then a difficult passage up the river, they anchored at Hobart on July 16. After they had waited for the storm to abate, favorable winds swept them on to Sydney.

Sydney to Port Essington

Sydney by 1838 was a booming, bustling town. Immigrants poured in weekly, as the volume of shipping in the harbor showed. Poor Helpman, the *Beagle*'s mate, who was desperately lovesick and frantic for news from his sweetheart in England, listed each ship in his diary. During the sixteen weeks they spent at Sydney, there were thirty-nine vessels from Britain alone (not counting arrivals from foreign countries). (Sad to say, only very few letters came for Helpman, and none from his girl, who had clearly deserted him.)

It was July when the *Beagle* arrived to find HMS *Britomart* and *Alligator* already in port, having come down from the new settlement at Port Essington. Captain Stanley reported that their expedition had arrived safely and was busy getting established.

As the season for bad weather was on them, Wickham decided to remain at Sydney for a complete refit and to work up the charts. The stay at Sydney was busy and cheerful. From Helpman's diary we gain an impression of the gay, if slightly confined, social life of the town. There was a steady round of parties, walks, picnics in the country, theatrical and musical performances, and a stream of new faces appearing and reappearing with tales of the outback, of farming life, or news from home. Sydney was no mere colonial outpost. It was already the center of a new way of life.

For Wickham and Stokes, one of the most important people they met in Sydney was none other than Captain Philip Parker King. They had followed King's charts from his explorations of the northern coast, and of course, King had previously commanded the first exploratory voyage of the *Beagle* (with HMS *Adventure*) from 1826 to 1830. King's father had been governor of New South Wales, and now King had settled just to the north, heading an agricultural development company, the Australian Agriculture Company. Although now a successful businessman, he lost no time in nostalgically treading the decks of the *Beagle* again and visiting with her officers. And they in turn were anxious for any new information he could give them about the country.

In early November the *Beagle* left Sydney to begin a survey of the Bass Strait, starting at Port Philip Bay, although she first visited the fledgling settlement of Melbourne upstream. After three weeks working on the north side of the strait, Wickham moved south via King and Hunter islands to the northern shore of Tasmania and the Tamar River. On the way, at Three Hummock Islands, Bynoe nearly lost his life in a brush fire that cut him off while he was collecting birds. All the while the *Beagle* was plagued by difficult weather, gales, and fog.

At first sight their track across the strait seems baffling. The ship zigzagged all over the place, for no sooner had she touched Tasmania than she set off back north to Port Philip Bay again. The purpose, however, was to obtain series after series of complementary fixes and meridional distances from landmark to landmark, landfall.

The ship was soon back at Hunter Island to continue the work around the western entrance to the strait until the end of February, when it was time once more to set off for Sydney, as the favorable time of year for work up in the Torres Strait was approaching. A survey (the first) of Port Philip Bay was quickly completed, and on March 10 all were back at Sydney, working up their charts.

They could not wait long, and two months later they left for the north. However, they left behind Usborne. His wound was still bothering him, although he tried very hard and had worked as well as could possibly be expected. Usborne "invalided out" and waited at Sydney for a passage home, bearing the precious new charts with him.

The *Beagle*'s first stop was at Port Macquarie, some eighty miles north of Sydney, the headquarters of King's agricultural venture, where the men were royally entertained. Here they discovered some important anomalies in their chronometer readings, and while work proceeded, Stokes took the opportunity to explore inland. Strangely, however, in his book Stokes does not mention that the crew of the *Beagle* also effected a valuable rescue mission at Port Macquarie. Helpman, in his diary, gives

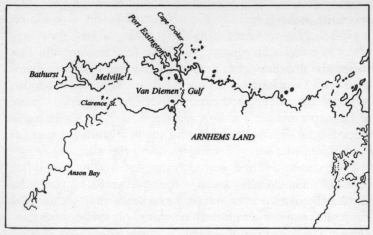

Redrawn detail of P. P. King's 1822 map of northern Australia showing the position of Port Essington; see Chapter 5, note 17.

a fuller account, perhaps because he was the focus of the salvage efforts.

They had spotted a cutter bearing a number of ladies who had been passengers on the *Francis Freeling,* a schooner out of Sydney headed to Port Philip. The ship was beached on the shore not far ahead. Helpman took a boat and picked up the rest of the passengers and crew who were "in a most miserable state." The vessel had evidently been in very poor shape, leaking badly even before they left Sydney. When the weather turned bad, the passengers were put to work at the pumps to keep her afloat. But it was a losing battle, and as the passengers kept at the pumps, the captain beached her. Helpman labored with some seamen for three or four days, diving to salvage what could be brought up from the holds of the *Freeling.*

For the next three weeks the *Beagle* passed inside the Barrier Reef, heading northward past Cape Melville until finally, on July 13, 1839, she reached Cape York. The trip along the reef was concerned mostly with charting dangers and noting the positions of safe anchorages. There was a serious divergence of opinion about passage north to the Torres Strait: whether inside or outside the reef was better. The outer passage was shorter because it was not necessary to anchor at night, but it was much more dangerous. The inner passage was much slower but on the whole safer for smaller vessels. In fact, the whole passage from Sydney north and then west toward the East Indies was a difficult one, not least of the major hazards being the Torres Strait itself. However, the *Beagle* had no opportunity to tarry. Pressed by shortage of water, she pressed on to the Cobourg Peninsula and Port Essington, the settlement upon which so many hopes had been pinned for the development of northern Australia.

The little settlement at Port Essington had become well established in eight months (since October 27, 1838). Governor Sir Gordon Bremer and the settlers had already erected a jetty, a church, a small Government House, and a series of small houses. The harbor itself looked fine as the *Beagle* arrived.

The Port is superb, about 5 miles wide and 10 deep, of a general breadth, but deeply indented, the shore is formed of Red Cliffs. Everything looks vastly pretty. At 3:30 we opened a point which brought the *"Britomart"* full in view. The Settlement has a most perfect appearance, at the top of the port and on one side of a Bay.

Shortened sail, and came to. Captain McVitty, Lieutenant Healy, and Hill came off, all looking vastly well. . . . We went ashore, and landed at "Victoria" on a Jetty that would not have disgraced a more antique Settlement; about 60 or 80 yards long, and 10 or 12 wide, well built, with numerous side landing places. A huge Flagstaff, and a regular Pier Lamp and Post are no mean symptoms of what is to be expected. At the end of this a good road well cut through the banks takes you up to the level. The first house is the Store, where the provisions, etc., are kept, it is one of the Sydney ones. Everything about it bore the appearance of being well ordered. Government House is quite a sight; neatly painted white, with green Venetian Blinds, and in an open space. It is on the highest part of the land, and is fronted about 200 yards off by a fort of 6 Guns, built on one of the Cliffs, it well defends every part of the Settlement, and has a good Flagstaff. The most ingenious and neatest part are the Cottages—one built by young Bremer is exceedingly neat, it is (as are all the rest) formed of Rushes over a light framing, a good height, with a veranda round the front, two excellent rooms and a servants place; a cleared garden. This is (since the *"Alligator"* left) Brewman's and Hammond's quarters. Priest's house is nearly as good outside and vastly superior in; inside it is evident he has a wife, neatness is observable. Two Wells, 30 to 50 feet deep and good water, are the proofs of Paul's ingenuity, they are called Peter and Pauls Wells—his name is Peter Paul. The Botanical Gardens have Melons, Pineapples, Bananas, and Cocoa Nut trees apparently flourishing. They have found no trouble with the Natives, on the contrary they are the most civil, friendly creatures imaginable. Nor have they had any trouble. One of the men was lost two days in the Bush, they sent out parties to look for him, but no purpose; however, the Natives found him and treated him exceedingly well, fed him, and took great care of him, and then brought him in safely. They now bring fish into them. The Botanist (Armstrong) has made some very good specimens of Wood, which he thinks good. There are a very great number of Alligators here, and they have been troublesome, one has been shot, after it had carried off a Dog and a Blanket, both of which were found in him. Stanley has fixed two Observatories, and has had numerous Transits. . . . [18]

In addition to the *Britomart* and *Alligator,* the settlement was served by the schooner *Essington,* whose captain and owner, Thomas Watson, hoped to make a livelihood supplying the new port. Among other items, he traded for tortoiseshell and beeswax from the islanders of the Torres Strait and the Arafura Sea. One of his more famous exploits was to rescue from Timor Laut an English sailor, Joe Forbes. Forbes had been kidnapped and enslaved from the schooner *Stedcombe,* the crew of which had been overpowered off Melville Island and murdered some seventeen years before, when that schooner had been involved in a previous unsuccessful effort to make a settlement on the Cobourg Peninsula. [19]

There were, however, two dark clouds on the horizon for the settlement. First a sister settlement at nearby Raffles Bay had already been abandoned, lasting only two years (1827–29). The reasons for the failure were debated. Certainly the climate was very difficult, and there had been a lack of enthusiasm on the part of the government officials. Bureaucratic bungling had caused a failure in imported East Indian labor. Perhaps no one really wanted to face the fact that contemporary agriculture was not yet advanced enough to be continued under such conditions by white European settlers completely unused to the tropics. At Port Essington nonetheless, with its one English cow and bull, two Indian heifers and two cows, about fifty goats, six working oxen, thirty buffaloes, six pigs, some chickens, five ponies, and "thirty half-greyhounds for catching kangaroos," the settlers were prepared to give it a good try.

The second damaging blow to the Port Essington settlers was the fact that the *Orontes,* their initial supply ship, struck a submerged reef right in the harbor entrance and sank. When this fact became generally known, merchant skippers in Swan River and Sydney were reluctant to accept freight for the Cobourg Peninsula.

Before the *Beagle*'s arrival, the port had been visited by the French polar expedition of J. S. C. Dumont d'Urville in the ships *L'Astrolabe* and *La Zelée.* They were very pessimistic about the chances of the settlement's surviving. They did, however, leave us two very nice lithographs of the port as it appeared in 1839.[20]

The day that the *Beagle* arrived at Port Essington, Crawford Pascoe of the *Britomart* was detailed to pilot her to an anchorage. His appearance was so unkempt, especially the long hair that had not been cut for months, that when he tried to come aboard the *Beagle,* Birch thought he was a Malay and called out, "You jumpee up; here, John." But Pascoe had recognized him and replied, "All right Tom, you catch hold of this chart. . . ."[21] Before the *Beagle* departed, Birch and Pascoe exchanged places; Pascoe's autobiography gives us another view of the Australian voyage.

Rather than become a burden on the dwindling supplies of the settlement, the *Beagle* quickly moved off to the west, toward Melville Island, Van Diemen's Gulf, and the Clarence Strait. At the eastern entrance of the Clarence Strait, they once again came across some promising signs. The mate, L. R.

Établissement Anglais à Port-Essington, the settlement at Port Essington in 1839; see Chapter 14, note 20.

Fitzmaurice, was dispatched to survey some small islands. Returning to the *Beagle,* his boat was suddenly forced off course, suggesting that there might be a river hidden behind the mangroves. Wickham was dubious but ordered two whaleboats to explore the next day.

Wickham took charge of one boat, and Helpman the other, but they did not return after two days, or three.

And when the fourth day came without bringing a sign of the boats, there was some anxiety as to the possibility of trouble having occurred with the natives.

The ship was therefore got under way and we moved towards the bight, intending to send other boats to their relief, but as the vessel approached the bight the boats were seen coming out, not, as we expected, short of provisions after being four days of two days' supply, but with a line stretched between the awning stanchions festooned with game, ducks and teal, while their stock of ship's provisions was untouched; and, what was of equal importance, they brought with them a good supply of fresh river-water.[22]

As this new and interesting river emptied into the Clarence Strait, it was named after Dowager Queen Adelaide, widow of the late king (formerly the duke of Clarence).

Fitzmaurice was evidently an alert young man, and this quickly showed itself again while Wickham's party was away from the *Beagle* exploring the Adelaide. Great difficulty had been experienced with the compasses in this region because of iron in the rocks, so Fitzmaurice and the clerk Charles Keys landed one morning to take some detailed observations. The two young men laid down their weapons and had just started to set up their equipment when a party of Aborigines, heavily armed, assembled on the cliffs about twenty feet above their heads. Fitzmaurice waved to them, and there was no problem until he opened the legs of the theodolite, which must suddenly have looked like a strange new weapon.

Stokes describes the Aborigines as "stamping on the ground, and shaking their heads to and fro, they threw out their long shaggy locks in a circle, whilst their glaring eyes flashed with

Dancing for Their Lives, from a drawing by L. R. Fitzmaurice (one of the dancers); see Chapter 13, note 10.

fury as they champed and spit out the ends of their long beards. . . ."[23] The problem became, how to get to the guns and retreat with the instruments. Fitzmaurice and Keys had to distract the Aborigines until the others could retrieve the gear. So they started to dance and shout, making themselves quite ridiculous. It worked, but whenever they slowed down, spears were aimed at their throats until eventually everything was recovered and everyone got back to the *Beagle*.

While this experience receded from frightening to funny in the minds of the *Beagle*'s crew, Wickham's exploration of the northern arm of the Adelaide was proceeding, reaching to some eighty miles inland. "For thirty miles of the upper part of the river the water was fresh; while the banks were low, being now more than five feet above the present level of the river, a circumstance very favorable for irrigation and the cultivation of rice. Fifteen miles from the mouth they were fringed with mangroves; and higher up many of the points were thickly wooded, while on either side stretched a vast extent of prairie country, dotted here and there with islands of timber. . . ."[24] The prospects for agricultural development here were indeed good, and the officers considered their discovery a major one. The southern arm of the river was shorter and less promising, although both branches were amazingly infested with "alligators." The fact that the first fifty miles of the rivers were navigable to vessels "of four and five hundred tons . . . and into fresh water . . . a thing hitherto unknown in Australia." At last their exploration had yielded a significant discovery. With water and provisions becoming low, and anxious to inform the settlers of the promising river so close to their west, they set off back for Port Essington, hoping that a ship might have arrived with supplies.

However, on their arrival (August 18) "we found no fresh arrival to greet our anxious gaze, the *Britomart* being the only guardian of the port."[25] The news of the discovery of the Adelaide did indeed cheer up the settlement, as did also some festivities that Captain Stanley had been working on. Everyone's spirits being distinctly low, "ever anxious to provide for the amusement of others, he had been for some time engaged in getting up a play." The play was *Cheap Living*, and it was much discussed in the settlement as the first theatrical performance in the whole north of Australia. Finally, on the appointed day:

> [A]s if to cause the first performance of a play . . . to take place under smiling auspices . . . HMS *Pelorus* arrived with supplies and letters from Sydney. The previous growing dearth of provisions had rendered it somewhat difficult to secure a very happily disposed audience, an empty stomach being apt to provoke fault finding; but the arrival of a ship on the very play day caused a crowded and contented attendance. Everything went off smoothly, and with hearty peals of laughter. All the characters being supported by men, the female personages of the drama presented a most grotesque appearance; moreover, the "act drop" being an old ensign, the ladies could be seen through it, regaling themselves, during these intervals, with a pipe.[26]

After a brief trip to Timor, on September 4, 1839, the *Beagle* was ready for sea again with her officers eager to fill a gap in their exploration: the coast between the Clarence Strait and Collier Bay. They explored the western entrance to the Clarence Strait briefly, finding a good passage for ships, and on September 7 anchored in a largish bay just to the west. The next morning they investigated the opening at the head of the bay but found only a swampy, alligator-infested area. It was very hot, and the sand flies and mosquitoes were bad. The harbor itself was a good one. Near its head they found cliffs with "talc shale . . . imbedded with quartz . . . the other rocks near it were of a fine grained sandstone—a new feature in the geology of this part of the continent, which afforded us an opportunity of convincing an old shipmate and friend, that he still lived in our memory; and we accordingly named this sheet of water Port Darwin."[27]

FIFTEEN

Routes to the Interior?

WITH NOTHING TO DETAIN THEM AT PORT DARWIN ("THIS dismal place"), after a brief fruitless exploration of the neighboring bays, the expedition headed southwest for a very large bay that King had reported, some 140 miles away, in Cambridge Gulf (Joseph Bonaparte Gulf).

King had visited this region in September 1819 but, having found the bay, could not enter it. His ship had been down to only one anchor, and he was unable to work in eastward against strong contrary winds. After two days, and several close brushes with disaster, he had given up. Now Wickham and the *Beagle* could pick up the thread. "Thus did the exploration of this wide and interesting opening fall to our good fortune; as we proceeded inward, several beautiful medusae passed the ship, and our hopes were roused to the highest pitch by the muddy appearance of the water."[1] Several small boats were put out to reconnoiter and find the main channel in the maze of banks and passages at the head of the bay.

They worked their way close to the wooded coastline, and two exploring parties were prepared. Wickham and Stokes took one boat to what seemed to be the main channel, and Fitzmaurice and Keys took another channel to the south. Wickham and Stokes left the ship in the evening of October 12,

1839, and sailed briskly "for the chasm in the high land, bearing S.20°E., twelve miles from the ship." As they closed the land, darkness fell, but "just as we found that the course we held no longer appeared to follow the direction of the channel, out burst the moon above the hills in all its glory, shedding a silvery stream of light upon the water, and revealing to our anxious eyes the long looked for river, rippling and swelling, as it forced its way between high rocky ranges." Here, in the most dramatic of moments, a truly great river had been found, running hard and full in a channel of eighteen to twenty fathoms. Stokes may perhaps be forgiven reporting a highly improbable conversation: " 'This is indeed a noble river' burst forth from several lips at the same moment; 'and worthy,' continued I, 'of being honoured with the name of her most gracious majesty the Queen. . . .' " This was the discovery of the Victoria River.[2]

The party stopped to camp for the night, but Wickham and Stokes were up before dawn and climbed a hill to see more of what might lie before them. "A rapid stream passing between barren rocky heights, there stealing in calm silence, there eddying and boiling . . . the boat lay in the mouth of a creek, which communicating with another four miles further down, formed an island on the eastern side of the river, which we called Entrance Island."[3] Quickly they broke camp and set off toward the gaps in the hills that showed where the main course of the river passed. The first few miles were difficult because of the extremely turbulent water, "violent eddies and whirlpools," and then there opened up a long splendid southerly reach that seemed, disappointingly, to end in very shallow water, probably limiting how far the ship could be brought up. They pressed upstream only to find that the course of the river soon became easterly rather than south toward the interior. After exploring for about another thirty miles, they turned back toward the ship for more reconnoitering and to plan a full-scale expedition. Fitzmaurice and his party also returned, having found a fine smaller river, which was named for him, just to the north.

On October 29 they brought the *Beagle* upstream as far as the head of the great southerly reach of the Victoria, some fifty miles from the coast. This would enable them to water the ship from the river rather than through the tedious business of digging wells. (Attempts to dig wells onshore had failed here probably because it was the end of the dry season and rain had not fallen for at least six months.)

A party of three boats under Wickham's command left the ship with all the watering casks, while Stokes followed on one of the whaleboats in which he and Wickham planned to take a small party as far as possible upstream. Wickham had ascertained that the point at which the river ran perfectly fresh was about seventy miles upstream, but before they could get that far, they were stopped by banks and shoals. The bigger boats could go no farther, and so the watering would have to be done by relay, using the smaller ones.

Leaving the watering party here, two boats set off upstream to explore, and by November 6 they were more than 75 miles from the ship and some 125 from the coast. Finally they were stopped by shallow water. Stokes climbed another hill and saw that the river kept going to the horizon, occasionally broad and deep, but frequently blocked again by bars and rocks. They called their position Reach Hopeless and decided that it would be worth trying at least a short expedition overland, despite the great heat. Stokes, Bynoe, Forsyth, and five men marched for four days in temperatures of up to one hundred degrees in the shade, tracing the course of the river eastward and southward. As seamen they were particularly unfit for this sort of trekking. One man was hit with sunstroke, but despite the lack of shelter and the inability to sleep because of the accursed flies and mosquitoes, they reached another 65 miles inland and some 140 miles from the coast—a significant penetration into the interior of Australia, the center of which lay still another 500 miles beyond.

The prospect before them, had they had the strength and facilities to go farther, was still good. "Far far away I could perceive the green and glistening valleys through which [the river] wandered, or rather amid which it slept; and the refreshing verdure of which assured me, just as convincingly as actual observation could have done, of the constant presence of a large body of water." Stokes was now convinced that the Victoria "will afford a certain pathway into the centre. . . ."[4]

The relatively green and fertile alluvial river valley they had followed was full of wildlife. Bynoe collected several new birds for his collections, and Stokes noted that the Aborigines they met, while menacing, seemed all well fed and healthy. Kangaroos, turtles, alligators, and fishes abounded, and Bynoe started to make some observations on the reproduction of kangaroos from dissections of the many dozens of specimens they shot. Of all the areas they explored, this seemed the most suitable for colonial development, as well as affording a route to the interior. Stokes began to develop a plan by which an expedition could trek inland using camels brought up the river by boats.

The party set off back to the boats, moving very carefully because their old tracks showed that they had been followed by Aborigines. They rejoined the rest of the party without serious mishaps except that the one sick seaman had to be carried most of the way. Then, after two more days, they reached the watering party, and they all headed to the ship, where a day and a half was spent trying to weigh the ship's anchor, which had become stuck fast in the "quicksand." They put out a second anchor, but soon, after "heaving down the ship nineteen inches by the head, and splitting the hawse pipes, we were ultimately obliged to leave both behind, and thirty fathoms of cables with one and fifteen with the other."[5] "The common notion among the crew in the forecastle was, that when we returned to Woolwich we should find the anchors had reached the dockyard before us."[6] (Here is an opportunity for the modern marine archaeologist: to find those anchors.)

The "alligators" of this region—actually two species of crocodile—are justly famous. On one occasion Wickham and some men were sleeping in a whaleboat at anchor in the river when he was pitched into the bottom of the boat. The man on watch was "so scared by what he saw that he was helpless . . . a huge alligator with his long nose resting on the gunwale, trying to throw his flipper over the side."[7]

Soon after this there was a more serious incident. Back in

Queens Channel, Bynoe and Stokes went ashore, Bynoe shooting more birds for his collections while Stokes checked errors in the chronometers. The morning passed uneventfully, except Bynoe got a new species of finch. In the afternoon Stokes returned to the same place, thinking it perfectly safe. He left his gun behind because he had to carry the chronometer across a long, low reef (it was low tide). While Master's assistant William Tarrant and one man followed with the rest of the instruments, Stokes set off for the observation point near a cliff "just glancing towards the cliff, which presented nothing to the view except the silvery stems of the never-failing gum trees.... I had just turned my head round to look after my followers when I was staggered by a violent and piercing blow about the left shoulder; and ere the dart had ceased to quiver in its destined mark a loud long yell...."[8] The cliffs were swarming with heavily armed Aborigines. A spear had penetrated a long way into Stokes's chest, puncturing a lung. Stokes pulled out the spear and started to stagger back to the beach, having the presence of mind not to drop the precious chronometer and to keep the spear—his only means of defense. Tarrant and his man had not yet noticed that Stokes had been hit.

Fortunately for Stokes, the Aborigines decided to come down from the cliffs, instead of following up their attack from above. This gave Stokes a chance to escape, and he "hurried on ... while at each respiration, the air escaping through the orifice of the wound, warned me that the strength by which I was still enabled to struggle through the deep pools ... must fail me soon." He fell twice, and the attackers, now down on the beach, were almost on top of him. At last Pascoe and Lieutenant James Emery spotted from the chart room of the *Beagle* that Stokes was wounded. Boats were manned, and a relief party dashed over the reef just in the nick of time to save Stokes, the Aborigines retreating in the face of superior force before they could get within spear's range again.

On board the *Beagle,* Bynoe probed the wound and decided that although deep, it was probably not fatal. For the next two days Stokes lay very ill while parties from the *Beagle* unsuccessfully scoured the shore for Aborigines with orders to kill or at least to destroy their huts. Stokes, Pascoe, and Helpman, however, each recorded their private relief that none could be found for punishment. This uncharacteristic attack probably came simply because the Aborigines, having never before seen Europeans or even a ship, were terrified at seeing the strange white figures on the beach with frightening "weapons" in their hands.

When Bynoe said it was safe for Stokes's health, the *Beagle* was under way again, with a course direct for Swan River with the news of their great discovery. During this long run the *Beagle* lost her cook, an old man named Mitchell, who had been a great favorite. He was buried at sea. According to Helpman, on Tuesday, January 21, 1840:

> Squally, with small rain, but no shift of wind. We have now only 14 days of water, and less of Provisions, even at half allowance. The nearest place is nearly 700 miles off, with a dead foul wind. Only 8 Candles left. . . . Buried Poor old Mitchell about 10:00 A.M. 'Tis very impressive; four weather-beaten rough messmates supporting a plank with the body on it, covered with a Flag— 'tis blowing fresh, with a nasty sea on—one plunge; the sound strikes the ear, and the next sea eddying over all that remains, closes for ever "the Scene of Life." The Funeral Service, always impressive and beautiful sounds doubly so and most awful when the very elements assist.[9]

The voyage to Swan River from the Victoria ended with a nice piece of dead reckoning. In view of the fact that they were depending on their own work, a modest boast was allowable. "We arrived at Swan River on the 31st, under circumstances which must forcibly illustrate to a landsman the precision with which a ship may be navigated. We had not seen land for fifty-two days, and were steering through a dense fog, which confined the circle of our vision to within a very short distance around the ship. Suddenly the vapour for a moment dispersed, and showed us, not more than a mile ahead, the shipping in Gage's Road."[10]

This time they stayed about ten weeks at Swan River, refitting and repainting the ship and working on their charts.

At the same time, men using small boats completed a survey of the harbor. Stokes steadily regained his strength with walks around Perth with the colonial officials who now were becoming their fast friends. During their walks he received news of the intrepid Grey's second, and even more disastrous, expedition from Lieutenant Roe, the surgeon general.

Grey Rescued Again

After returning to Swan River, Grey had discharged the *Lynher* and decided to explore the coast around Shark Bay. Using small boats this time, he cached a supply of stores on Bernier Island in Shark Bay. After a lengthy but fruitless attempt to explore in bad gales, the party returned to the cache, only to find they had not stored it high enough above water level. All their supplies were lost. "Grey retired to a distant rock, where, with the wild sea raging around him, he began to reflect the best way out of their dangerous predicament. Three courses were open to him: to seek the mainland, and remain there on the chance of seeing a colonial steamer pass; to start at once for the island of Timor; to make for Swan River. He chose the last, but not without some misgiving, and in order to restore his depressed spirits he 'sat down and read a few chapters of the Bible.' "[11]

The trouble with the route they chose was that the first 150 miles or more lay along an extremely dangerous coast, with no landing places. After three days of hard work at the oars they were off Gantheaume Island, exhausted. They tried to land but were wrecked instead. "The breaker we were on curled up in the air, lifting the boat with it, and when we gained the summit I looked down from a great height not upon water, but upon a bare sharp rock. . . ."[12]

They were now shipwrecked, stranded three hundred miles from Perth with very few provisions and no chance of any ship's passing by to rescue them. So they set out on foot. By the time they reached the region of Hill River, the party was half dead of thirst and starvation. They staggered a few more miles, and then Grey left them to go on alone to Perth. Roe headed a relief party in search of the rest, one of whom had died. They found the "poor fellow quite dead in a bush, with his blanket half rolled around him . . . reduced to a perfect skeleton; having in fact starved to death."[13]

Ironically, on his return to Perth, Grey found orders sent after the first expedition instructing him to stop. The reports he had sent home did not justify "the further prosecution of your researches." And it soon turned out that the mapping Grey had done in Western Australia was all wrong.

At about this time, unfortunately for our story, Frank Helpman, who had become more and more unhappy on the *Beagle,* quarreling with Wickham and his fellow officers, spotted a vacancy as captain of the colonial schooner *Champion* at Swan River. He applied for the post and got it, leaving the *Beagle* on March 4, 1840. With that his diary ends, and we lose the advantage that it gave us in reconstructing the details of the voyage.

Fully supplied, and with Stokes pretty much recovered, the *Beagle* left Swan River on April 6, 1840, heading north but just for 100 miles, in order to explore a group of islands called Houtman Abrolhos, lying north of Fremantle. Several early Dutch explorers had been wrecked here, including most notably Commodore François Pelsaert, who was wrecked here in the *Batavia* in 1627. Reaching the mainland in small boats, his expedition had been the first to land in Western Australia. Among the six or more other early vessels wrecked here was the *Zeewyck* (1727), and while exploring the islands, the *Beagle*'s officers found many relics of both ships, including a brass four-pounder gun,[14] brasswork, glass bottles, pipes, and coins.

On these islands, particularly on Wallabi Island, Bynoe continued his researches on the reproduction of kangaroos, following up work he had started on the Victoria River. The problem he wanted to solve was an old one. Many marsupials had been found with the young in the pouch, but never, or almost never, in the uterus. The young found in the pouch were at such amazingly immature stages and so very firmly attached to the nipples that the theory grew up that the young were actually born *through* the nipple. Bynoe was one of the first to find an embryo in the uterus, although its immature state did nothing to solve the puzzle, indeed what seemed the impossibility, of how such a "blob of jelly" reached the pouch.

What he found was "a small gelatinous mass, about the size of a pea. . . . I could distinctly perceive the rudiments of an animal. The Feet were not developed, but pulsation and motion were not only observed by me but by two of the men with me, both exclaiming 'look at the little animal' although I feel convinced they did not know what I was searching for."[15] Bynoe concluded that there must be an internal tube through which the embryo passed, but his anatomical preparations were not good enough to prove this. Eventually others showed that the real story is just as unbelievable. The marsupial embryo is "borne" ex utero in a very immature state and wriggles and "swims" in an incredible journey, along a pathway of saliva laid down in the mother's fur, to the pouch. If it survives this journey, the embryo then attaches to a nipple and remains in the pouch, passing through the equivalent of the second and third trimesters of human embryonic development outside the uterus. This is a sequence too incredible to be dreamed up by even the most fanciful of early biologists, but Bynoe at least played a part in putting down the theory that the young were born through the nipple.

After leaving Houtman Abrolhos, the *Beagle* went farther north to explore a small section of the northwestern coast omitted by King, between the Monte Bello Islands and Roebuck Bay. Here the officers had the opportunity of visiting the superb aboriginal drawings and carvings on the rocks of Depuch Island, some of which were copied by Wickham and published by him in the *Journal of the Royal Geographical Society*[16] and also in Stokes's narrative.

Depuch and the Turtle islands gave them a little respite from the tedium of surveying this dull coastline. The officers once again diverted themselves with natural history, collecting several new sorts of birds and wallabies during a long period of six months' coastal survey until July 14, when they headed out into the Sea of Timor. They skirted Scott Reef and made for

Rotee (Rote) Island and on to Timor and the port of Coepang (Kupang) on July 23.

Coepang

An aboriginal boy they had brought with them was astonished (as probably they were themselves delighted) at the lush tropical vegetation, the fruits, and all "the romantic scenery of Timor." The contrast with the barrenness of northern Australia was the more amazing considering the relatively short distances that separate Australia from Indonesia. They visited the Dutch resident for long discussions, including the problem of migration of Indonesian workers to settlements such as that at Port Essington, its now being clear that such workers would be a necessity for the ventures to succeed. They spent a few days exploring around Coepang, but they were unable to obtain complete provisions for the ship, a serious blow.

During a hunting trip a curious coincidence popped up, one of many that punctuate the history of the *Beagle*. One of the local men accompanying the military commandant of Coepang on this trip carried an old-fashioned British "Tower" musket. This type of gun had long since been out of service, and thousands been sold off by the British government as surplus. This particular gun, however, had once been issued to a marine serving on the *Beagle*'s first expedition, and his name (not recorded by Stokes) was still on the musket.

On August 6 they moved out of Coepang and, as they left Timor, carefully fixed the position of the various islands around the entrance to the harbor. Unfortunately they took with them an unwelcome present from the lush tropics: Practically every man had severe dysentery.

Shortage of provisions prevented them from attempting to link up the last remaining unexplored portion of the northwestern coast of Australia: from the Turtle Islands to Roebuck Bay. Instead they spent a shorter time surveying around the Monte Bello Islands before heading back to Swan River, which they reached on October 11. Here they reprovisioned, but "from the very debilitated state of some of the crew, from dysentery affections contracted at Timore, we were not able to leave Swan River before October 25th." Then they headed south for King George Sound, on their way to Sydney again.

A place they visited en route was the little settlement at Albany. "I was sorry to see that the infant town . . . had made so little progress, especially as it possesses by far the finest harbour in Western Australia." They stopped here "to obtain a meridian distance; and between the observations for rating the chronometers, made over several days, I availed myself of an offer of Lieut. Warburton, commanding the detachment of the 51st Reg., doing duty there, to accompany him on a visit to the out-stations."[17]*

When the *Beagle* left Albany, the next task was to stop in South Australia to obtain a meridian distance at a midpoint (Investigator Strait) between Swan River and Sydney. They were first sadly delayed by the burial at sea of a seaman who died of dysentery, only the second member of the crew to die during the voyage. Then, in working to the east, they stopped at Adelaide, where they found that "a noble city had in four years sprung, as if by magic, from the ground, wearing such an appearance of prosperity and wealth. . . ."[18] Stokes paid a visit to the port "distant from the town about 5 miles, made easy by an excellent macadamized road, carried, in some places, on a causeway over a swamp."[19]

Among those whom Stokes met at Adelaide on this visit was the explorer Captain Charles Sturt with whom Stokes exchanged views about the most popular topic of conversation in all of Australia: the way into the interior and what might be found there. This was, of course, some years after Sturt had

---

* Everywhere on the southern coast of Australia, in regions that had already showed themselves suitable for settlement and where sheep farming and some arable farming were becoming established, Stokes lost no opportunity to explore ashore and report back the conditions for his readers. In this respect his account of the voyage was an excellent aid to one interested in emigrating to Australia, being a mine of very careful, firsthand observations and predictions for future developments.

made his explorations of the Darling and just two years before he made his epic journey to the center of Australia (1843–45). The immediate excitement in Adelaide was the departure (not long before the *Beagle*'s arrival) of Edward J. Eyre's party, which was to make a fantastic exploration across the totally desert Nullarbor Plain westward to Albany, proving the total absence of any river along fifteen hundred miles of southern Australian coast.

December 23, 1840, found them off Sydney, where the news was also of explorations, the colonization of New Zealand, and the booming price of land in New South Wales. The *Beagle* had now been away from home for more than three years, with the prospect of two or more to go. With the most dangerous and exciting portions of their explorations seemed to be behind the officers and men, what remained was principally some residual exploration in the north and the long and difficult survey of the Bass Strait.

The years they had already spent had taken a heavy toll on the men of the *Beagle,* although only two had actually died. Now at Sydney Wickham left the expedition. He was worn out, never having fully recovered from the attacks of dysentery that had started even before they first left Swan River in 1838. Stokes, now fully recovered from his chest wound, was appointed to the command. He had served on the *Beagle* for every moment of her three commissions, starting as mate and assistant surveyor in 1826. Emery and Eden also left for England, and Lieutenant Graham Gore was promoted to Emery's place.

"This almost total change in the arrangements of the ship required some delay, and the season for passing through the Torres Strait, moreover, not having commenced, it was 3rd of June 1841 before the *Beagle* again rounded Breaksea Spit, having touched on the way for a meridian distance at Port Stephen.*

"As we were rounding Breaksea Spit, we met four merchant

---

* Six whole months are a long time to have spent here in Sydney. In part they must have had to wait for orders, and in part it would have been necessary to make sure that all the departing officers had worked up their contributions to the charts before they left.

ships, who gladly availed themselves of our convoy," and the *Beagle* set off north by the inner route again for Cape York. Seven weeks later she reached Booby Island, and the four merchant ships "soon disappeared in the western horizon, leaving the *Beagle,* that seemed to be destined to be a solitary roamer, once more alone at anchor. . . . In the same evening she was herself pursuing her lonely way towards the Gulf of Carpentaria, the eastern shore of which we saw on the morning of the 1st of July."[20]

Now they started a careful survey of the more southerly parts of the Gulf of Carpentaria, particularly the southeastern and southern shores. In all they explored some two hundred miles of coastline, largely from small boats, moving in among banks and shoals, probing the mangrove swamps, and finding a number of large inlets and small rivers. Mostly they worked to the east of the Flinders River, following in the tracks of the great Flinders himself. More exciting discoveries were ahead of them, but also two more serious accidents.

They came to a small inlet where the mangroves "were literally whitened with flocks of noisy cockatoos, giving the trees an appearance as if they were absolutely laden with huge flakes of snow . . . and soon the huge masses of white plumage began to float from tree to tree across . . . a fair challenge to the sportsman." The sportsman in this case was Gore, who, with Stokes and a seaman, was out in a small boat. "Mr. Gore accordingly resolved to secure a few of them for dinner," but there was a flash and an explosion, and "death came to our sides, as it were, and departed ere the report of the gun had ceased to roll. . . . Something whizzed past my ear . . . the next moment I saw my much valued friend Gore stretched at his length in the bottom of the boat."[21] Luckily, although Gore was shot in the hand, no bones were broken.

The Albert River

Here at the base of the gulf, Stokes now made up two exploring parties. One, under the command of Fitzmaurice, was to work east from the Flinders River while another under Stokes, with Forsyth, Gore (somewhat recovered), and Dring would explore to the immediate west of the mouth of the Flinders. The two parties left the ship in delightfully cool weather; hopes and spirits were high as Stokes started into a large bay which had two main arms. He selected the southerly-heading one first, but after about seventeen miles it petered out, still in salt water. On August 1 they headed up the westerly directed arm of the bay. By now the boat crews were tired of exploring hopeful-looking inlets, only to be disappointed, and they had begun to neglect the simple task of dipping a hand overboard every now and again to test the water. But after a few miles' winding back and forth between mangrove-lined banks, "it so happened that one of the whaler crew put his hand over, and gave us the delightful news that the stream was quite fresh."[22] As if by magic, all fatigue disappeared. They were convinced that they had discovered another important river, and they named it the Albert. After another day's rowing, the mangroves gave way to banks lined with gum and acacia trees, and the river turned south— always the hoped-for direction. Birds, especially ducks, were common, and the men ate in style. Soon they came upon the first signs of Aborigines and saw a party setting small brush fires to flush snakes and game. "The country was gradually becoming higher and the scenery extremely picturesque. Tall palm-trees and bamboos. . . ."

They entered a glorious reach: "[A] magnificent sheet of water lay before us in one unbroken expanse."[23] They were in a grassy plain stretching to the horizon as far as they could see. The water remained deep, the wildlife and vegetation well developed, and they moved steadily on until some fifty miles from the sea, where once again they found "bitter disappointment." Their way was blocked by fallen trees and vegetation. They tried a side tributary to no avail. So a small party set out on foot to see what might lie beyond. "Following up a short woody valley . . . a vast boundless plain lay before us, here and there dotted with woodland isles. . . . The river could be traced to the southward by a waving line of green trees. . . ."[24] Pressing on, Stokes calculated that he had reached to about four hundred miles from the center of the continent, to latitude 17° 58½'S longitude 139° 25' E of Greenwich. It was another wonderful place from which to set out to the interior.

However, when they got back to their rendezvous at the coast, they found Fitzmaurice seriously injured. A gun had gone off, and he had taken the full force of it, the shot remaining buried in his foot. At first Bynoe was afraid that he would have to amputate, but he managed to save the limb, although Fitzmaurice was disabled for the rest of his life and eventually retired from the service with a pension.

Their visit to the Gulf of Carpentaria, apart from the two serious accidents, had been a success, and they were satisfied with the results of their hard work as they set off back to Cape York to cross-check their positions before heading off west again to Port Essington. They had already heard that a hurricane that passed near them in 1839 had hit the settlement directly, and they were anxious to see how the settlers had fared.

Happily the small town still had a moderately prosperous air, the houses had been rebuilt, and new foliage covered the storm damage. But closer examination showed: "there was a careworn, jaundiced appearance about the settlers, that plainly revealed how little suited was the climate for Europeans to labour in."[25]

During the hurricane the *Pelorus* had been in the harbor, but poorly anchored, and before anything could be done, she had been driven on the rocks and lost, like the *Orontes* before her, adding more fuel to the rumors in Sydney and Swan River that the harbor was unsafe.

It was becoming apparent that if settlements like Port Essington, as then constituted, were to have any future, it must be as trading centers rather than in agricultural production. It was impossible to produce enough to support the town itself, let alone for export. But economical trading could not yet be established because of high import duties levied at all the Dutch ports in the region. Perhaps, as steam navigation developed between Singapore and Sydney, the port would become a coaling station. It had not fulfilled the goal of being a haven to vessels in distress in the Torres Strait; for that purpose a station at Booby Island would be needed, as many had thought originally.

As he prepared to quit Port Essington for the last time, Stokes was far less hopeful about the chances of the settlement's survival, and it was with many misgivings that the men of the *Beagle* set sail for Timor on September 7. A year later, when HMS *Fly* (which took over the *Beagle*'s work) visited the settlement the geologist Jukes looked about himself without any of the rosy optimism that Stokes and the others felt for the future of the place. Jukes found it depressing and totally unviable, with no future in trading or agriculture.

> The aspect of the place was anything but cheerful or inviting even to us, who had been so long at sea . . . the soil in and around the settlement seemed of the poorest and most sterile description . . . scarcely a blade of grass. . . . I do not think enough green stuff of any kind could at this time be found to keep a cow, a horse, or a sheep. . . . As the gardens are not equal to a constant supply of vegetables, they live during the greater part of the year pretty much as they would on board ship, on salt provisions, biscuit and rum, varied by an occasional kangaroo or a dish of fish. In the latter the harbour abounds, but there are commonly too many men sick to . . . form a party large enough to haul the seine.[26]

The last settlers pulled out in 1849. Today the last ruins of "Victoria" can still be found amid the mangroves.

At Timor they watered ship and sent off home all their rough charts. In an effort to reduce sickness, Stokes did not allow the crew ashore. Nevertheless, "the first lieutenant, the surgeon, the master, were seized with a violent attack of cholera which lasted twenty four hours—another evidence of the unhealthiness of Timor."[27]

The next stop was Roebuck Bay again to check one last inlet that had promise, but heavy seas prevented them from working from small boats. Doubting that any major river was to be found, they completed some chronometric and magnetic observations, took a supply of turtles on board, and left for Swan River, where they arrived on November 23, 1841.

More from Grey

At Perth, the Western Australia Company, ever anxious to continue colonization of the lands immediately to the north, showed the officers of the *Beagle* an encouraging report recently arrived from England, showing a fine safe harbor on the west coast at latitude 29°S, essentially inside the Houtman Abrolhos group of islands. The *Beagle* had already surveyed this whole area twice, and Stokes knew that the only even modest anchorage was at a place they called Champion Bay (site of modern Geraldton). The newly reported harbor was in essentially the same position but was now named Port Grey!

Of course, the report was based on no more reliable a source than Grey's second, disastrous expedition. Stokes was confident that the two places were the same and that Grey had wildly overestimated both the suitability of the harbor and the fertility of the surrounding land. Meanwhile, however, if the harbor was as good as Grey's report indicated, the company wanted to get settlers there as soon as possible. It was agreed that the best way to settle the matter was to send the *Beagle,* after a refit, up the coast to decide the question.

Of course, the harbor turned out to be nothing but Champion Bay, one of a series of errors that Grey later admitted. At least the careful work of the *Beagle* saved a whole party of settlers from a bleak fate marooned on that barren coast in another futile venture.

After putting back into Swan River to give the news, the *Beagle* immediately headed south, making for King George Sound once more, repeating the whole chain of measurements across the southern coast of Australia to Sydney. When the crew put in at Port Adelaide, they found that the energetic but controversial

Colonel Gawler had been replaced as governor by none other than "our brother explorer Captain Grey." *

At Adelaide they made the first full survey of the port, and in the process Stokes recommended that a railway be built alongside the road between Adelaide and the port in order to facilitate the considerable export and import trade that was developing, not only from agriculture but from the recent discoveries of the vast mineral wealth of southern Australia. Stokes also took time for a short inland exploration from Adelaide, and when the *Beagle* moved on to Portland, he made further explorations inland, reporting on the geology and farming potential of the land.

Hobart, Tasmania, was their next landfall, where Stokes needed to talk with the governor, Sir John Franklin, before starting surveys of the island and the Bass Strait.† He understood the situation and lent Stokes the colonial cutter *Vansittart* to help with the difficult inshore work. (If only Fitzroy had received this sort of generous governmental sanction and support.) Forsyth was put in charge of the cutter with Pascoe, and they set off on their work while the *Beagle* continued on to Sydney for supplies expected from England; because of foul weather, this journey took six days.

Expeditions to the Interior

At Sydney the latest talk was not of land prices so much as of the prospect for more journeys to explore the interior. "Two candidates for this important and deeply interesting undertaking had presented themselves—E. J. Eyre and Sir Thomas

---

* Evidently Grey had powerful connections who exploited the trumped-up fame of his explorations. He turned up next as the governor of New Zealand, a post in which he replaced none other than Captain Fitzroy.

† Franklin was already famous for his participation in Matthew Flinders's (his cousin's) exploration of the coast of Australia and his wreck there in HMS *Porpoise* in 1803, his service on the *Bellerophon* at the Battle of Trafalgar, and his first attempt to find the Northwest Passage. Not long after his meetings with Stokes he was recalled to England for his tragic second attempt for the passage and he died in the Arctic in 1847.

Mitchell, both experienced Australian explorers. The latter proposed to start from Fort Burke on the Darling; and the former from Moreton Bay. In my own humble experience, strengthened by recent experience, neither of these are practicable routes . . . ," reported Stokes.[28] Stokes still preferred a route starting at the north from one of his rivers, but no one tried it.

Victoria and New South Wales even began to vie for the honor of sending out the first expedition across the continent. In 1844 Ludwig Leichhardt managed to reach Port Essington in an epic journey from Sydney, but he disappeared in an attempt to strike all the way west to Perth in 1848. In 1845 Sturt made his famous trip north into the interior from Adelaide. It was not until 1860 that the expedition of Robert Burke and William Wills set off from Melbourne with the aim of striking north to the Gulf of Carpentaria. Burke, Wills, John King, and Charles Gray made the trek north to the sea from Cooper's Creek but without having waited for the rest of the party. When they returned to Cooper's Creek, the others had left, there were no supplies, and all perished.* In 1860 John McDouall Stuart started north from Adelaide but had to turn back. In 1861 he tried again, and on his third attempt (1862) he reached Van Diemen's Gulf. The same year J. McKinlay reached the Gulf of Carpentaria from Adelaide. These were some of the epic explorations of modern times. And their results were unequivocal. There could no more doubt about the essential nature of the interior: barren, desert, with shallow salt lakes but no rich grazing and no reliable water.

Last Days of the Voyage

Supplies had not yet arrived from England, so the *Beagle* headed back down toward the Bass Strait along the coast. "I was surprised to find by my observations here that this part of

---

* At the time of the Burke and Wills expedition, Crawford Pasco, having left the navy, was police magistrate at Swan Hill, north of Melbourne. He actively promoted Stokes's notion of either an expedition to the interior or a relief party working south along a river like the Albert. His advice was not followed.[29]

the coast is laid down ten miles too much to the eastward of Sydney, an error I found to be continued [from Twofold Bay] to Jervis Bay."[30]

A few days later there was a particularly lovely sunny day— almost the *Beagle*'s last. In a narrow channel between Wright's Rock and the Kent Group of islands disaster almost struck.

> The sea ... [after a recent winter storm] ... rolled in with solemn splendour ... each heaving swell carrying the ship nearer towards the almost fatal opening. Her motions, however ... were sluggish and slow, and she seemed unwilling to obey the impulse of the light southerly breeze that aided her progress. Indeed there appeared to be an opposing tide until we drew in between the high rocky sides of the channel, when suddenly the ship was hurried onwards with such rapidity that to prevent our being swept past a cove on the right it was necessary to close with its outer point, towards which a merciless eddy flung the ship's head. ...

The sails were thrown aback but did not slow the ship's way until the jib boom was almost touching the rocks. But then "the

HMS *Beagle Dangerous Situation*, from an original drawing possibly by J. L. Stokes; see Chapter 13, note 10. Courtesy of the National Maritime Museum.

Beagle's head was slowly paying off from the shore" when she went broadside on to the swell and was driven back on to the point. "Her stern went down before the swell." They were sure she would strike "the sensation was just as if my feet were under the keel . . . and I almost expected to feel the bones crushing."[31] But in the nick of time the sails were trimmed round, and she ponderously, hesitatingly, answered the helm and cleared the point. Within an hour they were safely anchored in East Cove.

The *Beagle* worked carefully southwest along the Bass Strait and started to look for the *Vansittart,* which they met near the mouth of the Tamar. Just below Yorktown they heaved the *Beagle* down (just as they had in 1834 in the Santa Cruz River) to examine her bottom and "found it so defective that 130 sheets of copper were required to make good the damage; in some places the two-inch protective sheathing was completely destroyed."[32]

While repairs were being made, Stokes made a trip to Launceston, "the second town in Tasmania . . . very pretty . . . perhaps there is no part of our southern colonies that more resembles England."[33] The repairs took all of July but did not prevent surveying from small boats and the *Vansittart.*

In August 1842 Stokes took the *Beagle* back to Sydney for the promised supplies, which were now waiting, and found in addition new orders—final orders: "return to England." In fact, the *Beagle*'s replacements, the 18-gun sloop HMS *Fly* and HMS *Bramble,* a 10-gun cutter, under the command of Captain F. P. Blackwood, were already at Sydney and preparing to start with an exploration of the Barrier Reef.

Far from being pleased with these orders, Stokes (at least) was disappointed. He wanted more time to complete the survey of the Bass Strait, and worse, he would now have no opportunity to make the last exploration planned for the voyage, New Guinea. His orders were to proceed directly home. New Guinea, "which we had always looked forward to as one of the most interesting parts of the voyage," had been held out to the officers and men as one last reward, one last piece of interesting work. Looking forward to it had helped them get over the dullest and hardest parts of the recent year's work. "On many occasions, during the heavy and monotonous parts of our labours, the anticipated delights of discovery refreshed our imaginations and elevated our spirits, imparting to our most irksome occupations an interest that did not belong to them, but was borrowed from those hoped-for scenes of adventure on the unvisited shores of New Guinea, to which we believed each dull day's hard work brought us nearer."[34]

Stokes was not one to leave something unfinished, and a period of several more months was spent working fast and hard at the survey of Bass Strait so that at least a complete general survey would be made.

Stokes's last observations on Tasmania concerned the state of the natives and their brutal treatment at the hands of the settlers. The Aborigines of the island were already well on their way to extermination, and a few desperate stragglers were being settled on Flinders Island. In fact, the *Beagle* and *Vansittart* were used to transport a pitiful few of the last Aborigines to Flinders in December 1842.

Then, leaving Forsyth and the *Vansittart* to a few last days of work, the *Beagle* left for Port Philip, where the indefatigable Stokes spent two more days on a survey of the harbor "of so great importance that I am induced to believe that Geelong will ultimately be the capital of Australia Felix." This done, Stokes left at Sydney "what stores were not absolutely required during the passage to England, for the use of the ships on the station...."[35]

"Our final arrangements were soon made; and on the 18th of February, the *Beagle* was turning out between the heads. ..." The thoughts of the men of the *Beagle* were full of the superb hospitality they had received at Sydney, "which had become to us as it were a second home."[36] They stopped at Hobart to pick up Forsyth and for Stokes to pay a last visit to Sir John Franklin. On March 15 they sailed for King George Sound and a few last meridian measurements, then went on to Swan River for more farewells, but still working hard: "Whilst waiting to rate our chronometers several soundings were taken...."[37]

Then, at last, "we left Swan River on the evening of the 6th of May, 1843, running out with a moderate N.E. breeze. Everything seemed auspicious. The water was smooth, and the sails, as they slept in the breeze, echoed back the sounds of the well known song, 'We are Homeward Bound,' that was sung with an earnestness that could not be mistaken."[38]

SIXTEEN

Home Waters

HMS *BEAGLE* FINALLY CAME HOME ON SEPTEMBER 30, 1843, this time after a voyage of six years. After she had been paid off, the copper was removed from her bottom at Sheerness. Over the next twelve months she lay in ordinary, being surveyed and patched up somewhat (the "Admiralty Progress Book" records work costing a total of £522).

Promotions came through for all the officers except Gore, who subsequently gained his by a distinguished voyage to the Arctic in the *Erebus* with Sir John Franklin. Stokes's promotion to captain came in July 1846, and in 1847 he was appointed to command the *Archeron* (paddle sloop of five guns), surveying in the East Indies and New Zealand. Parts of his journal of this voyage were published in a New Zealand newspaper in 1926.[1] In 1859 he was sent to survey the south coast of Devon, England, and the river Tamar. Eventually promoted to admiral, in 1863 he was seriously considered for the post of hydrographer, but the appointment was given to George Richards (whose distinguished career marked the first crucial developments of modern oceanography).[2]

While her young former officers continued with their new careers, the familiar, comfortable *Beagle* now lay cold and silent in the black waters of the Thames. Stripped down by the dockyard workers and without even the hum of activity from a work detail, suddenly she looked old, worn, and very small. Stokes took one last look:

> After giving the men their certificates, I loitered a short time to indulge in those feelings that naturally arose in taking a final leave of the poor old *Beagle* at the same place where I first joined her in 1825. Many events have occurred since my first trip to sea in her. I have seen her under every variety of circumstances, placed in peculiar situations and fearful positions, from nearly the antarctic to the tropic, cooled by the rigid clime of the extreme of South America, or parched by the heats of North Australia; under every vicissitude, from the grave to the gay, I have struggled along with her; and after wandering together for eighteen years, a fact unprecedented in the service, I naturally parted from her with regret. Her movements, latterly, have been anxiously watched, and the chances are that her ribs will separate, and that she will perish in the river where she was first put together.[3]

The *Beagle* was now twenty-five years old and had covered perhaps a quarter of a million miles in the course of an eventful career. Most of her sister ships had long since left the service, either cut down as barges and hulks around the coast or dispatched to the breaker's yard. The hull of the *Beagle* was relatively sound, however, and there was one last role for her to play.

On June 14, 1845, at Sheerness, her bottom was coppered again, and on July 11 she set sail on her last voyage. It was a short trip. She headed out of the Thames and passed cautiously along the Essex coast, past the tiny fishing village of Southend with its long jetty where vessels could moor at low tides without being caught on the vast mud flats of the Thames estuary. Then north, past Shoeburyness and Maplin sands, around Foulness Point, taking care not to ground on the dangerous Foulness sands. She was piloted by a man who knew this area well: George Wrake, the skipper of the revenue cruiser *Dispatch*, based at Burnham-on-Crouch. He guided the *Beagle* into the mouth of the river Crouch and then turned her south into the river Roach, which is the landward definition of Foulness Island. When they came to the small arm of the Roach called Pagelsham Pool, which leads north to the little village of Pagelsham, sitting in the marshland of coastal Essex, they dropped the anchors.

The last phase of the *Beagle*'s career had begun; she was now the *Beagle Watch Vessel,* assigned to the Coast Guard Service. She would never sail again.

In 1845 the glamorous days of smugglers and the coast guard were already over. Their legends served British children for generations in the same way that "cops and robbers" are the focus for the games of children everywhere. The riding officers galloping along the foreshore, the lookout cottages on the bluffs, the cargoes of silks carefully wrapped and floated in on the tides from armed luggers offshore, the pig-tailed cutthroats, the secret passages leading from lonely taverns on the marshes: These were now fading into memory. Since the Napoleonic Wars, smuggling had been put down severely, and in the new era of expansive world trade, the number of items that it was profitable to smuggle had declined. Tobacco and spirits still could be brought in at a small profit, but the great days of the illicit trade with the Continent had gone. In the old days ... well, everything they could say about the old days was more or less true, and Pagelsham had once been one of the most notorious of all smuggling centers in this maze of marsh and creeks.

The collector of customs at Maldon, Essex, was in charge of a very large area of formerly prime smuggling territory. His authority reached from Tilbury to Colchester. Within this large collectorship there were several coast guard stations, including principally those of Leigh, Crouch River, Gillingham, Southend, Shoeburyness, Rochford Creek, and Burnham.

There was a great deal of paperwork associated with the duty, principally in the registry of boats, large and small, fishing gear, and all incoming and outgoing cargoes. Luckily a small sample of the record of the Maldon Collectorship has survived, having been discovered and saved by Edward Carson, librarian and archivist at Customs House in London. The Maldon letter books are mostly intact for the period we are interested in, although Mr. Carson had no luck in discovering other documents (full list, Appendix G).

In 1845 the role of the watch vessel was something relatively new, as the older mobile coast guard service was replaced in part by a chain of fixed stations moored along the waterways and coasts. These fixed watch stations were all former naval vessels, used by the coast guard as observation stations, living quarters, office and storage space, and so on. There were six such watch vessels on the Maldon station. When the *Beagle* was moored off Pagelsham Pool, a man standing on her deck could easily have seen the tips of the lower masts of another vessel two miles away across the marsh at Burnham. And by a curious coincidence, two famous surveying vessels were meeting again, for the watch vessel at Burnham was none other than HMS *Chanticleer*. At Haven Hole there was another sister ship, HMS *Emulus*.

At Pagelsham a permanent mooring was prepared for the *Beagle*, using chains obtained from another watch vessel, the *Dove*, which was moored in the Crouch. Life on the Essex marshes was rather quiet and dull. For the great majority of the period in question, the active vessels at Maldon were two small-ish revenue cruisers, *Dispatch* and *Onyx*, the workhorses of the port, constantly on patrol in the estuaries keeping an eye on things. The Maldon letter books give lists of vessels registered and ships inspected, but very little smuggling is reported, or at least very little contraband was intercepted. Most of the quarterly reports mention only the seizure of small quantities of cigars, silks, and spirits from coasting and fishing vessels.

Among the more noteworthy events recorded in the letter books for the *Beagle*'s period was the boarding of a yacht flying the Royal Yacht Club colors that refused to identify herself properly (presumably there was a possibility of some spirits being brought in during a jaunt to the Continent). Nothing daunted by the prestige of his target, the second mate in charge of the revenue cruiser boarded her and thus set off a flurry of angry letters back and forth.

More commonly recorded in the letter books was the confiscation of unregistered boats and cargoes and supervision of the oystermen. The coast guardsmen had to keep their eyes open for small quantities of liquor and tobacco being brought over from the Continent and then dumped overboard inshore to be picked up later. For example, a great brouhaha ensued in 1846, when two fishing vessels were found with large quantities of unmanufactured tobacco on board. This turned out to have come from a wreck (by law the property of the crown) and had been picked up at sea. Many letters were exchanged before the conflicting accounts of the episode were adjudicated. The customs suspected the fishermen of trying to smuggle, while the fishermen (at least once they had been spotted) claimed that they were merely bringing the tobacco into port, having found it washing around in the swim. The owner of the vessel involved even had the gall to sue the customs for a reward for having salvaged the tobacco. This same vessel was the one that had made off at speed when the *Dispatch* appeared and had to be stopped with a warning shot. But all this is another story.

All in all, apart from occasional alarms and excursions, life in the port of Maldon had become rather sober by 1850, and paperwork was beginning to supersede the chasing of smugglers. Taxes, in their inexorable way, were being applied to every conceivable commodity, and the service had lost its glamour. Occasionally a visiting revenue cruiser would put in for a while to show the flag when a "run" was suspected. The names of the revenue cutters *Vigilant, Ranger, Adelaide, Fox, Lapwing, Vulcan,* and *Lively* appear briefly in the records. But the *Beagle* took no part in any of this, remaining moored at Pagelsham, every year becoming more run-down.

Although we have no direct evidence about the people who lived on board the *Beagle* here at Pagelsham, on the nearby *Cadmus* accommodations were set up for a commander and seven men, each with his family. It was considered a real hardship posting as they were isolated from shore. They formed their own tight little community, the wives teaching the children (who could not get to school). Someone had to row off each day for the mail, and there were weekly shopping trips. Wives "were allowed on shore on Fridays and Saturdays."[4]

The records show when supplies and a new stove and hearth were provided for the *Beagle*. In September 1845 a caboose was installed, cluttering up the decks of which Fitzroy and Wickham had been so proud. Orders for painting, headlights, and many minor repairs are quite frequent in the record book for the next few years, but then mention of the *Beagle* declines. This is in part due to a change in the nature of what was recorded in the letter books, but no doubt also it reflects a gradual decrease in the attention paid to the *Beagle,* slowly becoming a rotten hulk.

When the *Beagle* had first been established at Pagelsham, she was stripped down, and her upper masts and spars had been taken away, for she was not expected to be moved again. However, in 1850 there was a small flurry of activity. On June 12, 1850, a group of "Oyster Company Captains" of the Burnham area petitioned the collector at Maldon that the *Beagle* be moved. The problem was that she was moored in the middle of a rather narrow river and vessels had difficulty getting around her at low tide, often falling foul of her moorings. This was

Ship breaking on the foreshore at Southchurch Manor (Thorpe Bay) near Southend-on-Sea, 1883. The brig at left is larger than HMS *Beagle* would have been, probably an old 18-gun brig or a merchant brig of similar type. Watercolor painting by J. G. Ford, courtesy of Southend Museums Services.

confirmed by the "chief officers of the *Beagle*," and it was suggested that she be moved to the shore. Eventually, after much correspondence, this was done, and she was tied up on the Pagelsham side of the river.

Five years pass before the next reference to the *Beagle* in the Maldon letter books, and now it turns out that although an official agreement had been drawn up for the use of the land adjoining the *Beagle,* the fees had never been paid. Lady Olivia Sparrow's lawyers naturally were suing for payment, which, after more delays, was made. This is the last we find of the *Beagle* in the customs records.

In 1859 the navy took over the operation of the coast guard although, of course, many of the vessels and nearly all of the commissioned officers were already part of the Royal Navy. Following the change, the watch vessels were stripped of the last vestiges of their former individuality and character. On May 25, 1863, all the watch vessels were given numbers and HMS *Beagle* became *W.V.7.* The *Chanticleer* became *W.V.5.*

In 1870 even the decaying hulk of *W.V.7* was superfluous, and on May 13 she was sold to "Murray and Trainer" (presumably dealers in scrap) for £525. What became of her after that is unknown. Perhaps she was cut down to be used as a barge, but most probably the fifty-year-old vessel was towed from Pagelsham around onto the mud flats of the Thames estuary, and there, alongside the exposed ribs of a hundred other old ships, the *Beagle* was broken up for scrap.

It would be nice to think that some remnant of her still exists, perhaps that the great ship's wheel is still intact, with Augustus Earle's painting of Neptune at its center hidden under coats of black paint.[5] Or that the great table of the poop cabin where Darwin, Wickham, Pringle Stokes, John Lort Stokes, Fitzroy, Sulivan, Usborne, Philip Gidley King, and Forsythe all worked has been saved somewhere. But the *Beagle,* "not a particular ship," was not destined for a special resting place, and the last remains of her timbers lie somewhere undisturbed, all her life gone except where it is preserved in the pages of books and the thousand memories we call history.

Endnotes

CHAPTER 1

1. L. Darling, "The *'Beagle'*—a Search for a Lost Ship," *Natural History* 69 (1960), 5–13.
2. K. S. Thomson, "HMS *Beagle*, 1820–1870," *American Scientist* 63 (1976), 664–72.
3. D. Stanbury, "HMS *Beagle*," *Mariner's Mirror* 65, (1979), 355–57.
4. J. Edye, *Calculations Relating to the Equipment, Displacement, etc. of Ships and Vessels of War* (London: Hodgson, 1932).
5. L. Darling, "HMS *Beagle*," *Mariner's Mirror* 64 (1978), 315–25.
6. L. Darling, "HMS *Beagle*, 1820–1870," *Sea History* 31 (1984), 27–42.

CHAPTER 2

1. W. James, *The Naval History of Great Britain* (London: Macmillan, 1902), v. 6, p. 298.
2. J. Fincham, *History of Marine Architecture* (London: Whittacker, 1851), p. 163.
3. B. J. Sulivan unpublished letter to J. D. Hooker, c. 1882. Cambridge University Library.
4. Fincham, op. cit., p. 163.
5. C. R. Darwin, diary entry for March 24, 1833. Published in N. Barlow, *Charles Darwin's Diary of the Voyage of the Beagle* (Cambridge: Cambridge University Press, 1923), p. 141.

CHAPTER 3

1. "Carronade," *Encyclopaedia Britannica*, 11th ed. (New York, 1910).
2. J. Briggs, *Naval Administrations, 1827–1892: The Experience of 65 Years* (London: Sampson, Low, Marston, 1897), p. 9.
3. J. J. College, *Ships of the Royal Navy: An Historical Index* (Newton Abbot: David and Charles, 1969), vol. 1.
4. W. James, op. cit., vol. 4, p. 484.
5. Private builders of the 10—gun brigs were as follows: Pitcher at Northfleet, Brent at Rotherhythe, Barnard at Deptford, Perry, Wells at Blackwall, Dudman at Deptford, King at Upmoor, Brindley at Freindsbury, List at Fishbourne, Bailey at Ipswich, Muddle at Gillingham, Rowe at Newcastle, Warwick at Ealing, and Guillaume at Northam. All these were noted builders of small vessels for the merchant trade.
6. Of the thirty-three privately built brigs, ten were lost through sinking or being wrecked, and one was lost in action with a pirate. Of the seventy-three built by the navy, only sixteen were lost at sea, admittedly mostly in peacetime conditions.

CHAPTER 4

1. James, op. cit., vol. 6, p. 409.
2. Briggs, op. cit., p. 23.
3. B. J. Sulivan. *Life and Letters of the Late Admiral Sir B. J. Sulivan, KCB, 1810–1890*, ed. H. N. Sulivan (London: Murray, 1896), p. 24.
4. A. Day, *The Admiralty Hydrographic Service, 1795–1919* (London: HM Stationery Office, 1967).
5. G. S. Ritchie, *The Admiralty Chart* (New York: Elsevier, 1967).
6. W. F. W. Owen, *Narrative of Voyages to Explore the Shores of Africa, Arabia, and Madagascar*, ed. H. B. Robinson (London: Bentley, 1833), p. 9.
7. Ibid., p. 34.
8. Ritchie, op. cit., p. 163.
9. W. H. Webster, *Narrative of a Voyage to the Southern Atlantic Ocean, in the Years 1828, 1829, and 1830, performed in H. M. Sloop Chanticleer, under the command of Captain Henry Foster, F. R. S. etc.* (London: Bentley, 1834).
10. J. H. Boteler, *Recollections of My Sea Life from 1808–1830* (London: Navy Records Society, 1942), vol. 82.
11. London: Webster, op. cit., vol. 1, p. 208.
12. B. Hall, *Account of a Voyage of Discovery to the West Coast of Corea and the Great Loo-Choo Island* (London: Murray, 1818).
13. M. A. Lewis, *The Navy in Transition* (London: Hodder and Staughton, 1965).

CHAPTER 5

1. A. Villiers, "Queries." *Mariner's Mirror* 57 (1975), 446–47.
2. Sulivan, op. cit., p. 28.
3. E. Belcher, *Transactions of the Institution of Naval Architects* (1871), p. 204.
4. Owen, op. cit., p. 9.
5. Darling, "The *Beagle*," loc. cit.
6. C. R. Darwin, *The Voyage of the Beagle,* rev. ed. (London: Murray, 1890).
7. Barlow, op. cit., pp. 9,12.
8. R. D. Keynes, *The Beagle Record* (Cambridge: Cambridge University Press, 1979).
9. Thomson, op. cit.
10. Darling, "HMS Beagle,, 1820–1870," loc. cit., p. 36.
11. A. Earle. Drawing *Crossing the Equator on Board the Beagle.* First published in R. Fitzroy and P. P. King, *Narrative of the Surveying Voyages of His Majesty's Ships Adventure and Beagle, 1826–1836* (London: Murray, 1839).
12. G. Barsala, "The Voyage of the *Beagle* without Darwin," *Mariner's Mirror* 59 (1956), 42–48.
13. Ibid.
14. A. R. Roussin, *Navigation aux Côtes du Brésil* (Paris: 1821).
15. Barsala, op. cit., p. 47.
16. Fitzroy and King, op. cit., vol. 1, p. xi. All subsequent references to the Fitzroy and King *Narrative* are cited as "Fitzroy."
17. P. P. King, *Narrative of the Survey of the Intertropical and Western Coasts of Australia* (London: Murray, 1827).
18. Ritchie, op. cit., p. 173.
19. Webster, op. cit., p. 210.
20. Fitzroy, op. cit., vol. 1, p. 78.

CHAPTER 6

1. J. Weddell, *A Voyage towards the South Pole* (London: Longman, Rees, Orme, Brown and Green, 1825).
2. Fitzroy, op. cit., vol. 1, pp. 150–51.
3. Ibid., pp. 152–53.
4. This and following quotations from Stokes's log are recorded in Fitzroy, op. cit., vol. 1, pp. 154–81.
5. J. Thomson, *The Seasons* (Edinburgh: Robertson, 1768).
6. Fitzroy, op. cit., vol., 1, p. 188.
7. Sulivan, op. cit., p. 33.

CHAPTER 7

1. Ibid., p. 16.
2. Ibid., p. 33.
3. Ibid.
4. Fitzroy, op. cit., vol. 1, p. 217.
5. Ibid., p. 225.
6. Ibid., p. 232.
7. Ibid., p. 241.
8. Ibid., p. 257.
9. A. C. F. David, "Discovery of Relics on Mount Skyring of *Beagle*'s Survey of Magellan Strait, *Mariner's Mirror* 68 (1982), 40–42.
10. Fitzroy, op. cit., vol. 1, p. 313. Curiously, although Fitzroy went to some lengths to accumulate a vocabulary of the Fuegian languages (see Fitzroy, op. cit., vol. 4, Appendix, p. 135), nowhere is this apparently significant word translated. However Fitzroy included in some drawings of Fuegians (*Narrative*, v. 2, facing p. 141) an individual *named* as "Pecheray man," indicating that "Pecheray" was a group name.
11. Ibid., vol. 2, p. 5 (see also vol. 1, pp. 391–404).
12. Ibid., vol. 1, p. 410.
13. Ibid., vol. 2, p. 5 (see also vol. 1, pp. 415–16).
14. Ibid., vol. 1, pp. 426–27.
15. Ibid., p. 444.
16. Ibid., vol. 2, pp. 4–7.

CHAPTER 8

1. Ibid., pp. 91–92.
2. Ibid., p. 13.
3. Ritchie, op. cit.
4. Fitzroy, op. cit., vol. 2, p. 17.
5. Ibid., vol. 2, p. 18.
6. Fitzroy, quoted in Darling, "HMS *Beagle,* 1820–1870," loc. cit., p. 29.
7. Fitzroy, quoted ibid.
8. E. P. Brenton, *Naval History of Great Britain,* rev. ed. (London: Colburn, 1837), p. 41.
9. Fitzroy, op. cit., vol. 2, p. 18.
10. Ibid.
11. Ibid., p. 82.
12. Ibid.
13. Ibid.
14. R. M. Bloomfield, Note, *Mariner's Mirror* 2 (1916), p. 8.
15. Anon., Note, *Mariner's Mirror* 16 (1920), 199.

16. Fitzroy, op. cit., vol. 2, p. 24.

17. Ibid., vol. 4 (Appendix), p. 325.

18. C. Martens, watercolor painting, *Port Desire: Christmas Day, 1833* (1833), figured in Keynes, op. cit. (cover).

19. Owen Stanley, watercolor painting, *The Beagle at Sydney Harbour* (1841), reproduced in A. Moorehead, *Darwin and the Beagle* (London: Penguin, 1969).

20. Sulivan quoted in F. Darwin, *The Life and Letters of Charles Darwin* (London: John Murray, 1896), vol. 1, p. 192.

21. Keynes, op. cit., p. 67.

22. Stanbury, "HMS *Beagle*," loc. cit. p. 357.

23. Darling, "HMS *Beagle*, 1820–1870," loc. cit., p. 35.

24. Ibid.

25. Fitzroy, op. cit., vol. 2, p. 21.

26. Benjamin Francis Helpman, manuscript diary of service in HMS *Beagle*, 1837–40. Latrobe Library, State Library of Victoria, Australia.

27. Webster, op. cit. vol. 1, p. 214.

28. Helpman, op. cit.

29. Sulivan, op. cit., p. 38.

30. N. A. Sulivan, "Management of Ships under Sail," *Mariner's Mirror* 37 (1951), 243–44.

CHAPTER 9

1. There have been many biographies of Darwin, the most notable being A. Desmond and J. Moore, *Darwin* (London: Joseph, 1992).

2. A. P. Martin, *Life and Letters of the Rt. Honorable Robert Lane, Viscount Sherbrook*. (London: Longmans, Green, 1893), p. 19.

3. All the following extracts of letters in this chapter are quoted from the standard work: F. Burkhardt, ed., *The Correspondence of Charles Darwin* (Cambridge: Cambridge University Press, 1985), vol. 1. Hereafter referred to as *Correspondence*.

4. R. McCormick, *Voyages of Discovery in the Arctic and Antarctic Seas, and round the World* (London: Sampson Low, Marston, Searle and Rivington, 1884).

5. J. W. Gruber, "Who Was the *Beagle*'s Naturalist?," *British Journal for the History of Science* 4 (1969), 266–82.

6. H. L. Bursten, "If Darwin Wasn't the *Beagle*'s Naturalist, Why Was He on Board?," *British Journal for the History of Science* 8: (1975) 62–69.

7. Darwin, *Correspondence*, p. 143.

8. Ibid., p. 136.

9. Fitzroy, op. cit., vol. 2, p. 22.

10. A. Friendly, *Beaufort of the Admiralty: the Life of Sir Francis Beaufort, 1774–1857* (New York: Random House, 1977).

CHAPTER 10

1. Darwin, *Correspondence*, p. 179.
2. Darwin, *Diary*, p. 6.
3. Ibid., p. 9.
4. Ibid., p. 11.
5. Ibid.
6. Ibid., pp. 12–13.
7. Ibid., p. 18.
8. Fitzroy, op. cit., vol. 2, p. 43.
9. Darwin, *Diary*, p. 262.
10. Darwin, *Correspondence*, pp. 204, 220.
11. Sulivan, *Life and Letters*, p. 47.
12. Darwin, *Correspondence*, p. 203.
13. Fitzroy, letter to Beaufort, quoted in Keynes, op. cit., p. 42.
14. Darwin, *Correspondence*, p. 238.
15. N. Barlow, *Charles Darwin and the Voyage of the Beagle* (New York: Philosophical Library, 1946), p. 34.
16. Darwin, *Correspondence*, p. 393.
17. Fitzroy, op. cit., p. 45.
18. Earle, op. cit.
19. Darwin, *Diary*, p. 36.
20. Ibid., p. 39.
21. Ibid., p. 57.
22. Darwin, *Correspondence*, p. 176.
23. Ibid., p. 238.
24. McCormick, op. cit., pp. 218–22.
25. Fitzroy, op. cit., v. 2, p. 94.
26. Darwin, *Diary*, p. 85.
27. Ibid., p. 87.
28. Fitzroy, op. cit., Appendix, p. 329.
29. Fitzroy, letter to Beaufort, quoted in H. E. L. Mellersh, *Fitzroy of the Beagle* (London: Rupert Hent-Davis, 1968), p. 131.
30. Fitzroy, op. cit., vol. 2, p. 111.
31. Ibid., p. 116.
32. Ibid., p. 117.
33. Fitzroy, op. cit., Appendix, p. 99.

CHAPTER 11

1. Ibid., vol. 2, p. 119.
2. Darwin, *Correspondence*, p. 306.

3. Fitzroy, op. cit., vol. 2, p. 124.
4. Ibid., p. 125.
5. Ibid., p. 127.
6. Ibid., p. 203.
7. Ibid., p. 206.
8. Ibid., p. 208.
9. Ibid., p. 219.
10. Ibid., p. 220.
11. Keynes, op. cit., p. 159.
12. Beaufort, quoted in Mellersh, op. cit., p. 132.
13. Fitzroy, letter to Beaufort, in Keynes, op. cit., p. 170.
14. For details on this interesting experimental ship, see Fincham, Brenton, or James, op. cit.

CHAPTER 12

1. Sulivan, *Life and Letters,* pp. 42–43.
2. Ibid., p. 45.
3. Fitzroy, op. cit., vol. 2, p. 322.
4. Ibid., p. 324.
5. Ibid., p. 327.
6. Ibid., p. 331.
7. Weddell, op. cit., p. 199.
8. Darwin, *Correspondence,* p. 564.
9. Conrad Martens, drawing *The Beagle Laid Ashore, River Santa Cruz.* First published in Fitzroy, op. cit., vol. 2.
10. Fitzroy, op. cit., vol. 2, p. 336.
11. Ibid., p. 339.
12. Ibid., p. 362.
13. Darwin, *Correspondence,* p. 418.
14. Fitzroy, op. cit., vol. 2, p. 370.
15. Darwin, *Correspondence,* p. 434.
16. Fitzroy, op. cit., vol. 2, p. 425.
17. Ibid., p. 429–30.
18. Darwin, *Correspondence,* p. 458.
19. Anonymous (possibly J. MacDonald), *A Diary of the Wreck of His Majesty's Ship Challenger, on the Western Coast of South America, in May, 1835* (London: Longman, Rees, Orme, Brown, Green and Longman, 1836). See also C. Pasco, *A Roving Commission* (London: Robertson, 1897). Pasco, who was serving on the *Blonde* at the time of the wreck, later joined the *Beagle* on her third voyage, see Chapter 12.
20. Fitzroy, op. cit., vol. 2, p. 483.
21. Ibid., p. 496.
22. Darwin, *Voyage of the Beagle,* p. 474.

23. Fitzroy, op. cit., vol. 2, p. 508.
24. Ibid., p. 563.
25. Ibid., p. 621.
26. Ibid., p. 624.
27. Darwin, *Correspondence*, p. 496.
28. Darwin, *Diary*, p. 415.

CHAPTER 13

1. Darwin, *Correspondence*, p. 506.
2. Ibid., p. 508.
3. Sulivan, *Life and Letters*, p. 46.
4. H. P. Douglas, "Fitzroy's Hydrographic Surveys," *Nature* 129 (1932), 200.
5. The only existing complete account of Fitzroy's life is that of H. Mellersh, op. cit., but while this is an extremely sympathetic study, it contains many errors of detail, including what may be the start of the false story that the *Beagle* was sold to Japan as a training ship. (H. E. L. Mellersh is a descendant of Arthur Mellersh, who served on the *Beagle*.)
6. Darwin, *Correspondence*, p. 496.
7. R. B. Freeman, *The Works of Charles Darwin: an Annotated Bibliographical Handlist*, 2d ed. (Hamden, Conn.: Archon, 1977).
8. W. Irving, *Apes, Angels and Victorians* (London: Weidenfeld & Nicolson, 1955).
9. King, op. cit., vol. 1, p. 92.
10. J. L. Stokes, *Discoveries in Australia* (London: Boone; 1846), vol. 1, p. 25.
11. Ibid., p. 6.

CHAPTER 14

1. Ibid., p. 43.
2. Ibid., p. 47.
3. Ibid., p. 50.
4. Ibid., p. 72.
5. Ibid., p. 80.
6. Ibid., p. 81.
7. Ibid., p. 84.
8. J. J. Keevil, "Benjamin Bynoe, Surgeon of the *Beagle*," *Journal of the History of Medicine* 3 (1949), 90–111.
9. During the voyage Bynoe and his many willing helpers collected thousands of specimens of birds and hundreds of mammals, all of which were sent back to London. The birds were particularly useful to J. Gould, who was at that time preparing his *Birds of Australia* (London:

R. and J. E. Taylor, 1840–48). Curiously, although many of the species Bynoe collected were new to science, none was named after him. Of the mammals (see, for example, Gould in *Proceedings of the Zoological Society of London* [1842], pp. 57–58), *Halmaturus bynoe* was named for Bynoe. This kangaroo is now considered a subspecies of *Dama pademelon* (see Iredale and Troughton, *Checklist of the Mammals of Australia*, ([Sydney: Australian Museum, 1934]).

Most regrettable is that Gould did not name a single new Australian bird species after Bynoe, who collected so many of the orignal specimens upon which Gould's descriptions are based. For example, Bynoe's most spectacular discovery—the blazingly multicolored little finch *Chloebia gouldiae*—became the Gouldian finch; Gould disingenuously named it after his *wife!*

10. Stokes, op. cit., vol. 1, p. 121.
11. Ibid., p. 124.
12. Dampier's famous remarks on the flies of Australia, quoted ibid., p. 99.
13. Ibid., p. 129.
14. Ibid., p. 134.
15. Ibid., p. 150.
16. Ibid., p. 219.
17. Helpman, op. cit.
18. Ibid.
19. The rescue of Joe Forbes is a tale often retold. A complete contemporary account is given in an Appendix to the first volume of Stokes, op. cit. See also Pasco, op. cit.
20. J. S. L. Dumont d'Urville, *Voyage au pole sud et dans l'oceanie par les corvettes L'Astrolake et la zelec. executé par l'ordre du Roi Bendant us Années, 1837–1840* (Paris: Gide, 1842–54).
21. Pasco. op. cit., p. 103.
22. Ibid., p. 105.
23. Stokes, op. cit., vol. 1, p. 413.
24. Ibid., p. 416.
25. Ibid., p. 432.
26. Ibid., p. 434.
27. Ibid., vol. 2, p. 6.

CHAPTER 15

1. Ibid., p. 31.
2. Ibid., p. 40.
3. Ibid., p. 41.
4. Ibid., p. 82.
5. Ibid., p. 102.

6. Pasco, op. cit., p. 106.
7. Ibid., p. 94.
8. Stokes, op. cit., vol. 2, p. 108.
9. Helpman, op. cit.
10. Stokes, op. cit., vol. 2, p. 124.
11. G. C. Henderson, *Sir George Grey: Pioneer of Empire in Southern Lands* (London: Dent, 1907), p. 32.
12. G. Grey, *Journals of Two Expeditions of Discovery in North-West and Western Australia* (London: Boone, 1841), vol. 1., p. 412.
13. Stokes, op. cit., vol. 2, p. 126.
14. Ibid., p. 149.
15. Ibid., p. 159.
16. J. C. Wickham, "Notes on Depuch Island," *Journal of the Royal Royal Geographical Society* 12 (1842), 78–83.
17. Stokes, op. cit., vol. 2, p. 227.
18. Ibid., p. 234.
19. Ibid., p. 235.
20. Ibid., pp. 250–51.
21. Ibid., pp. 281–82.
22. Ibid., p. 307.
23. Ibid., p. 312.
24. Ibid., p. 316.
25. Ibid., p. 354.
26. J. B. Jukes, *Narrative of the Surveying Voyage of HMS Fly* (London: Boone, 1847), pp. 249–53.
27. Stokes, op. cit., vol. 2, p. 367.
28. Ibid., p. 414.
29. T. Bonyhady, *Burke and Wills: From Melbourne to Myth* (Balmain, Australia: Ell (1991), pp. 62, 93.
30. Stokes, op. cit., vol. 2, p. 417.
31. Ibid., p. 420.
32. Ibid., p. 433.
33. Ibid., p. 435.
34. Ibid., p. 437.
35. Ibid., p. 497.
36. Ibid., p. 499.
37. Ibid., p. 516.
38. Ibid., p. 518.

CHAPTER 16

1. *Evening Star* (New Zealand), "Early Days; New Zealand in 1849–50; "Journal of First Surveying Ships"; "Captain Stokes Visits Infant Settlements," May 1, 8, 15, 22, 29; June 5, 12, 19, 26; July 3, 10,

17—all 1926.

2. Ritchie, op. cit.
3. Stokes, op. cit., vol. 2, p. 526.
4. W. Webb, *Coastguard* (London: Her Majesty's Stationary Office, 1976), p. 44.
5. N. DuSowsky and S. M. Dubowsky, "The Final Mission of HMS *Beagle*," *British Journal of the History of Science* 27 (1994), 105–11.

Appendix A

	Length	Diameter
Lower Masts		
Fore	46 feet 6 inches	16 inches
Main	54 feet 6 inches	17¾ inches
Topmasts		
Fore	13 feet	10 inches
Main	13 feet	10 inches
Topgallant masts		
Fore	7 feet 6 inches	6 inches
Main	7 feet 6 inches	6 inches
Bowsprit	12 feet	17 inches
Yards		
Fore-lower	16 feet	11 inches
Fore-topsail	13 feet 6 inches	8 inches
Fore-topgallant	10 feet	6 inches
Main lower	16 feet 11 inches	11 inches
Main topsail	13 feet six inches	8 inches
Main topgallant	10 feet	6 inches

Booms

Main driver	18 feet, 8 inches	11 inches
Driver gaff	10 feet 4 inches	7½ inches
jibboom	9 feet	8 inches
spritsail-yard	13 feet 6 inches	8 inches

In addition, when converted to bark:

Mizzenmast-lower	15 feet	16 inches
Mizzen-topmast	10 feet	10 inches
Mizzen driver boom	10 feet	7½ inches

Sail Plan

For the 10-gun brig, the basic sail plan was: jib (560 square feet), fore course (916), fore-topsail (962), fore-topgallant (478), main course (1,288), main topsail (962), main topgallant (478), main driver (1,200). To these were added: flying jib, royals, foretop staysail, forestaysail, fore and main trysails, together with lower, top, and topgallant studding sails.

For the *Beagle* converted to bark there were the following sails: standing and flying jibs, foretop staysail, fore staysail, fore course, fore topsail, fore topgallant, fore royal, fore trysail, main course, main topsail, main topgallant sail, main royal, main trysail, lower studding sail, top studding sails, mizzen driver, and mizzen gaff topsail.

Miscellaneous

The typical 10-gun brig carried three bower anchors plus stream anchor, and kedge anchors. The guns weighed a little over 8 tons, with 6 tons of shot and 1½ tons of gunpowder. The iron ballast and tanks weighed 25 tons. A full store of water weighed 19 tons. There were 6½ tons of provisions, spirits, and slops and 6 tons of coal and wood. The ship also carried 8½ tons of bos'n's and carpenter's stores, rope, etc. Two or 3 tons of spare masts and booms were stowed on deck. At the load line, 4½ tons of weight displaced the ship one inch. The total weight of the ship, loaded, was 282½ tons, of which 156½ tons were the actual weight of the hull. The displacement of the ship, loaded, was 297 tons.

Sources. John Edye, 1832. *Calculations Relating to the Equipment, Displacement, etc. of Ships and Vessels of War* (London: Samuel and Richard Hodgson) David Stanbury, 1979. "Notes; HMS *Beagle*." *Mariner's Mirror* 65: 355–57.

Appendix B

Some of the uncertainty about the history of the *Beagle* has stemmed from confusion between the *Beagle* on which Darwin sailed and her immediate successor. It may be worthwhile, therefore, briefly to summarize the history of the name Beagle in the Royal Navy.

1. The first *Beagle* was an 8-gun gallivat from Bombay Marine, built approximately 1766.
2. An 18-gun brig-sloop of the Cruiser Class, built in 1808 by Perry, Wells, and Green. She was of 383 tons (builders' measurement) and was nicknamed the Golden Beagle from her success in taking prizes during the Napoleonic Wars. She earned battle honors at Basque Roads and at San Sebastián. Sold 1814.
3. The *Beagle* of our story was the third *Beagle*. A Cherokee Class 10-gun brig-sloop. She was of 235 tons (builders' measurement) before conversion. Sold 1870.
4. The next *Beagle* was a screw-driven steam vessel of 477 tons (builders' measurement). She was 160 feet long and $25\frac{1}{2}$ beam, armed with four guns, including two 68-pounder mortars. Launched at Blackwall in 1854, she saw active service in the Crimean War of 1854 and in 1863 was sold, at Hong Kong, becoming the Japanese training ship *Kanko* (1865). She was broken up in 1889. Battle honors: China and the Black Sea.
5. A 120-ton schooner of one gun, built at Sydney, Australia, in 1872, carrying one 12-pounder. She was sold in 1883 at Sydney.

6. A large sloop of 1,170 tons, 195 feet long, built in Portsmouth in 1889. She carried eight guns and was driven by twin screws. Sold in 1905.
7. A destroyer of 950 tons, 269 feet long and armed with two torpedo tubes, a four-inch gun, and 2 12-pounders. Built by John Brown in 1909 and sold in 1921. She gained battle honors in the Dardanelles.
8. A destroyer of 1,360 tons, 312 feet long and armed with four 4.7-inch guns and eight torpedo tubes. She was built by John Brown in 1930 and sold in 1946. She gained battle honors in Norway, the Atlantic, North Africa, the Arctic, English Channel, and Normandy.
9. The last bearer of the name was, appropriately enough, a survey vessel of 1,050 tons, built in 1967.

Sources: T. D. Manning and C. F. Walker, *British Warship Names* (London: Putnam, 1959); J. J. College, *Ships of the Royal Navy* (Newton Abbot: David and Charles, 1969), vol. 1 (rev. ed., Annapolis: Naval Institute Press, 1987).

Appendix C

On May 17, 1809, the *Goldfinch* (Captain Fitzherbert George Skinner), cruising in the Atlantic well out off the coast of Portugal, attacked and chased the distinctly superior French corvette *Mouche* (sixteen guns and 1,880 men). The chase took fifteen hours, and the firing started at 3:00 A.M. the next day. At 7:00 A.M. the corvette had her foremast shot away and made off to windward, easily outsailing the *Goldfinch*. The *Goldfinch* suffered three men killed and three wounded and was much more heavily damaged, especially in the masts and rigging. The difference in damage occurred because the brig was unable to get close enough to use her carronades while the corvette picked her off with her long eight-pounders. (Later in the month the *Mouche* was in action with the British armed lugger *Black Joke* and then was captured by the frigates *Amelia* [38] and *Statira* [38] in the Spanish harbor of San Andero.)

On January 10, 1810, the *Cherokee* (Captain Richard Arthur) attacked a group of seven French lugger-privateers at anchor under the batteries of Dieppe Harbor. In a daring attack at 11:00 A.M. the *Cherokee* ran between two of them. One, the *Aimable* (16 guns, sixty men) was captured and taken out as a prize while the *Cherokee* was under heavy fire. The brig suffered only two wounded.

These first instances of the 10-gun brigs in action capture the flavor of their contribution to the fighting over the whole war period. When they were in single light actions, they were either evenly matched with or slightly outgunned by their opponents. When they were involved in larger fleet actions, their role was to carry messages and pass signals far from the actual fighting.

I have been able to find records of twenty-three actions in which the 10-gun brigs played a part that was worth recording. During war we find them mostly deployed on patrol in the North Sea or in the Atlantic off the Spanish coast and the entrance to the Mediterranean. Very often as barges of shallow draft that could move about beyond the range of any larger vessel compelled to stand offshore they worked close inshore against coastal shipping. On March 27, 1812, the captain of the *Rosario* showed the possibilities of such inshore work.

The *Rosario* (Captain Harvey), while off Dieppe, spotted the 14th Division of the Boulogne coastal flotilla making its way along the coast to Cherbourg. The flotilla consisted of twelve fully loaded brigs (each armed with three long 24-pounders and one 8-inch howitzer) escorted by a fast armed lugger. When the *Rosario* swept in to pick off the rearmost brig, the whole flotilla formed a line and bore down on her. The *Rosario* bore off to join up with another British brig, the *Griffon* (18, Captain George Trollope). The two together then set on the rear of the French flotilla as it tried to run into Dieppe. The *Rosario* ran right among the French ships, cutting the running rig of two and making them collide, then attacking a third which lost her mainmast and fore-topmast. The *Rosario* next set on the next brig in line, running it onto the shore. Although they were now only three-quarters of a mile from shore, the *Rosario* boarded and captured another brig. All this happened before the *Griffon* had got within gunshot. The *Griffon* now attacked one of the damaged brigs and drove it onshore while coming under very heavy fire from the shore batteries. Next, while the *Rosario* was making emergency repairs to her rigging, the *Griffon* attacked the rest of the flotilla, now at anchor under cover of the batteries, and captured one of the brigs. The *Rosario* then went back to board the brig that had been dismasted and abandoned. The result of all this action was that three French brigs were taken as prizes, and two were driven onshore. Incredibly, the only British casualties were one midshipman and four men wounded, all on the *Rosario*. Captain Harvey was promoted, as was one midshipman.

On several occasions, of course, ten-gun brigs were drawn into tackling an overwhelming superior enemy ship. On September 2, 1811, the *Chanticleer* (Captain Richard Spear) and the twelve-gun brig *Manly* (see p. 41) spotted three Danish 18-gun brigs (with long 18 pounders) off the coast of Norway. Instead of running, the Danish vessels prepared for battle, and it turned out to be a fierce one. First the *Chanticleer* took on one brig (the *Sampsoe*) while the other two (*Loland* and *Alsen*) attacked the *Manly*. Next two broke off, and all three Danish shipps attacked and chased off the *Chanticleer* before turning on the *Manly* again. Although outnumbered three to one, the unfortunate *Manly* fought on, but she was cut to pieces and surrendered although (remarkably enough, despite all the damage to her running gear) her casualties were light (one killed, four seriously injured). The *Chanticleer* escaped.

A case where a heavily outnumbered British squadron performed very successfully was a famous encounter that started with the adventures of HMS *Shearwater*. On July 15, 1810, the *Shearwater* (Captain Edward Reynolds Sibly) was part of a group detached from Admiral Cotton's fleet blockading Toulon. The small squadron, consisting of the 74-gun *Warspite*, *Ajax* and *Conqueror* and the 36-gun frigate *Euryalus* had been left in charge of the blockade duties when bad weather forced the rest of the fleet off to the east. On several subsequent days the French sent out groups of ships to test the British. On the morning of the twentieth, the tiny *Shearwater* was reconnoitering off Cape Sepet and the *Euryalus* off Toulon, when six ships of the line and four frigates came out from Toulon apparently to escort a convoy of merchant ships bottled up in the nearby harbor of Bandol. The *Shearwater* was recalled by the British commodore, but while the rest of the British ships were forming a defensive position, both the *Shearwater* and the *Euryalus* became cut off. The huge French 74-gun *Ajax* (not to be confused with the British 74 of the same name) together with the *Amelie* (40 guns) took them on. The British vessels managed to squirm away and join up with the rest of their squadron without being hit. Now the British ships in line of battle—*Warspite, Conqueror, Ajax*—engaged the French, and after a short and inconclusive action the French ships returned to Toulon. As James notes, the action is interesting because on the face of it, "one French 130-gun ship, five French two-deckers, 80's and 74's, and four 40-gun frigates, were driven back into their port by three British 74's, a 36-gun frigate and a 10-gun brig" (there is something about the last in the list that invites derision). It was the subject of heated correspondence in British and French papers at the time.

The remarkable fact is that despite the intensity of naval warfare at the level of the smaller vessels, no 10-gun brig was sunk or captured.. Many incurred heavy damage and casualties, but they inflicted more damage than they suffered, and all survived the war. In view of the criticisms that were leveled at them—that they were poor sea boats, not fast sailers, difficult to handle in bad weather—they had a surprisingly good war record.

There is no record of any 10-gun brig being involved during the war with the United States (1812–14); they were probably too weak to be risked against the American superfrigates.

Once peace had been concluded both in Europe and with the United States, the role of the Royal Navy began to change again. Pax Britannica was based upon freedom of the seas, and one of the first tasks was to deal with the problem of piracy. During the wars various governments had been happy to encourage predation by "privateers" on rival shipping. The typical pirate vessel was a fast schooner, well armed and prepared to fight tenaciously. When the peace came, naturally enough, these pirates were not keen to give up a highly profitable activity, especially as a booming period of world merchant trade was developing. Furthermore, one of the major activities of the privateers was slaving, which was already illegal in most countries. It fell to Great Britain, having the largest navy and the most mercantile interests at stake, to assume the role of policer of the seas. And the success with which this was accomplished is manifest in the growth and strength not only of the great British Empire, built as it was upon trade, but of international commerce in general.

One of the major British actions against pirates was the Battle of Algiers. Although the Algerians had previously been forced to free some seventeen hundred slaves and had signed treaties agreeing not to enslave Christians, on May 23, 1816, "the crews of between 300 and 400 small vessels engaged in the coral-fishery, while on their way to celebrate mass (it being Ascension Day), were barbarously massacred" off Algiers. The British government mounted a punitive expedition against the town of Algiers, led by Admiral Lord Exmouth. Included in the British fleet were three 10-gun brigs: *Britomart* (Captain Robert Riddell), *Cordelia* (Captain William Sargent), and *Jasper* (Captain Thomas Carew). A Dutch squadron joined in the attack (July 28, 1816), which was totally successful. As usual, the brigs were not involved in much of the fighting, the *Jasper* (as probably the others) being used for carrying dispatches.

As a footnote to this action, in 1823 it was again necessary to send a punitive expedition to Algiers because the new dey had reverted to the old ways. The 10-gun brig *Cameleon* (Captain James Ryder Burton) was sent with the *Naiad* (fifth rate, 38 guns, under the command of Captain the Hon. Sir Robert Spencer. Spencer delivered his government's letters to the dey and got the British residents and officials on board secretly. As they left, they attacked and boarded the Algerian corvette *Tripoli* (18 guns), rescuing seventeen Spanish sailors and taking the vessel as a prize. The captured dey declared war but quickly gave in without fighting. No more "should Christians be made slaves."

Piracy continued to be a problem, however. The *Redpole* (as a packet vessel) was sunk by the American pirate *Congress* off Cape Frio in 1828. The *Icarus* was part of a squadron in West Indian waters acting against pirates off Cuba in April 1832.

Perhaps the only other prominent naval action in which 10-gun brigs were involved was the Battle of Navarino, in OCtober 1827. The occupation of Greece by the Turks created such problems in the Mediterranean that Britain, France, and Russia resolved to impose some sort of settlement by force if necessary. Despite treaty negotiations, Turkish and Egyptian fleets assembled in Navarino Harbor, evidently preparing for trouble. A combined British, French, and Russian force engaged them right within the harbor. The loss of life was high on both sides, and the Turkish fleet was almost totally destroyed. In the British part of the allied fleet were the *Musquito* (two killed and four wounded), the *Brisk* (one killed, four wounded), and the *Philomel* (one killed and seven wounded). This was the last significant naval action until the beginning of the Crimean War although, as we shall see, even HMS *Beagle* got into a few scrapes and had to run out her guns in South American waters.

Source: W. James, *The Naval History of Great Britain* (London, Macmillan, 1904).

Appendix D

THE MISSION OF HYDROGRAPHIC SHIPS WITH
RESPECT TO GENERAL NATURAL HISTORY

As has been noted many times, the Royal Navy expected all its vessels, especially those in the Hydrographic Service, to bring back information on an enormously wide range of subjects beyond those specific missions outlined in detail in the Admiralty orders. Very often the expectations in terms of natural history were not explicitly laid out. However, in the case of King's expedition to the northern coast of Australia in 1817–22, a memorandum issued by the Admiralty neatly summarizes the subject:

> The following will be among the most important subjects, on which it will be more immediately your province, assisted by your officers, to endeavour to obtain information on any occasion which may offer.
>
> The general nature of the climate, as to heat, cold, moisture, winds, rains, periodical seasons; the temperature regularly registered from Fahrenheit's thermometer, as observed at two or three periods of the day.
>
> The direction of the mountains, their names, general appearance as to shape; whether detached or continuous in ranges.
>
> The animals, whether birds, beasts, or fishes; insects, reptiles, &c., distinguishing those that are wild from those which are domesticated.
>
> The vegetables, and particularly those that are applicable to any useful purposes, whether in medicine, dyeing, carpentry, &c.; any scented or ornamental woods, adapted for cabinet work and house-

hold furniture, and more particularly such woods as may appear to be useful in ship-building; hard woods for tree-nails, blocksheaves, &c., of all which it would be desirable to procure small specimens labelled and numbered, so that any easy reference may be made to them in the journal, to ascertain the quantities in which they are found; the facility or otherwise of floating them down to a convenient place for shipment, &c.

Minerals, any of the precious metals, or stones; how used, or valued by the natives.

The description and characteristic difference of the several tribes or people on the coast.

The occupation and means of subsistence, whether chiefly, or to what extent by fishing, hunting, feeding sheep or other animals, by agriculture or by commerce.

The Principal objects of their several pursuits, as mentioned in the preceding paragraphs.

A circumstantial account of such articles growing on the sea-coast, if any, as might be advantageously imported into Great Britain, and those that would be required by the natives in exchange for them.

The state of the arts, or manufactures, and their comparative perfection in different tribes.

A vocabulary of the language spoken by every tribe with which you may meet, using in the compilation of each the same English words.

Source: Philip Parker King, *Narrative of the Survey of the Intertropical and Western Coasts of Australia* (London: Murray, 1832).

Appendix E

THE LIGHTNING CONDUCTORS OF WILLIAM SNOW HARRIS

Every American is, of course, familiar with Benjamin Franklin's experiments with electricity and his observations of the protection of buildings from lightning by the use of metal "conductors" that safely "ground" the lightning discharge (B. Franklin *Experiments and Observations on Electricity Made at Philadelphia* [1769]). The usefulness of lightning conductors is now well established, but needless to say, acceptance of these newfangled devices came slowly. The trouble was that empirical evidence showed that one should do everything possible to avoid "attracting" lightning. Today's golfers know better than to wander around in the open carrying metal golf clubs in a thunderstorm, for example. The trick was to persuade people that mounting a metal rod on the roof of the house would be a safety measure *if the rod were properly grounded to earth.*

In Europe both British and French scientists made early experiments with lightning conductors. In 1769, at the request of the dean and chapter of St. Paul's Cathedral, the Royal Society recommended a way of protecting the building by connecting the ball and cross on the top of the dome to the lead sheathing of the dome and roofs, to iron rods driven into the ground, via the lead downspouts. All possible gaps were bridged with metal. While another Wren church—St. Martin's-in-the-Fields—suffered lightning damage as late as 1842 (because it was unprotected), St. Paul's was safe.

The British and French did not like to install the projecting metal "lightning rod" that Franklin recommended—and is still seen on almost all American buildings. They preferred the more indirect route used at St. Paul's or the installation of copper tapes from roof to ground.

Lightning storms were as dangerous to ships at sea, before, say, 1850, as they are to modern golfers (the principal human victims of lightning these days). Not only were the ship's masts a hundred feet or more higher than anything for miles around, but the masts were soaked in salt water much of the time—an excellent conductor of electricity. The ships themselves were wooden (a poor conductor) but full of combustible pitch and tar, let alone barrels of gunpowder. No wonder that lightning at sea was universally feared.

By the 1830s British ships were equipped with a crude sort of lightning protective device advocated by Martyn Roberts. This took the form of a length of chain, one end of which was to be triced up to the signal hall-yards in the event of a storm. The other end was supposed to reach the water. In principle this should have been effective. However, the chain usually remained in its box. When a storm struck, people were usually too busy managing the sails to have time to set up a newfangled gadget.

W. Snow Harris's conductors solved the problem. A continuous strip of copper tape was let into the masts and yards and grounded at the base of the mast to the keel and thence the water. Like any lightning conductor's, its efficacy depended on the line of conductors' not being broken.

While all this seems perfectly obvious to us today, and was made in part obsolete with the adoption of steel masts and hulls, as late as 1842 the *Nautical Magazine* was still conducting (so to speak) a campaign, and Mr. Harris was still touring the country, lecturing and making his demonstrations, all to persuade shipowners to install lightning conductors.

For example, on May 22, 1842, the merchant brig *Frisk,* en route from Buenos Aires to Cork, was struck by lightning. Her main royal and top-gallant masts were splintered to pieces, shredding her main topgallant sail, and her rigging caught fire. "From the main-top-gallant mast the lightning descended by the chain topsail-tye, and afterwards by the [steel] chain topsail-sheets, without doing any further damage until about three fathoms from the deck, where the topsail-sheets were frapped together with some rattlin stuff, when it exploded, completely shattering the remainder of the topsail-sheets, and showering the pieces about the deck; it then descended by the chain cable into the chain locker, and from thence it is supposed it made its escape into the sea by the copper bolts which run through the kelson and keel. When the vessel was put on the gridiron here for examination no damage had been sustained in her bottom, but one of the copper bolts had a *bright* drop of copper about half an inch long, hanging from it '*just like* a drop of rain,' said the mate."

Two men were half paralyzed. The chronometers and compass were set badly off (A. Livingston, "Effects of Lightning," *Nautical Magazine,* enlarged series, n. 9, [1842], 641–42).

By contrast, the experimentally equipped *Beagle,* twenty years before, had survived worse storms with no damage at all.

Appendix F

It is only too easy to make fun of people like Sir George Grey (see Chapters 14 and 15), whose ambition to make a heroic name for himself (preferably not posthumously) by exploring northwestern Australia readily outstripped his experience, his common sense, and the zeal of his companions. Missionaries readily fitted into the same category. Fitzroy's missionary efforts with (essentially at the expense of) the Fuegians, alas, were not the end of the story as far as fanatics in Tiera del Fuego were concerned.

Commander Allen Gardiner was a naval officer who first heard the call to a missionary life when visiting Tahiti on a navy vessel. In 1826, aged thirty-two, he retired from the navy and looked for a likely target for his Christian services. He tried South Africa and Chile, to no avail. He founded the Patagonian Mission and tried to work in the Gran Chaco, where his opposition was not the heathen but the Catholic Church. Nothing daunted, in 1848 he set off for Tierra del Fuego, where he tried to set up a small outpost at the eastern end of the Beagle Channel. Having started out hopelessly poorly equipped and prepared, six months later his party was back home, having lost everything, either to the weather or to the nimble-fingered, religion-resistant Fuegians.

A second expedition was attempted, once again poorly equipped and poorly planned. Soon they all were dead, of scurvy, starvation, and exposure. But instead of this being the end of the matter it was a challenge. Hardy souls stepped forward who would do the job *properly* via a base on the Falklands. Fitzroy was consulted and halfheartedly approved the idea. Captain Parker Snow was put in charge of a ship (the *Allen Gardiner*) and set off in 1853, carrying two missionaries to the Falklands. The new plan was to find Jemmy Button first. He would open the doors, so to speak, for a party to settle among the otherwise hostile Fuegians.

Eventually, after leaving the missionaries in the Falklands, Snow reached Ponsonby Sound, and just as with Fitzroy in the *Beagle,* twenty years before, two canoes approached the ship. Snow shouted, "Jemmy Button, Jemmy Button," and amazingly enough one of the Fuegians answered, "Yes, James Button." When they approached, "A stout wild and shaggy looking man" asked, "[w]here's the ladder?"

The official plan was to induce Jemmy to travel with them back to the missionaries, ensconced in the Falklands—shades of Fitzroy's hostages. But Snow disapproved of the idea, and the Fuegians were obviously very suspicious. Snow gave them food and clothes, thus inducing even more begging and, once more, some nasty incidents. Snow left, but his arrival at the Falklands without the Fuegians led to much quarreling, accentuated by the arrival of a new senior missionary, G. Packenham Despard (one could scarcely *invent* better names) with his wife, children, piano, and the usual paraphernalia of chamber pots for the Fuegians, plus as an assistant none other than the son of Allen Gardiner, all of which (together with a herd of wild cattle) he instructed Snow to ferry to the missionary base on Keppel Island. Snow quit instead.

Where all others failed, the young Gardiner promptly succeeded in getting Jemmy Button, with wife and three children, to Keppel Island for six months. Then Despard returned the Fuegians and started building a house at Woolya. More Fuegians went off to Keppel Island, and eventually Gardiner went home. In October 1859 the latest group of Fuegians returned in the *Allen Gardiner* to the new settlement. Many loaded canoes arrived. On the first Sunday a service was to be held in the new hut. Everyone went ashore except one man, the cook, who was left on board the ship. He watched helplessly as the Fuegians first removed the oars from the boats onshore so as to prevent any escape and then killed all the Europeans.

Several months later a rescue party found the *Allen Gardiner* intact and the cook living with Jemmy Button's family. A court of inquiry back in England found almost everyone to blame. Further missionary efforts were discouraged.

Today the true Fuegians are all extinct, as a result of both European diseases and direct extermination.

Sources: J. W. Marsh and W. M. Stirling, *The Story of Commander Allen Gardiner* (London: 1874); Nesbit, H. E. L. Mellersh, *Fitzroy of the Beagle* (London: Rupert Hart-Davis, 1968).

Appendix G

Customs Letter Book 101/66 1847

Board to Maldon
157 estimates for repairing mooring shackles, 30 Oct 1847
Customs Letter Book 101 / 66 1850

Board to Maldon
60   repairing Beagle, material supplies, £14.5.2, 1 June 1850

Customs Letter Book 101 / 22 1847–1853

Maldon to Board
211–212 letters requesting and petitioning moving Beagle to new
         position because of blocking navigation, 29 July 1850
         (original petition from oystermen not preserved)
321   approval of request, 25 Sept 1850

Customs Letter Book 101 / 68 1851

Board to Maldon
48   correspondence on lease from Lady Sparrow for *Beagle* moor-
         ing, 12 June 1851
50   materials for repair *Beagle,* £1.18.4, no date
56   refit of *Beagle* by S. Read, £7.7.2, 16 Aug 1851
Customs Letter Book 101 / 23 1859

Maldon to Board
154   complaints with respect to nonpayment of rent for Beagle's
         mooring from Lady Sparrow, 7 March, 1856

Index

Page numbers in *italics* refer to illustrations.

Index

Index

Index